Philosophy and Sport

ROYAL INSTITUTE OF PHILOSOPHY SUPPLEMENT: 73

EDITED BY

Anthony O'Hear

CAMBRIDGE
UNIVERSITY PRESS

PUBLISHED BY THE PRESS SYNDICATE OF THE UNIVERSITY OF CAMBRIDGE
The Pitt Building, Trumpington Street, Cambridge, CB2 1RP,
United Kingdom

CAMBRIDGE UNIVERSITY PRESS
The Edinburgh Building, Cambridge CB2 8RU, United Kingdom
32 Avenue of the Americas, New York, NY 10013–2473, USA
477 Williamstown Road, Port Melbourne, VIC 3207, Australia
C/Orense, 4, planta 13, 28020 Madrid, Spain
Lower Ground Floor, Nautica Building, The Water Club, Beach Road,
Granger Bay, 8005 Cape Town, South Africa

Printed in the United Kingdom at Bell and Bain Ltd.
Typeset by Techset Composition Ltd, Salisbury, UK

A catalogue record for this book is available from the British Library

ISBN 9781107647695
ISSN 1358-2461

Contents

List of Contributors   v

Preface   1

Ways of Watching Sport
STEPHEN MUMFORD   3

The Martial Arts and Buddhist Philosophy
GRAHAM PRIEST   17

Sport as a Moral Practice: An Aristotelian Approach
MICHAEL W. AUSTIN   29

A Plea for Risk
PHILIP A. EBERT AND SIMON ROBERTSON   45

Not a Matter of Life and Death?
ANTHONY O'HEAR   65

Sport and Life
PAUL SNOWDON   79

Glory in Sport (and Elsewhere)
TIMOTHY CHAPPELL   99

Conceptual Problems with Performance Enhancing
Technology in Sport
EMILY RYALL   129

Is Mountaineering a Sport?
PHILIP BARTLETT   145

Rivalry in Cricket and Beyond: Healthy or Unhealthy?
MICHAEL BREARLEY   159

In the Zone
DAVID PAPINEAU   175

Olympic Sacrifice: A Modern Look at an
Ancient Tradition
HEATHER L. REID   197

Chess, Imagination, and Perceptual Understanding
PAUL COATES   211

Index of Names   243

List of Contributors

Stephen Mumford – University of Nottingham and Norwegian University of Life Science

Graham Priest – University of Melbourne, St. Andrews, City University of New York

Michael W. Austin – Eastern Kentucky University

Philip A. Ebert – University of Stirling

Simon Robertson – Cardiff University

Anthony O'Hear – University of Buckingham

Paul Snowdon – University College London

Timothy Chappell – Open University

Emily Ryall – University of Gloucestershire

Philip Bartlett – Greenhead College

Michael Brearley – British Psychoanalytical Society

David Papineau – King's College London

Heather L. Reid – Morningside College

Paul Coates – University of Hertfordshire

Preface

Philosophy and Sport brings together the lectures given in the Royal Institute of Philosophy's annual lecture series for 2012–13. In the Olympic year, it seemed fitting to consider some of the many philosophical and ethical questions raised by sport, and to bring together contributors from both philosophical and sporting worlds. This ground-breaking volume considers many different areas connected to sports and its practice. These include the watching of sport, drugs in sport, the Olympic spirit, sport and risk, sport as a moral practice, rivalry and glory in sport and the importance of sport in human life more generally.

On behalf of the Royal Institute, I would like to thank all the contributors both for their lectures and for their published papers, and also Adam Ferner for preparing the volume for publication and for the index.

Anthony O'Hear

doi:10.1017/S1358246113000374   © The Royal Institute of Philosophy and the contributors 2013
Royal Institute of Philosophy Supplement **73** 2013

Ways of Watching Sport

STEPHEN MUMFORD

1. Sport and how it is watched

There are many ways that we can watch sport but not all of them are philosophically interesting. One can watch it enthusiastically, casually, fanatically or drunkenly. One might watch only because one has bet on the outcome. Some watch a friend or relative compete and have a narrow focus on one individual's performance. A coach or scout on the lookout for new talent may have completely different interests to a supporter of a team. But what of the ways of watching sport that are of philosophical interest?

I am going to defend the distinction between partisan and purist ways of watching sport. In doing so, I will opt for a strong distinction between these two ways of watching: they are different to an extent that a partisan and purist looking at the same event may literally see different things. And I will then proceed to explain the substantial basis for the distinction between these two ways of watching. This comes down to what we see sport as being about. Is sport ultimately aimed at victory or is it about something else? I argue that our partisan and purist spectators are watching sport for different purposes and looking for different things. These two purposes are not necessarily in conflict, however. Indeed, one can assist the other. When we ask what sport is about, we could answer that it is about victory. But I will argue that the purist is looking for an altogether different kind of answer to this question, demanding a different level of explanation. This will also constitute a defence of the purist way of watching sport against the charge that it is in some way inferior because it misses the essence of sport. On the contrary: I argue that it captures the essence of sport perfectly.

2. Victory

What does the athlete aim to do when they engage in sport? An obvious answer is that they aim to win, or at least to do their very best. Some participants will realise that they have no chance of

doi:10.1017/S1358246113000222   ©The Royal Institute of Philosophy and the contributors 2013
Royal Institute of Philosophy Supplement **73** 2013

victory, such as an also-ran in a marathon with hundreds or thousands of runners. But even here there is some goal: to do their best, to complete the race within a certain time limit, or just to complete at all. In the high-level competitive sports, we want to see each competitor strive for success. If they deliberately do less than their best, they are often seen as betraying a central norm of sport. This could be a form of cheating, if part of match-fixing for instance. But even a legitimate winner could be criticised if they have not given their all for it could be seen as insulting or patronising to their opponents. Suppose a runner is so far ahead in the home straight that they stop and light-up a cigar? This, I suggest, conflicts with a norm concerning regard for one's opponents, even though there are some sports such as boxing which flirt with the disregard of this norm. My suspicion, however, is that in all sports athletes tend to have a mutual respect, born out of a shared understanding of the demands of the sport and a common interest in its flourishing, even if there are minor antagonisms that are sometimes encouraged.

Victory as the aim of sport *prima facie* conflicts with its aesthetic interpretation in which sport is often likened to art and athletes to artists. In some sports, its best competitors are thought of as maestros, concerned with the higher value of producing beauty rather than with the vulgarities of victory and defeat. But how literally should we take this? Is it still not the case that unless the competitor is aiming to win, they are not properly engaging in sport? If, for example, a footballer stops trying to win and instead juggles the ball as a show of skill, then they may be in the business of pure entertainment but they are no longer playing football. If a sportsman or woman really does wish to create art, then while they may have become an artist, they will have done so at the expense of sport.

Philosophers of sport have understood this. Elliot affirms it in the following:

> The goddess of sport is not Beauty but Victory, a jealous goddess who demands an absolute homage. Every act performed by the player or athlete must be for the sake of victory, without so much as a side-glance in the direction of beauty.[1]

And this is surely how many sports fans see it too. While a beautiful win might be preferred to an ugly one, an ugly win is always preferred to a beautiful defeat. Beauty may be a by-product of victory, and of

---

[1]   R. Elliott, 'Aesthetics and Sport', in H. Whiting and D. Masterson (eds) *Readings in the Aesthetics of Sport*, (London: Lepus, 1974), 107–16, 111.

playing for victory, but it never should itself be the primary aim. It may become an optional extra only once victory is secure. Two ugly goals always beat one beautiful one and only if an unassailable lead is acquired would the fan feel comfortable with their team 'turning on the style'. Dick Fosbury's innovative high-jump technique was far from graceful. It was even called a 'flop'. But such was its effectiveness that very soon all the contestants were jumping the Fosbury flop. Were it an aesthetic contest, this jump would have lost. But it is of course a contest merely of how high one can jump, by any style, and height is all that matter for the win.

Apart from the feeling that our athletes ought to be trying their best, the idea has an underpinning in the philosophical theory of what constitutes sport. The somewhat grandiosely titled ontology of sport deals exactly with this. And the most progress on the matter is made by Bernard Suits in *The Grasshopper*.[2] Suits attempts to define what it is to play a game but it is pertinent here because sport may be understood as the institutionalised form of games.[3] To play a game is, according to Suits:

> to engage in an activity directed towards bringing about a specific state of affairs, using only means permitted by the rules, where the rules prohibit more efficient in favour of less efficient means, and where such rules are accepted just because they make possible such activity.[4]

A simpler way of summarising the account is that 'playing a game is a voluntary attempt to overcome unnecessary obstacles'.[5] I say that sport is an institutionalised form of game-playing in that it is a status bestowed upon certain games by the institutions of sport, such as world governing bodies, the biggest of which is the International Olympics Committee. Such institutions grew historically around certain forms of practice with aims among others of codifying them, but one might also say commercially exploiting them.[6]

It follows from this that to watch sport is to watch someone voluntarily attempting to overcome unnecessary obstacles. If one considers a sport picked at random, such as the shot put, one sees that to play

---

[2]   Bernard Suits, *The Grasshopper: Games Life and Utopia*, 2nd edn, (Peterborough, Ontario: Broadview Press, 2005).

[3]   Stephen Mumford, *Watching Sport: Aesthetics, Ethics and Emotion*, (London: Routledge, 2011).

[4]   Suits, op. cit. note 2, 48–9.

[5]   Suits, op. cit., note 2, 55.

[6]   Mumford, op. cit., note 3, ch. 4.

this sport is to accept certain artificial constraints in attempting to complete a certain task. The aim appears to be to get the shot as far as possible from a fixed point. Suits calls this the prelusory (pre-game) goal of this particular sport. This is only superficially the aim, however. If one really wanted to get the shot down the field, there would be more efficient means of achieving it than propelling it in one throw without leaving a small circular area. One could carry it down the field, or construct a catapult, or at least take a run-up before the throw. But to play the sport is to accept the constraints of the rules, and one does so, according to Suits, precisely because they make game playing possible. They make the shot put a sport. Without the constraints of the rules, we would have no game. Hence the aim within the game – its lusory goal – is to propel the shot by a single unaided throw from within a seven-foot diameter circle. Now if one opts out of this – if one ceases to take a lusory or game-playing attitude to this activity – then one ceases to play the sport. If one gains the longest throw by taking a run up, starting outside the circle, then one has not played the sport of shot put.

We can generalise this to other sports. One has not played high jump if one gets to the other side of the bar by walking under it rather than jumping over it. And one has not competed in a running race if one gets to the finishing line first by cutting across the infield. Sometimes the unnecessary obstacles are physical impediments, such as the high bar. In some sports they are provided by other competitors: football would be so much easier if it wasn't for the other team trying to stop you getting the ball in their net. And sometimes the unnecessary obstacles come in the form of rules that make the prelusory goal harder to achieve, such as the rule that the baton within a relay has to be passed within a small bounded stretch of the track.

This is by way of justifying the claim that if one aims to do anything other than voluntarily attempting to overcome the unnecessary obstacles circumscribed by the sport, one has thereby ceased playing the sport. And the case that interests us here is if one instead seeks to produce beautiful movements or moves within the sport that are not assisting one's lusory goals. Hence, my aim could be to get over as high a bar as possible. I don't mind if my movement is beautiful as I jump, as long as it does not hinder me. But my focus has to be entirely on the lusory goal and any beauty I produce in my sport is incidental.[7]

[7] See David Best, 'The Aesthetic in Sport', *British Journal of Aesthetics*, **14** (1974): 197–213, for example.

We have here a putative philosophical underpinning to the idea that the goal of sport is victory. If I aim during the game to produce aesthetic value, for instance, I have ceased playing that sport. And as watchers of sport, the spectators have come to see that voluntary attempt to attain the lusory goals. The spectators are thus thwarted in their aim if a player of football starts aiming to please in aesthetic rather than competitive ways. If the spectator is happy to see that, then they may have ceased being a sports fan and instead they have become an art-appreciator, perhaps.

The partisan watcher of sport can claim, therefore, that the way they watch sport, looking for victory, is the appropriate and right way to watch sport. They are not art appreciators. They understand the goals of sport, what it is all about, and in watching to see a win, they have tapped into the essence of sport.

This would seem to offer a vindication of partisanship as the fit and proper way of watching sport. The partisan is a supporter of a sports team or an individual. He or she watches sport in the hope of seeing his or her favoured team or individual win. It does not matter so much if the opponents underperform as this assists the favoured team to victory. And a win is always preferred to a defeat, even if it is an ugly win. Aesthetic pleasure will be accepted in sport as long as it provides no impediment to the favoured team's triumph.

3. The aesthetic way

Thus far, all seems in favour of the partisan way of watching sport. But there is another. Dixon[8] distinguishes the partisan from the purist and although I characterise these kinds of sport spectator differently from him,[9] I think the initial distinction retains use. While a partisan is a supporter of one side and wishes to see them win, a purist is someone who watches sport for its own sake, taking an aesthetic pleasure in it. A purist need not care which teams wins. She may enjoy a dramatic victory but be indifferent as to which of the sides attains it. Coming into the last few minutes of a tied game, she may hope for a victory just for the sake of the drama, not minding which team wins it. The aesthetic enjoyment of the sport can be found in its higher values being realised during the competition. The purist takes pleasure in seeing the sport played well. And it

[8]   Nicholas Dixon, 'The Ethics of Supporting Sports Teams', *Journal of Applied Philosophy*, **18** (2001): 149–58.
[9]   Mumford, op. cit., note 3, ch. 2.

follows that the purist wants to see all competitors play their very best so that as good a game as possible is witnessed. This could contrast with a partisan who may on occasion be happy for the opposition to underperform insofar as it increases the chance of their own side's success.

What we have considered in relation to the striving for victory has been presented as a challenge to the purist. The allegation is that they are watching sport in the wrong way, looking for beauty rather than the competition to win. But insofar as this is an attack on the purist spectator, it seems premised on an assumption of the incompatibility of beauty and competition. This should be challenged, and it can be.

Imagine that we were admirers of the human physical form and the extent of human capabilities generally, whether this concerns our physical or mental causal powers as free agents. Perhaps we have seen dance and had found that there are certain aesthetic values that are to be found in human shape and movement. A fully extended limb, for example, may be more appealing than one that hangs loose. And dance performance has at times demonstrated dramatic movements. Suppose we had seen all of this but lived in a world in which there was no sport. People had run and jumped and swam but not competitively. Nevertheless, the possibility of the aesthetic admiration of these practices had already come to our attention. Jumping can look good, and perhaps the higher someone jumps the more spectacular it looks. Having seen these activities, and more variety of human movement in dance, then our aesthetic sensibilities have become attuned to the athletic human form and its potential. In such circumstances, I suggested, it would make perfectly good sense for us to invent sport for the purposes of providing us with even better aesthetic experiences.

If we think how we should go about doing that, it would seem a perfectly reasonable supposition that we need to find ways to force people to instantiate the aesthetic forms that interest us. And we can note that speed is an aesthetic category in relation to the human body. When a runner runs faster, it is more aesthetically appealing to us that a runner who runs slower. What we need, therefore, is an incentive for our runners to push themselves to their limits. The same would apply to swimming. In other cases, the aesthetic categories that interest us might be strength, stamina, dexterity, flexibility, power, height, length, extension, smoothness, grace, fluidity, and so on. And we might note that the more we get under these categories, the better. Hence a more fluid motion appeals to us more than a less fluid one.

The thinking could be, therefore, that it would be good to set up contests that were largely meaningless, in terms of their useless prelusory goals, but which incentivised the display of these physical attributes to their maximum limits. And this fits well with the account of sport we have inherited from Suits. The participants have to overcome unnecessary obstacles in their quest to win. But why have we put these obstacles in their way? Why do we make them jump over a bar rather than walk under it? To accept the lusory goal of the sport is to accept that the contest is to be staged on certain grounds, grounds that will require the exhibition of certain bodily aesthetic qualities.

The purist can be defended, therefore, on the grounds that far from not getting the idea of sport as being essentially about victory, such a quest for victory within the sport is precisely the thing that secures the aesthetic features that we admire. Sport makes us run faster, jump higher, exhibit the maximum strength. It is an entirely artificial contest, insofar as its prelusory goals tend to be worthless or worth little. But what is important about them is that their pursuit creates the athletic beauty we seek: fully-exerted human bodies, graceful style, intricate tactics and real drama.

I say that the drama is real for a couple of reasons. Sport is full of twists and turns when it is at its best. Defeat can rapidly turn to victory and vice versa. The incredible and improbable can occur. We can have all of this in fiction, of course, in a novel or play. But there the drama is contrived. The author determines it from outside the form. Except in rare cases, the writer is not part of her own novel, manipulating it as a character from within. In sport, however, the outcomes, including the dramatic ones, are determined by the participants in the course of their striving for victory. The competitors bring their athletic and other virtues to the contest so that they can battle it out. The outcome is not contrived but the result of this competition of skill and strength. Were we to find that the sporting outcome was scripted, as occasionally occurs with fixed or staged contests, we immediately feel cheated and realise that the drama was illusory.

A second reason to say that sport provides real drama, however, is that its reality has been doubted elsewhere in the aesthetics of sport.[10] It is suggested that there are various disanalogies which tell us the hackneyed cliché of sport as unscripted theatre is wide of the mark. Nobody is injured on the stage when the character of Caesar is stabbed, for the stabbing occurs to the character rather than the

---

[10] Best, op. cit., note 7.

actor. But in sport, people really do break legs. Victory and defeat is real in sport whereas in drama it occurs only to the characters.

The analogy can nevertheless be rescued. When sport is played correctly, the participants do adopt roles as opponents. Injuries may occur but they are inflicted on the other *qua* opponent not *qua* human being. In that case, it looks as if one adopts a character when one plays sport. One takes on an adversarial role in which it is accepted that injuries may occur but these are not inflicted directly against the person. Hence, friends playing football against each other may enter into some tough, hard challenges and as a result an accidental injury may occur. The friendship is not threatened if this was inflicted in the context of sport. Hard tackles are an integral part of some sports. Hence the analogy holds between sport and the stage. The actor playing Caesar similarly does not mind if even the fake dagger hurts his skin, for it was pain inflicted on his character rather than on him as an actor and human being.

But sport is not always played right. If one player has been holding a grudge against another, for whatever reason, and goes into the tackle not with the aim of winning the game but of injuring his opponent, then that injury is inflicted on the opponent *qua* other person rather than on the opponent *qua* opponent. In that case, the fouling player has stopped playing the sport. They have swapped their lusory goal for some other: revenge, perhaps. But then exactly the same could occur on stage. The actor playing Brutus may hate the actor playing Caesar and may deliberately dig his fake knife much further into his fellow actor than is required of his part. Our Brutus had thus stopped acting his required role and instead had sought a petty revenge. Because of that, the injury was to the actor, not to the character of Caesar. The analogy holds, therefore, for the cases of sport and theatre look the same and the drama of sport looks as real as any.

The purist has therefore a perfectly reasonable way of viewing sport: one which is in line with the purpose and essence of sport. Sport's contests force its contestants to exert their full power, to stretch, jump, run and swim to their maximum capability, or to exhibit some skill as well as they are able. Doing so instantiates aesthetic qualities. And striving for victory creates real drama which pleases the viewer. Far from the purist's aesthetic quest being incompatible with sports requirement of victory, this very quest is exactly what produces its positive aesthetic content. The purist is someone who understands this. But they appreciate the drama without worrying as to who emerges from that drama victorious. And they want all sides to play to their full capability because that adds to the aesthetic.

Hence, the purist has an interest in all contestants flourishing in a way that the partisan does not.

Partisanship requires allegiance to a single object: wanting one team to flourish at the expense of others. It can be likened to a monogamous relationship, forsaking all others. It is a love with a jealous lover: to favour any other team is tantamount to a betrayal. But when the purist wants all to flourish, they exhibit a love that is like the love of a parent to all their children. They love them equally. They want them all to do well and they cannot choose favourites.

4. Ways of Seeing

I have spoken of there being different ways of watching sport and the partisan and purist watching sport in different ways. How literally should we take this? My view is that we should take it wholly literally. A partisan and a purist can see sport in different ways: they can even see the very same event in two different ways.

One way of making this claim clear is to distinguish between accompaniment and perception theories of ways of seeing. The accompaniment theory would say that

> (T$_A$) two persons a and b looking at the same event E, with similar angles on E and equally reliable perceptual faculties, have indistinguishable perceptions of E but they may have different thoughts, beliefs and intentions accompanying those perceptions.

Applied to the case of the purist and partisan, we would then say on the accompaniment theory that when watching the same game, the partisan and purist see the same but what they see is accompanied by different thoughts. The purist thinks that what they see is beautiful, for example, while the partisan seeing virtually the same thing thinks that it's a chance to score. At least in theory, our partisan and purist could have intersubjectively indistinguishable perceptions and their difference in their way of seeing rests only in them having different thoughts alongside those perceptions.

The accompaniment theory might seem *prima facie* to be the easy theory to defend. The perception theory, in contrast, tells us that

> (T$_P$) two persons a and b looking at the same event E, with similar angles on E and equally reliable perceptual faculties, may nevertheless have distinguishable perceptions of E.

Stephen Mumford

Where we are concerned with purist and partisan ways of watching sport, perception theory tells us that the ways of watching sport amount to literally seeing different things. We rule out cases of difference in perceptual organs. A short-sighted person's view on an event could be blurry, but the perception theory is more than a claim about that. And two viewers with different angles on the same thing could of course see it entirely differently. The perception theory aims for more substance than that. Two partisans, rooting for the same side, could see this event E exactly the same. Their perceptions could be intersubjectively indistinguishable, so says the philosophical theory (we could never check this empirically). But if we substitute the place of one of those partisans with a purist, looking at exactly the same thing, the purist could have a distinct perception from the partisan.

We are tempted to resist the perception theory, I think, to the extent that we believe perception is something that occurs prior to cognition. The suggestion would be that one sees and can then think about what one sees but thoughts do not interfere with what is seen. But there is also tradition that goes back at least to Hanson and has more recent proponents such as Dennett in philosophy and Gregory in psychology in which what one sees is at least in part determined by what one thinks.[11] And if we accept that our perceptions can be cognitively laden or merely influenced, then a perception theory looks more plausible.

This is indeed what I urge to be the case. The partisan sees sporting situations in terms of dreaded defeat and longed-for victory. When a success is close, the fan wills it to be so. They hope for it and they believe that their team deserves it. And where the belief is strong, they see that it is so. They see that the ball has crossed the line, that the jump is the longest, or that their team is playing best. The purist instead has no such willing in relation to a particular team. But they will also have beliefs that influence what they see. Indeed, if they train their aesthetic sensibilities, they are able to see all sorts of things as beautiful. They contemplate, they are disinterested[12] in

---

[11]   Norwood Russell Hanson, *Patterns of Discovery: An Inquiry into the Conceptual Foundations of Science*, (Cambridge: Cambridge University Press, 1958); Daniel Dennett, *Consciousness Explained*, (London: Penguin, 1991); Richard Gregory, *Eye and Brain: The Psychology of Seeing*, 3rd edn, (London: Weidenfeld and Nicholson, 1977).

[12]   Alan Goldman, 'The Aesthetic', in B. Gaut and D. McIver Lopes (eds) *The Routledge Companion to Aesthetics*, 2nd edn, (London: Routledge, 2005, 255–66), 263.

that everything is not seen as being for victory. Their perception is an aesthetic rather than competitive one. And it also follows once we take the perception theory seriously, that two partisans of opposing teams can see things differently. Many calls in sport are contested by opposing fans. Need one of those fans always be disingenuous? Not once we grant the perception theory. The two fans could by honestly declaring what they have seen, looking at the same incident, but they simply had very different perceptions of that event.

While this sharp distinction has been drawn between the two ways of watching sport – the purist's aesthetic perception and the partisan's competitive perception, we must also concede that these two ways of watching sport may be limiting cases.[13] The majority of sports fans are doubtless neither absolute partisans nor absolute purists. They may have simply a mild preference for a team or they may support a team only on the condition that they play beautifully. There are doubtless many complex things that could be going on in the mind of a moderate sports fan – one who finds some middle ground between partisanship and purism. But the simplest way I have of accounting for the moderate case is that such a fan is someone who likes to switch between aesthetic and competitive perceptions of sport, sometimes rapidly and frequently. Looking for beauty, they might see a particular move in aesthetic terms. But as soon as their team scores, they see it as a competitive advantage.

5. What's it for?

We have two different ways of watching sport, therefore. Which is right? Which is appropriate? Purism has faced attack. We saw Elliott claiming that sport was about victory. Consequently, he thought that the right way to watch sport was a competitive, partisan one. He went on:

> the ordinary spectator … does not fully enjoy a football match unless he has an interest in the victory of one side or the other. We have no right to tell him that he ought to adopt a detached aesthetic attitude unless we can assure him that by doing so he will gain more than he loses. In fact, he will gain very little and lose a great deal.[14]

[13] Stephen Mumford, 'Moderate Partisanship as Oscillation', *Sport, Ethics and Philosophy* 6 (2012): 369–75.
[14] Elliott, op. cit., 110, note 1.

Stephen Mumford

We should watch for the excitement of victory, it is alleged. Dixon even goes so far as to suggest that a purist exhibits a character flaw and – lacking in empathy – may have trouble forming interpersonal relationships.[15]

Elliot's claim that victory is the aim of sport is right only in one respect. It is the aim of every competitor, if they truly are playing the game, to do their best at it. This may not always be possible but it is at least what they try to do. Although this is the aim within sport, however, we can still raise the wider question of what sport is for. And here we can think more metaphysically. What need within us does sport satisfy? Is it slaking our thirst for victory? If that's what it was meant for, it does not seem exactly appropriate. Given that for every win there are at least as many defeats, and in some sports there are far more losers than winners[16] – consider a marathon race, for instance – then sport does a pretty bad job of satisfying that desire.

While the competitors aim to win, it is arguable that sport itself aims at beauty. Its competitions set up situations in which it is likely to manifest, by pushing our bodies to their extremes. This, instead, could be the need it satisfies, just as we imagined those interested in bodily aesthetics setting sport up for that purpose. As some minor confirmation of this view, consider how many rule changes in sport are designed for the purpose of making it more pleasurable to watch. The goalkeeper was banned from picking up a backpass, for instance, because it slowed the game down and was a recipe for time-wasting. We need to distinguish, therefore, between the aim of sport within the sport – its lusory goals – and its external purpose. And if we are asking why sport exists at all, it is arguable that our purist is more in tune with sport's essence.

There is something about sport that might be missed by the competitive perception. It is pleasurable for us as embodied agents to exercise our physical and mental abilities. Sport allows us to do this: and to the greatest degree. It is also pleasurable to watch others exercising their abilities. Although sport is superficially pointless, and its victories meaningless, there may be something deeply profound underlying it. It gives us an insight into the nature of embodied existence as free agents with causal powers. Sport teaches us what it is to be a human being. And it is surely the purist more than the partisan who is in a position to contemplate this deeper meaning. Elliot's

---

[15] Dixon, op. cit., note 8.

[16] Anthony Skillen, 'Sport is for Losers', in M. McNamee and S. Parry (eds) *Ethics and Sport*, (London, Routledge, 1998), 169–81.

claim that the purist would gain very little can be challenged. For the purist, sport can be a deep and edifying experience, which is quite a gain.

Although the aesthetic perception of sport is different from a competitive one, as I have argued, it is not clear that it is an inferior experience. While one loses out on some possible experiences, one gains the possibility of other kinds of experience. Two valid ways of watching sport exist, therefore. I have argued that they are sharply distinguished. The moderate sports fan will argue that they get the best of both worlds.

University of Nottingham and Norwegian University of Life Science
stephen.mumford@nottingham.ac.uk

The Martial Arts and Buddhist Philosophy

GRAHAM PRIEST

1. East Asian Martial Arts

My topic concerns the martial arts – or at least the East Asian martial arts, such as karatedo, taekwondo, kendo, wushu. To what extent what I have to say applies to other martial arts, such as boxing, silat, capoeira, I leave as an open question. I will illustrate much of what I have to say with reference to karatedo, since that is the art with which I am most familiar;[1] but I am sure that matters are much the same with other East Asian martial arts.

Karatedo is a style of martial art that developed in Okinawa. It evolved from a fusion of a local martial art (te) with empty hands and farm implements as weapons, and wushu techniques imported from the Chinese mainland. (A number of historically significant karate masters either came from China, or trained there.) It migrated to the Japanese mainland at the start of the 20th century, and thence, because of increasing Western involvement with Japan post Second World War, to the West.[2]

Karetedo, and the East Asian martial arts in general, teach many things. But one thing they undeniably are is a training how to be violent to others. Karate jutsu (techniques) are designed to stop an attacker in various ways, varying from restraint and temporary disablement, to maiming, and even killing. The training in the dojo (training-place) is both physical and mental. The physical training

---

[1]   A brief autobiographical note: I have been practicing karatedo now for well over 20 years. I am 4th dan in Shitoryu (Yoshukan) and a 3rd dan in Karatedo Shobukai. I am also an Australian national kumite referee and kata judge. I have trained for substantial periods of time at dojo in Australia, Japan, the US, and the UK (the dojo in the last two countries being with styles other than my own).

[2]   Karate has traditionally been passed on by direct transmission of practice. There are hardly any written records before the 20th century. Good (objective and reliable) histories of karate are therefore hard to find. One of the most authoritative I know is M. Bishop, *Okinawan Karate*, revised edition (Boston, MA: Tuttle Publishing, 1999).

doi:10.1017/S1358246113000246   ©The Royal Institute of Philosophy and the contributors 2013
Royal Institute of Philosophy Supplement **73** 2013

concerns learning the techniques and how to apply them (though obviously a number of them have to be practiced in a restrained way with training partners). The mental training is in the psychological discipline necessary to apply the techniques effectively, should this ever be required. It is worth noting that many East Asian martial arts, karate included, have evolved sports forms in the last 100 years. These involve competition governed by strict rules. Thus, in sporting fights, only a limited number of techniques are permissible: those which can maim or kill an opponent are not allowed. Unlike real fighting, people must play by rules; and the point becomes just to win a medal. Many clubs now concentrate on this kind of practice; in the process, essential parts of 'traditional karate' are often lost. Though I do not want to denigrate sports karate (it's alright in its place), it is clearly a deviation from the tradition of the art; and it is the 'traditional art' of which I shall be speaking.[3]

2. Two Puzzles

This is sufficient background for me to explain two puzzles which frame the rest of this essay.

Puzzle Number 1

> There is undeniably a close connection between the East Asian martial arts and Buddhism – especially Zen Buddhism. Legend has it that the first patriarch of Zen Buddhism was Bodhidharma, an Indian missionary who took up residence at the Shaolin Temple. Legend has it that the same Bodhidharma was the founder of the Shaolin wushu. Whatever the history, the Shaolin Temple is famous for producing Zen Buddhist monks who are also wushu practitioners. The connection goes far beyond this, though. Many samurai, such as the legendary Musashi Miamoto (who also practiced Zen calligraphy), were Buddhists, and saw their Buddhism and their martial practice as deeply connected.[4]

[3] Some styles of karate allow full-contact competition, which is obviously more realistic than 'non-contact' forms. But even in these, certain techniques are forbidden as too dangerous. Sporting competition was never a part of traditional karate.

[4] See W. King, *Zen and the Way of the Sword* (New York, NY: Oxford University Press, 1993). On Musashi specifically, see the last chapter of his

The Zen Buddhist Monk Takuan Sōhō is well known for having written letters to martial practitioners giving them Zen advice.[5] Indeed, in traditional dojo, training sessions begin and end with short zazen (kneeling meditation) sessions. The Buddhist connection is also evident in popular martial arts books,[6] and Buddhist ideas are evident in the thought of many great karate masters.[7]

Now, this connection is certainly puzzling.[8] Buddhism is a religion and philosophy that is strongly anti-violence. Indeed, it has a number of Precepts (codes of conduct), the first of which expresses the principle of ahiṃsā, non-violence.[9] The major rationale of Buddhism is the elimination of duḥkha – a Sanskrit word whose meaning is hard to translate, though it certainly includes physical suffering. Clearly, the cause of a good deal of physical suffering is violence. How can those on a Buddhist path train to inflict violence on others, or give advice to others about effective ways of doing so?[10]

Puzzle Number 2

People trained in these martial arts are frequently more peaceable than ordinary people. Indeed, it is not uncommon for people who take up such an art in order to learn how to fight to lose

---

Book of Five Rings, 'The Book of Emptiness'. (T. Cleary (tr.), *The Book of Five Rings* (Boston: Shambhala, 1993).)

[5] See T. Cleary (tr.), *Soul of the Samurai* (North Clarendon, VT: Tuttle Publications, 2005).

[6] Such as such as J. Hyams, *Zen in the Martial Arts* (New York, NY: Bantam Books, 1982).

[7] See, e.g, G. Funakoshi, *The Twenty Guiding Principles of Karate* (Tokyo: Kodansha International Ltd., 2003).

[8] Historically, there are many political connections between Buddhist institutions and state power, including military power. (For a survey, see P. Harvey, *An Introduction to Buddhist Ethics* (Cambridge: Cambridge University Press, 2000), 264–70. The dynamics of power-structures makes *this* anything but puzzling.

[9] See, e.g., P. Harvey, *An Introduction to Buddhist Ethics* (Cambridge: Cambridge University Press, 2000), 69.

[10] It is clear why martial practitioners might want to *receive* advice concerning certain Buddhist mental practices. These can have effects that improve fighting, as we will note in due course. However, that hardly explains why a Buddhist should want to *give* such advice.

the desire to do so. It is hard to get documentary evidence of this;[11] but it is folklore, and certainly gels with my experience. And legend has it of many great karate masters that they refused to fight, even when they knew they would win easily.[12] Again, this is odd. Training to climb mountains makes you *more* likely to climb mountains. Training to speak a foreign language makes you *more* likely to speak the language. How is it that training in how to be violent makes you *less* likely to be violent?

A caveat here. Not all training in an East Asian martial arts produces peaceful people. Some martial arts clubs are quite prepared, for example, to turn out bouncers who are only too happy to apply their martial skills on unsuspecting victims. A more guarded way of putting my point is, therefore, that there is something about certain kinds of martial training that can have this effect on people. What and why?

Doubtless, answers to both of these questions are complex and multi-faceted. Thus, one reason, one might suppose, that Buddhists train in a martial art is for self-defence. Buddhism *per se* is not against this. And one reason that a training in violence might make you less violent is that violence and aggression are often driven by gut-reaction fear. If you know that you have the ability to defend yourself, fear may well be reduced, or at least controlled.

But these can hardly constitute sufficient answers. To learn to defend yourself, it is hardly necessary to practice hours a week, year after year – long beyond the point where any casual attacker is a serious threat. A short self-defence course with a readily available weapon such as a stick (or, in modern terms, a can of mace), is probably just as good at this. And though decreasing one's fear may make

---

[11]   Some can be found in C. Layton, 'The Personality of Black-Belt and Non-Black-Belt Traditional Karateka', *Perceptual and Motor Skills* **67** (1988): 218; C. Layton, 'Anxiety in Black-Belt and Non-Black-Belt Traditional Karateka', *Perceptual and Motor Skills*, **71** (1990): 905–6; T. Nosanchuck, 'The Way of the Warrior: the Effects of Traditional Martial Arts Training on Aggressiveness', *Human Relations* **34** (1981): 435–44; T. Nosanchuck and L. M. C. MacNeil, 'Examination of the Effects of Traditional and Modern Martial Arts Training on Aggressiveness', *Aggressive Behavior* **15** (1989): 153–9; A. Rothpearl, 'Personality Traits in Martial Artists: a Descriptive Approach', *Perceptual and Motor Skills* **50** (1980): 391–401.
[12]   See, e.g., the anecdote in J. Hyams, *Zen in the Martial Arts* (New York, NY: Bantam Books, 1982), 131–3.

one less aggressive, this hardly explains why trained martial artists should not be violent just for the love of it (in the way that people play the piano just for the love of it). There must be more going on than these things.

In what follows, I want to suggest a more profound explanation: that a training in the martial arts of the appropriate kind can itself be a way of treading the Buddhist path.[13] In what follows, I will explain some of the basics of this path. I will then explain how a martial training can implement at least certain important aspects of it. I will end by returning to our two puzzles.

3. Basic Buddhism

There are many forms of Buddhism, just as there are many forms of Christianity. And there are significant differences – metaphysical, ethical, and practical – between the different forms. Thus the metaphysics of emptiness (śūnyatā), to be found in all the Mahāyāna Buddhisms, is quite different from the reductionism of the earlier Abhidharma traditions. The central importance of the virtue of compassion, again in Mahāyāna Buddhisms, is quite different from the stress on self-enlightenment of the pre-Mahāyāna forms. And the tantric practices of Tibetan Buddhisms are a million miles away from the kōan practice of Rinzai Zen Buddhism.[14]

There are, however, some general ideas common to all forms of Buddhism. These are based on the direct pronouncements of the historical Buddha (Siddhārtha Gautama, c. 6th century BCE) and his first teachings, known as the Four Noble Truths. These generic considerations will be sufficient for our purposes.[15] I emphasize that I am not here concerned to defend the views – though I do assume (and I think, justifiably) that Buddhist practices have a certain causal efficacy. My aim is simply to explain the ideas, so that I can make the relevant points about martial arts practices.

The Buddha's teachings present a picture of what one might call the human condition, and how to ameliorate it. All people get ill,

---

[13]   For a light-hearted expression of the idea, see G. Priest, 'An Interview with Bodhidharma', ch. 2 of G. Priest and D. Young (eds), *Martial Arts and Philosophy* (Chicago, IL: Open Court, 2010).

[14]   On the variety of Buddhisms, see D. Mitchell, *Buddhism: Introducing the Buddhist Experience* (Oxford: Oxford University Press, 2002).

[15]   On the following, see, e.g., M. Siderits, *Buddhism as Philosophy* (Farnham: Ashgate, 2007), chs. 2, 3.

age (if they are lucky enough), may lose limbs, loved ones; many suffer at the hands of tsunamis, nuclear disasters, and other 'acts of god'; they are maimed or traumatized by war. And so the catalogue of unhappinesses goes on. Of course, people do derive pleasure from many things in life; but the natural consequence of this is that they are not content with such impermanent pleasures, and desire more – generating more unhappiness. As Hume observed, then, if the world is designed by a god, human happiness was not his purpose.[16]

There is, according to Buddhism, something that can be done about this situation, however. The first thing is to realise that, though we cannot really control what fate brings our way, we can control our *attitude* to it. When bad things happen, we get upset because we *make* ourselves so. It is the mental clinging and attachment, that we bring to events, which generate the unhappiness. Moreover, the world we live in is one of impermanence. Nothing lasts forever; all things will eventually pass. Once one realises this, the folly of clinging becomes patent.

A particularly pernicious case of attachment concerns the self. A person is like a car, whose parts come together at a certain time, interact, wear out sometimes and are replaced, and finally fall apart. Our parts are not mechanical or electronic in the same way as those of a car: they are psycho-biological; but the point remains the same. Indeed, just as, in reality, there is nothing more to the car than the sum of its parts, there is nothing more to a person than the sum of their parts. There is no essential self or soul which holds them all together.[17] We certainly have the illusion that there is, though. We all think that there is an essential 'me-ness', something which is present throughout my existence, which defines me as me. The attachment to this non-existent object is an especially strong source of grief.

4. The Noble Eightfold Path

An upshot of all this is that it makes sense to get rid of the attitude of attachment, which is the one source of unhappiness that is largely

---

[16] See his *Dialogues Concerning Natural Religion*, Part X.

[17] Which is not to say that the *person* does not exist, any more than that the car does not exist – though some Buddhist schools, notably the early Abhidharma schools, do endorse the thought that a partite object does not have the same reality as its ultimate parts.

under our control. If one can do this, then one will be left with a resulting peace of mind, whatever slings and arrows of outrageous
fortune arrive.[18] Getting your head around the kind of world you
live in and the kind of thing you are (not), certainly helps. But
simply knowing the facts is not enough. One has to break ingrained
and powerful psychological habits. Illusions can be hard to shake
off, even when one knows that they *are* illusions.

To this end, the Buddha suggested a number of fields of attention
that, when suitably pursued, can help. This is the fourth of the Noble
Truths, itself called the Noble Eightfold Path.[19] The eight fields are
usually broken up into three groups.

1. Cognitive: *right view*; *right intention*. Having the right view is,
    as I have said, a good start. But just as important is the deter-
    mination to dig oneself out of the hole one is in. Without
    that, nothing will happen.[20]

2. Ethical: *right speech, right action, right livelihood*. Cutting this
    cake into three is, to a certain extent, artificial. The point is
    that one should treat others appropriately. Don't lie, steal,
    kill, or do other things that are wont to inflict suffering on
    others. No doubt an important part of the idea here is that if
    one does not like to suffer at the hands of others, one should
    not inflict suffering on them. But more important is the fact
    that the practice of putting the interests of others before one's
    own is an important step in ridding oneself of the self-
    centred grasping which destroys peace of mind.

3. Attitudinal: *right effort, right mindfulness, right concentration*.
    Right effort is the realisation of the right intention. Akrasia is
    all too easy, and self-discipline is required. Right mindfulness
    is the ability to be aware of what one's mind and body are doing.
    How are you going to be able to control your mind if you are not
    aware of what it is up to? The same goes for your body. Not that

---

[18] One can find views similar to this in various Hellentistic philos-
ophies, such as Stoicism and Epicureanism. See, e.g., T. Irwin, *Classical
Thought* (*A History of Western Philosophy: 1*) (Oxford: Oxford University
Press, 1989), chs. 8, 9.

[19] See, e.g., J. M. Koller, *Asian Philosophies* (4th edn.) (Upper Saddle
River, NJ: Prentice Hall, 2002), ch. 12, or D. Mitchell, *Buddhism:
Introducing the Buddhist Experience* (Oxford: Oxford University Press,
2002), ch. 2.

[20] Note that determination is not the same as attachment. The former is
a resolute decision to act in a certain way. The latter is about the attitude one
has to the results of our actions when things go right or wrong.

these two things are unconnected. Mind and body interact. How can you expect your mind to work at its best if you abuse your body smoking heavily, over-eating, or living in inebriation? Conversely, how can you expect your body to work properly if your mind is a mess? The Latins who popularised the slogan 'mens sana in corpore sano' knew what they were doing. Finally, right concentration is the ability of mental focus. Right mindfulness is not going to be achieved if one's mind is all over the place.

Of course, how best to implement these steps is not entirely obvious. (And that is where many of the variations in Buddhist practices come in.) But all forms of Buddhism agree that some kinds of meditative practices are important. There are various kinds of such practice. This isn't the place to go into the variety;[21] suffice it here to note that mental focus – mindfulness and concentration – are central to all of them.

5. Martial Training

We are now in a position to see how a martial training can be taken to implement some of these Buddhist ideas.

Start with the Noble Eightfold Path. There is little in a martial training which addresses the cognitive aspects of this. I have never trained at a dojo where any Buddhist (or other) philosophical ideas about impermanence, the self, attachment, and so on, were discussed.[22] But this is perhaps the least important aspect of the Path. In most Māhāyana Buddhisms, the fundamental truth about reality is ineffable, a simple tathatā ('thatness');[23] any description of how things are, is ultimately inadequate. Buddhist doctrines may be helpful en route, but they are themselves just as inadequate in the last instance. They are just a skilful means (upāya), to be discarded when they have done their job. Indeed, in Zen, great stress is placed on the fact that enlightenment can be arrived at only by

---

[21]   See, e.g., O. Leaman, *Key Concepts in Eastern Philosophy* (London: Routledge, 1999), 200 ff.

[22]   Though of course there may be *some* Buddhist practitioners who also teach a martial art, and who talk their students about Buddhist ideas. Thus, see K. Furuya, *Kodo: Ancient Ways: Lessons in the Spiritual Ways of the Warrior/Martial Artist* (Santa Clarita, CA: Ohara Publications, 1996).

[23]   See, e.g., D. Keown, *Dictionary of Buddhism* (Oxford: Oxford University Press, 2003), 296.

direct wordless transmission.[24] Actions speak louder than words. (And there is certainly plenty of action in a dojo!)

The connections between a martial training and the other parts of the Path are more evident. Take ethics, to start with. Again, this is rarely discussed in a dojo, but a good training embeds in people crucial ethical values. One bows with respect on entering and leaving a dojo, at the beginning and the end of a kata performance, and of training with a partner. One has respect for one's teacher and the senior students from whom one learns.[25] One has concern for the well-being of one's training partners and those whom one teaches. Anger, ill will, and lack of self-control are not tolerated. And one learns respect for oneself as well. Nor is this something that stops when one leaves the dojo: one takes it out of the dojo too. In the dojo, one learns how to interact with other people, not just with other karateka. And one thing that goes with this respect is a determination not to use violence unless absolutely necessary. In karate, all kata begin with a defensive movement. This is often taken to be symbolic of the fact that karate techniques should only ever be used in self-defence. There is a traditional saying: 'karate ni sente nashi' (in karate there is no first strike).[26]

Effort and self-discipline are also required and developed in a martial training. For a start, these are required in exercises that build up strength and stamina. Training routines also have to be re-peated many times until them become reflexive. One has to discipline oneself to do what one is told immediately and without reservation. And one learns the self-discipline of patience. For many things (such as the results of grading exams) one just has to wait. One aspect of self-discipline is particularly germane in the present context. In the dojo, things will often happen that you don't like:

[24] See, e.g., A. Welter, 'Mahākāśyapa's Smile: Silent Transmission and the Kung-an (Kōan) Tradition', S. Heine and D. S. Wright (eds), *The Kōan: Texts and Contexts in Zen Buddhism* (Oxford: Oxford University Press, 2000), 75–109.

[25] On the importance of respect in the martial arts, see D. Young, 'Bowing to Your Enemies: Courtesy, Budo and Japan', *Philosophy East and West* **59** (2009): 188–215; and, for a more light-hearted account, D. Young, 'Pleased to Beat You' ch. 1 of G. Priest and D. Young (eds), *Martial Arts and Philosophy* (Chicago, IL: Open Court, 2010).

[26] See, e.g., G. Funakoshi, *The Twenty Guiding Principles of Karate* (Tokyo: Kodansha International Ltd., 2003), 23 ff. On the theme of vio-lence, Buddhism, and the martial arts, see C. Mortensen, 'Budo for Buddhists', ch. 14 of G. Priest and D. Young (eds), *Martial Arts and Philosophy* (Chicago, IL: Open Court, 2010).

you get hit in sparring, you make a mistake in a kata when everyone is watching, you fail a grading exam. You have to learn to shrug this off, put it behind you – to just carry on and focus on what comes next.

For the final two parts of the Path, one has to know something about kata. A major part of a martial training is the learning of sequences of movements, kata. These can be long or short, fast or slow, but are repeated over and over again until one does them without thinking. Developing a kata can be done only with great mindfulness of one's body, the position of one's limbs, the angle and speed of movements. Moreover, a kata should be performed with complete focus and concentration. When one performs a move of the kata, that and only that is where one's being is. In the context of Buddhist meditation practices, this would be called 'one-pointedness' (citta-ekagratā).[27] I think, in fact, that it is not fanciful to see kata performance as a kind of moving meditation. (In Buddhist traditions, meditation does not have to be done sitting or kneeling: it can be done walking, for example.[28])

6. Kumite

Another central part of a martial training is kumite. This is fighting with a training partner to develop one's skills in practice. Kumite can be of many kinds, from simple prearranged exercises, to free sparring, where both people can attack or defend in any way they like (though always with control).

For many people, this is the hardest part of the training. Being attacked by someone (often someone who is better than you), naturally brings out fear, and aggression naturally comes in its wake. One must learn to conquer these – if only because fear and aggression make one much less efficient in performing: they slow down one's reactions, and make one's techniques wild and inefficient. It's an old adage, but a true one, that one's true opponent in this situation is not one's attacker but oneself: one's own mental dispositions, which need to be controlled.

[27] See D. Keown, *Dictionary of Buddhism* (Oxford: Oxford University Press, 2003), 62.
[28] See, e.g., T. N. Hahn, *The Long Road Turns to Joy: A Guide to Walking Meditation* (Berkeley, CA; Parallax Press, 1996). Indeed, some Zen Buddhist masters, such as Hakuin, held kneeling meditation to be somewhat useless. See T. P. Kasulis, *Zen Action Zen Person* (Honolulu, HI: University of Hawai'i Press, 1981), 111.

What one must learn to do is to empty the mind of all thoughts, emotions, and react purely spontaneously (a spontaneity based, of course, on routines hard wired in by constant repetition). This is what is called 'mushin' (no mind) in Japanese.[29] Naturally, one thing that goes in the process is any sense of self. Getting rid of the sense of self is, as I noted, one of the most important things in Buddhism. Perhaps for evolutionary reasons, in a situation where one has to fight, one's sense of self is particularly strong. If it can be overcome in this particularly stressful situation, it ought to be much easier to overcome it in more mundane situations.

A final word on kiai. This is a shout used at various times in both kumite and kata. The point is to increase the effectiveness of one's action. It does this by focusing mind and body into a single undiluted present. Shouts may be used in the Zen tradition for exactly the same reason.[30]

7. The Puzzles Revisited

There are probably other important connections between a martial training and Buddhism that I have missed. But I hope that I have said enough, anyway, to demonstrate that an appropriate martial training can be a way of implementing a Buddhist path, even though one may not be consciously aware of this, or even if one has never even heard of Buddhism.

Let me end by returning to the two puzzles with which I started. Why has Buddhism often been connected with a martial training? That should now be obvious. It is one way of following the path. It is no accident that most martial arts are called 'do': ways. They are not simply learning to fight, but training in a path of much greater import. (Of course, I am not suggesting that a training in a martial

---

[29] As described by Takuan Sōhō in his letters of advice. See the translations in T. Cleary (tr.), *Soul of the Samurai* (North Clarendon, VT: Tuttle Publications, 2005). For a light-hearted commentary, see B. Finnegan and K. Tanaka, 'Don't Think! Just Act!', ch. 3 of G. Priest and D. Young (eds), *Martial Arts and Philosophy* (Chicago, IL: Open Court, 2010). A more extensive discussion of mushin can be found in E. Herrigal, *Zen and the Art of Archery* (New York, NY: Random House, 1981). The similarity between Zen and the martial arts, in that both require unmediated response, rather that premeditated action, is noted by T. P. Kasulis, *Zen Action Zen Person* (Honolulu, HI: University of Hawai'i Press, 1981), 121.

[30] See T. P. Kasulis, *Zen Action Zen Person* (Honolulu, HI: University of Hawai'i Press, 1981), 122.

art is the only way to follow the path, or even the best way. It seems entirely plausible that different ways are appropriate for different people.)

And why should those who undergo this kind of training become more peaceful people? If I am right, the training is effective in inculcating those attitudes important to Buddhism – in particular, in freeing oneself from attitudes that result in mental dis-ease, and allowing one to be in a state of inner peace. Greater inner peace leads naturally to greater outer peace. Those with inner peace have less desire to be aggressive or violent to others (or themselves). I am not suggesting that all this is a conscious matter. Many things we do have an effect on our mental states in ways of which we are unaware. Nor am I suggesting that accomplished martial practitioners are Buddhist saints. That would be absurd. They usually have the same human failings as anyone else. But as Aristotle observed, it is in our practices that we develop the sort of person we are.[31] This is certainly true of religious practices, such as those of Buddhism, and, it might now appear, of an appropriate martial training.[32]

Departments of Philosophy, Universities of Melbourne,
St Andrews, and the Graduate Center,
City University of New York
g.priest@unimelb.edu.au

[31] *Nichomachean Ethics*, Book 2, Ch. 1.
[32] A version of this paper was given under the title 'Karatedo and Buddhism', at the Royal Institute of Philosophy, London, October 2011, in their series of lectures on Philosophy and Sport. I am grateful to the audience there for their helpful comments. I am grateful, also, to two anonymous referees for their comments, and, especially, to Damon Young for his.

Sport as a Moral Practice: An Aristotelian Approach

MICHAEL W. AUSTIN

Sport builds character. If this is true, why is there a consistent stream of news detailing the bad behavior of athletes? We are bombarded with accounts of elite athletes using banned performance-enhancing substances, putting individual glory ahead of the excellence of the team, engaging in disrespectful and even violent behavior towards opponents, and seeking victory above all else. We are also given a steady diet of more salacious stories that include various embarrassing, immoral, and illegal behaviors in the private lives of elite athletes. Elite sport is not alone in this; youth sport has its own set of moral problems. Parents assault officials, undermine coaches, encourage a win-at-all costs mentality, and in many cases ruin sport for their children.

Is the claim that sport builds character, then, merely a myth? The belief that there are important connections between sport and morality has been shared across a variety of cultures, both past and present. For example, the claim that sport can have instrumental value with respect to moral development can be found as far back as Plato's *Republic*. For Plato, physical training has important moral and intellectual benefits. It promotes the harmonization of the soul, prepares one for the rigors of philosophy, and also helps cultivate the moral strength required for public servants in the city-state.[1]

The claim that I will articulate and defend in this paper is that sport should be approached as a moral practice. For my purposes, this means that a chief though not sole function of sport should be the cultivation of moral and intellectual virtue. My claim is not that the value of sport lies solely in its potential to foster the development of virtue. Sport serves other useful ends, such as enjoyment and physical health, and it may also have intrinsic value. However, sport should also be approached as a moral practice, which means that athletes, coaches, administrators, and other relevant parties should take advantage of the significant opportunities it provides

---

[1] Heather Reid, 'Sport and Moral Education in Plato's *Republic*', *Journal of the Philosophy of Sport* **34** (2007), 160–175; see also Plato, *Republic* 410bc, 411e.

doi:10.1017/S1358246113000301   ©The Royal Institute of Philosophy and the contributors 2013

Royal Institute of Philosophy Supplement **73** 2013

for cultivating and displaying virtue. This will likely necessitate not only changes in the attitudes of many toward sport, but also changes in how it is practiced and administered.

In what follows, I will give an account of moral development in the context of sport, which will be largely consistent with other neo-Aristotelian accounts of the moral purpose and functions of sport.[2] My intent is not to be strictly faithful to or solely draw from Aristotle's views; I will also make use of some of the relevant thought of Plato and Aquinas. Next I defend the account and then conclude with a discussion of some of its many potential practical implications.

Sport can bring out the worst in us, but it can also bring out our best. If we approach sport as a moral practice, as a context for cultivating and displaying the virtues, then we can at least begin to more fully realize its potential for helping us become excellent human beings. In other words, sport can build character, if we approach it in the right manner.

1. On the Philosophical Importance of Sport

Before I explain and defend this thesis, I will make a few brief points with respect to the philosophical importance of sport. Some will be skeptical that sport is worthy of the attention of philosophers. They may reject philosophy of sport because sport is an element of so-called 'low' culture.[3] Others may be concerned about the violence, anti-intellectualism, fascistoid hero worship, and morally problematic tribalism that can be found in sporting contexts. And perhaps others simply find sport uninteresting as a context for doing philosophy.

However, there are many reasons why sport merits the attention of philosophers. First, many of the foregoing reasons for rejecting philosophy of sport are examples of the type of reflection upon sport done by people working in the field. Philosophers of sport engage the morally and socially troubling aspects of this realm of human life. Given the centrality of sport across numerous cultures, philosophers can provide a useful and important corrective to the excesses of sport

---

[2]   See, for example, M. Andrew Holowchak and Heather L. Reid, *Aretism: An Ancient Sports Philosophy for the Modern Sports World* (Lanham, MD: Lexington Books, 2011); Carwyn Jones, 'Teaching Virtue through Physical Education', *Sport, Education, and Society* **13** (2008), 337–349; and Mike McNamee, *Sports, Virtues and Vices: Morality Plays* (New York: Routledge, 2008).

[3]   For a sustained argument against this view, see William J. Morgan, *Why Sports Morally Matter* (London: Routledge, 2006).

and sporting culture. Fortunately, however, there are more hopeful reasons for engaging in philosophy of sport related to its more positive aspects, including the numerous connections that exist between morality and sport.

Second, philosophical work done in the context of sport is relevant to other areas of philosophy. It can illuminate issues in metaethics, normative ethical theory, philosophy of law, medical ethics, and issues related to race, gender, and social justice.[4]

Finally, moral philosophers should not only be concerned with a conceptual analysis of morality, seeking to understand the sources of our obligations, and elucidating a sound normative ethical theory. They should, in the tradition of Aristotle, also be concerned with becoming virtuous. Philosophical reflection upon sport and a philosophical approach to it can help us understand and engage in the process of moral development via the cultivation of virtue in our sporting lives which we may then transfer to the rest of our lives. It is to this Aristotelian approach to sport that I now turn.

2. Approaching Sport as a Moral Practice

To conceive of and engage in sport as a moral practice means that one of the primary functions of sport should be to cultivate and display moral and intellectual virtue. From an Aristotelian perspective, in order to flourish, we must be virtuous and act from virtue. It is reasonable and even incumbent upon us, then, to make use of sport for moral development, given its potential for developing some of the particular moral and intellectual virtues. In order to clarify how this is the case, consider one way of understanding the structure of sport. One reason that sport can foster moral development has to do with some of the positive values that are embedded within the structure of its traditions. In order to understand this point, consider Alasdair MacIntyre's description of a *practice*:

> any coherent and complex form of socially established cooperative human activity through which goods internal to that form of activity are realized in the course of trying to achieve those standards of excellence which are appropriate to, and partially definitive of, that form of activity, with the result that human

---

[4]   For example, see Jan Boxill (ed.), *Sports Ethics: An Anthology Anthology* (Malden, MA: Blackwell, 2003); and William Morgan (ed.), *Ethics in Sport,* 2nd. (ed.) (Champaign, IL: Human Kinetics, 2007).

powers to achieve excellence, and human conceptions of the good and ends involved, are systematically extended.[5]

According to MacIntyre, football, chess, music, architecture, and the work of a historian are all examples of a practice. When a person decides to participate in an established practice, she at least tacitly agrees to be governed by the standards of excellence and traditions within that practice, even as those practices sometimes undergo change. Many who have been influenced by MacIntyre think of sports as practices, and believe that in developing skills such as speed, strength, and tactical imagination, moral development occurs:

> ...the cultivation of certain virtues, such as trust, courage, and fairness, is paradoxically both a necessary condition and a consequence of proper engagement. In such an account we can think of sports in terms of a human, or moral, or character laboratory... where one tests oneself and one's competitors in order to find one's limitations in pursuit of the ends of the game.[6]

The upshot is that in many sports, the standards of excellence in operation include not only the physical and athletic skills relevant to the sport, but also moral values and virtues such as sportspersonship, courage, and fairness.

Given the structure of sport as a practice, it can also foster humility in both athletes and coaches, who must submit themselves to the standards of their sport if they wish to excel or even just participate in their chosen sport. These standards not only include the formal rules, but the informal ones as well. Humility can also be acquired via sport as an athlete reflects on the numerous causes of his success. While it is true that an athlete is responsible in part for success at the elite level, given all the work and dedication that this requires, the properly reflective athlete will also see that there is reason to be humble even in the midst of success. As 2006 Olympic gold medalist speedskater Joey Cheek put it, 'a lot of people... don't realize the sheer dumb luck that goes into being born into a country and a family that has the means and resources to allow you to chase your dreams'.[7]

While the structure of sport is in some sense conducive to the development of virtue, the connection in actual practice between sport and moral

[5]   Alasdair MacIntyre, *After Virtue*, 2d. ed. (Notre Dame: University of Notre Dame Press, 1984), 187.
[6]   Carwyn Jones and Mike McNamee, 'Moral Development and Sport: Character and Cognitive Developmentalism Contrasted', *Sports Ethics*, Jan Boxill, ed. (Malden, MA: Blackwell, 2003), 42.
[7]   http://youtu.be/8MAXCWLWx3U; accessed September 13, 2011.

development is perhaps tenuous at best. In fact, one can abide by the traditions of her particular sport and act in accord with any particular virtue but not truly possess it. Perhaps her motives are directed at more egoistic ends such as fame and fortune. In Aristotle's terms, with respect to an individual trait she may fail to meet the other conditions of being virtuous, by having the wrong motives, desires, and emotions. However, a connection between sport and the cultivation of virtue is present; the *potential* for significant moral development in and through sport does exist. Sport offers the opportunity to cultivate character as one repeatedly engages in virtuous actions. Given this, I will next offer a brief commonsense account of how sport can be employed for developing the cardinal virtues of prudence, courage, temperance, and justice.

First, consider the virtue of prudence. The practically wise person is able to make good judgments about what to do and then carries out the proper actions based on those judgments. Athletes can cultivate this trait in the context of their sport and then apply it to other areas of life. For example, a good football player will ideally learn that his welfare as an athlete and the fortunes of his club are both bound up with the welfare of his teammates. Beautiful and excellent football requires individual team members to work together on the pitch. Sometimes this also requires that he forego what his in his narrow self-interest for the sake of the team, such as when he lays the ball off to a teammate who is in a much better position to score rather than taking a more difficult shot himself in a quest for individual glory. A thoughtful athlete should realize that a similar interdependence exists in his other relationships and in the broader community, and that he must sometimes sacrifice his narrow self-interest in these contexts as well. When he does come to know these things and then seeks to act accordingly, he is displaying prudence.

Second, consider a character trait more often associated with and admired in sport, the virtue of courage. For Aristotle, the courageous person '...stands firm against the right things and fears the right things, for the right end, in the right way, at the right time, and is correspondingly confident'[8] as prescribed by reason. Aristotle also takes courage to involve 'standing firm against what is painful'.[9] Consider cycling as it relates to the formation of courage. Given the pain of a four hour ride as well as the danger from automobiles, human error, mechanical failure, and the environment, cyclists have the opportunity to develop courage in the context of their sport. If a cyclist is approaching the sport in part as a way to cultivate moral excellence, then this can

---

[8]   Aristotle, *Nicomachean Ethics* 1115b15–20.
[9]   Ibid., 1117a30–35.

Michael W. Austin

foster the growth of courage in the context of cycling. And there is reason to think that this can also help foster courage in other contexts of life, as we will see.

Third, temperance, or self-control, can be developed in the context of sport. According to Aquinas, temperance is the character trait that 'directs our desires for bodily pleasures so that all these movements of the appetite support, rather than detract from, our pursuit of what reason has judged is good'.[10] The temperate person is not controlled by her desire for such bodily pleasures, but rather has and exercises self-control in her pursuit of the good.

Sport is related to the cultivation and practice of self-control in a variety of ways. In Plato's *Republic*, for example, physical training has instrumental value in part because it can train the rational part of the soul to rule over the other parts of the soul.[11] There are many temptations in the context of sport to fail to display self-control. An athlete is presented with many opportunities to lose control – or in Plato's terms, let spirit or appetite rule the soul – with a dishonorable opponent, disrespectful fans, or a coach who makes a choice with which she disagrees. There are many other high-pressure situations in sport which can make exercising self-control difficult. However, it is just these situations which give the athlete an opportunity not only to display self-control, but to cultivate it as well.

Some contemporary science affirms this, as there is significant empirical evidence in support of the view that self-control can be developed.[12] One model takes the capacity for self-control to be similar to a muscle. On this model, an individual's capacity for self-control becomes fatigued immediately after exertion, but over the long-term it becomes stronger as a result of exercise. When people engage in activities which require them to exert self-control, they are more likely to have less ability to exercise it immediately afterwards. But over time they gain increased stamina with respect to self-control. As the authors of one study put it, 'In the short run, exertion makes self-control tired and

---

[10]   Rebecca Konyndyk DeYoung, Colleen McCluskey, and Christina Van Dyke, *Aquinas's Ethics: Metaphysical Foundations, Moral Theory, and Theological Context* (Notre Dame, IN: University of Notre Dame Press, 2009), 139.

[11]   Op. cit. note 1, 164–165. See also Plato, *Republic*, 411e, 441e, 442a.

[12]   Mark Muraven, Roy Baumeister, and Dianne Tice, 'Longitudinal Improvement of Self-Regulation Through Practice: Building Self-Control Strength Through Repeated Exercise', *The Journal of Social Psychology* **139** (1999), 446–457.

diminishes its power; in the long run, exercise makes self-control stronger and increases its power'.[13]

This helps to explain why some elite athletes exhibit failures of self-control in other realms of life. Perhaps at certain moments they have exhausted their self-regulatory resources as athletes and are therefore more susceptible to such failures in other realms. However, research also shows that when an individual has sufficient motivation, the effects of this depletion can be overridden.[14] It follows that athletes can strengthen their capacity for self-control while avoiding the dangers of depleting their resources for self-regulation if they are sufficiently motivated to do so. If this model is correct, then it seems clear that sport is one context in which there is significant potential for individuals to cultivate self-control.

In fact, there is empirical evidence in favor of this very claim.[15] In one longitudinal study, individuals who began an exercise program increased their self-control over a two month period. They watched less television, smoked fewer cigarettes, consumed less alcohol, caffeine, and junk food, engaged in less impulsive spending and overspending, and procrastinated less. In addition, they studied more, were more faithful in keeping their commitments, and reported an increase in their emotional control. The participants exhibited better self-control in behaviors that are both related and unrelated to exercise, as well as their performance on a self-control task in the laboratory. The findings of this study 'suggest that our regulatory "stock" is not set; it can be increased by a number of behaviors'.[16] While it is true that sport is not merely physical exercise, it does include it, and so it is plausible to think that these benefits will also accrue to the athlete. The implication for our present purposes is that while athletes can build their physiological muscles via their sport, there is also the opportunity to cultivate the 'muscle' of self-control. Psychologists consistently find that self-control is a crucial trait for predicting positive outcomes in the lives of individuals.[17] Given this, and given the potential for developing self-control via sport, it would be wise to approach sport as a moral practice, as I am arguing in this paper.

---

[13] Ibid., 453.

[14] Megan Oaten and Ken Cheng, 'Longitudinal Gains in Self-Regulation from Regular Physical Exercise', *British Journal of Health Psychology* **11** (2006), 717–733.

[15] Ibid.

[16] Ibid., 731.

[17] Roy Baumeister and John Tierney, *Willpower* (New York: The Penguin Press, 2011), 1. The other one is intelligence.

Michael W. Austin

Finally, consider the cardinal virtue of justice. According to Aristotle, there is more than one variety of justice.[18] For our purposes, consider Aristotle's notion of *general justice*. An important aspect of this type of justice for Aristotle is that he who possesses it will engage in actions that benefit other members of the community. Justice seeks the good of another. This form of justice is relevant to sport in many ways. It can be developed as a player befriends teammates and seeks their good. It is also present when an athlete treats opponents, coaches, officials, and fans with respect. It is exemplified when an elite athlete makes use of whatever fame and fortune he receives to contribute to the common good, as Joey Cheek did when he donated the bonus he received from the United States Olympic Committee for his gold and silver medals at the 2006 Olympic Games to Right to Play, an organization that uses sport to improve the lives of children in disadvantaged areas of the world.[19]

Admittedly this is a brief treatment of how particular virtues may be cultivated in the context of sport, but the general idea that sport builds character in such ways is familiar and has intuitive appeal. It is also consistent with Aristotle's view that in order to become virtuous, one must practice by intentionally performing virtuous actions, or, as he puts it, 'we become just by doing just actions, temperate by doing temperate actions, brave by doing brave actions'.[20] And there is empirical evidence from contemporary psychology which affirms Aristotle's views of moral development and my application of them to sport. But can the notion that sport can be effectively put to use for cultivating virtue stand up to philosophical scrutiny?

The claim that sport ought to be approached as a moral practice is likely to be met with skepticism by some. In what follows, I will consider and respond to objections to this claim.

3. The Moralism Objection

A possible objection to the claim that one of the primary purposes of sport ought to be the cultivation of virtue is that such a view is

---

[18] Aristotle, *Nicomachean Ethics* 1129a–1137b.

[19] http://www.righttoplay.com/International/about-us/Pages/mission.aspx; accessed September 13, 2011. The mission of Right to Play is 'To improve the lives of children in some of the most disadvantaged areas of the world by using the power of sport and play for development, health and peace.'

[20] *Nicomachean Ethics*, 1103b.

moralistic. If I am guilty of moralism, then that would be a significant problem for my argument, given that moralism is generally thought of as a vice in which one 'overdoes morality' (though there are several different ways of understanding the details of this trait).[21] One variety of moralism that is relevant to my argument is moralism of scope. This form of moralism 'involves seeing things as moral issues that aren't, and thereby overmoralizing the universe'.[22] The charge against my argument might be that in it, I am guilty of over-moralizing the sporting universe. Sport is primarily about physical and tactical excellence in service of victory, not the cultivation of virtue.

While one person's *illicit moralism* is another person's *moral exhortation*, there are good reasons for thinking that the charge of moralism fails. First, it is clear that victory is not the sole end of sport. The common notion in sport of a hollow victory points to this fact. This fact is also recognized by practitioners at the elite level. For example, in a 1999 Football Association Cup match between Arsenal and Sheffield, a Sheffield player went down with an injury and his goalkeeper intentionally kicked the ball out of bounds.[23] Customarily, Arsenal would put the ball back in play to Sheffield, and the match would resume. In this instance, however, a newly acquired player from Nigeria who was perhaps unaware of this unwritten rule took the throw-in and passed it to a teammate who shot and scored. Members of both teams were upset, and after the game ended with a 2-1 victory for Arsenal, manager Arsène Wenger declined the victory and chose to replay the match, saying 'It wasn't right to win that way'.

Moreover, as I have argued above, certain moral values are embedded within the traditions and structures of sport. There are moral considerations that limit what may legitimately be done in the pursuit of victory. Various forms of cheating, for example, are unjustifiable. Values such as fairness, sportspersonship, and respect for persons are deeply embedded in the traditions of many sports. Nevertheless, in many ways, sport is what we make of it. We can seek to uphold these and other values as we participate in sport, or not. We can abide by these values in our sporting lives, but not in

---

[21] C.A.J. Coady, *What's Wrong with Moralism?* (Malden, MA: Blackwell, 2006), 1.

[22] Ibid., 25.

[23] David Cruise Malloy, Saul Ross, and Dwight Zakus, *Sport Ethics: Concepts and Cases in Sport and Recreation* (Toronto: Thompson Educational Publishing, 2003), 188–189.

Michael W. Austin

the rest of our lives. However, given its potential for the cultivation and display of not only athletic excellence, but moral excellence as well, we ought to take sport to be and engage in it as a moral practice which can contribute to our flourishing in all of life.

4. The Emotivist Cheerleading Objection

In a recent paper, Alan Bäck argues that while many make claims about the moral excellence of sport, such claims are false:

> A lot of the discussion on the goodness of sport amounts to emotivist cheerleading: we like sports and feel that being involved in sports has been a positive influence on our lives; therefore sport is good. Yet philosophers, like academics in general, are supposed to be lovers of truth. I shall suggest that, although such claims for the moral excellence of sport have much popularity, they have little truth...Rather, practicing sport promotes more vices than virtues.[24]

Bäck's proposed solution is the abandonment of sport for one of the traditional martial arts, which he claims provide the moral benefits many wrongly attribute to participation in sport.

While it is true that much of the empirical research in the history and psychology of sport appears to support the claim that sport promotes vice more than virtue, there are reasons to question how much this research shows about the actual impact of sport as well as its potential for character development.[25] For instance, some of the research supports the claim that participation in sport can evoke egocentric reasoning. However, the assumption that moral interaction in the context of sport is reducible to moral judgment ought to be challenged. There is more to morality than the application of universal rules. Character is also important, and sport can contribute to both the improvement and deterioration of character, depending in part on the context in which a particular athlete finds himself. In fact, some of the research supports the view that sport can be employed for the development of character.[26] When the motivational climate emphasizes excellence rather than victory, values such as

[24]   Alan Bäck, 'The *Way* to Virtue in Sport', *Journal of the Philosophy of Sport* **36** (2009), 217.
[25]   Op. cit. note 6, 40–52.
[26]   For example, see David Light Shields and Brenda Light Bredemeier, *True Competition* (Champaign, IL: Human Kinetics, 2009).

respect, sportspersonship, and sound moral reasoning are fostered.[27] There is evidence that elite athletes also prefer a motivational climate where excellence is emphasized over victory.[28] Ultimately, the moral impact of participation in sport, like most other realms of life, is dependent in a variety of ways upon the beliefs, desires, attitudes, intentions, and character of the relevant persons. Sport is a human creation. It is up to us to make of it what we will.

Lastly, the objection that sport in fact does not yield virtue, but rather vice does not count against the argument I am making, which is that great *potential* for the cultivation of virtue exists and ought to be realized. The realization of this potential may require wholesale changes in how many of us approach sport at all levels. Given the prevalence of sport across cultures, I believe we should seek to transform sport if this is necessary for realizing its potential for character development, rather than abandon it. Nothing in the empirical research or in Bäck's case for the superiority of martial arts with respect to the cultivation of virtue necessitates abandoning the thesis that we ought to approach sport as a moral practice. However, there is another point raised by Bäck which constitutes a different sort of objection to my argument, to which we now turn.

5. The Restricted Virtue Objection

Bäck points out that it is common for a person who is excellent at a particular sport not to excel in other spheres of life, including the moral sphere. Perhaps this is due to the artificiality of the sport environment, as any excellence cultivated in an artificial environment may be restricted to that environment.[29] It is clearly the case that there are athletes who appear to have certain virtues in the context of their sport, but in few other contexts. One might conclude that

[27]   See Y. Ommundsen, G.C. Roberts, P.N. Lemyre, and D. Treasure, 'Perceived Motivational Climate in Male Youth Soccer: Relations to Social-Moral Functioning, Sportspersonship, and Team Norm Perceptions', *Psychology of Sport and Exercise* **4** (2003), 397–413; Blake Miller, Glyn Roberts, and Yngvar Ommundsen, 'Effect of Motivational Climate on Sportspersonship among Competitve Youth Male and Female Football Players', *Scandinavian Journal of Medicine and Science in Sports* **14** (2004), 193–202.

[28]   A.M. Pensgaard, and G.C. Roberts, 'Elite Athletes' Experiences of the Motivational Climate: The Coach Matters', *Scandinavian Journal of Medicine and Science in Sports* **12** (2002), 54–59.

[29]   Op. cit. note 24, 221.

in such cases the athlete does not really possess the virtue in question, or at best has only a truncated version of it. How is it that a person can display courage, self-control, and even justice on the field of play, but not off of it? The objection here is that even if sport does foster certain character traits in that limited context, the artificiality of the environment seems to restrict the scope of the virtues that are cultivated.

Given one way of understanding the structure of any particular virtue, it is not surprising that some individuals will display virtue in one context, but not others. In this book, *A Theory of Virtue*, Robert Adams discusses the idea that there are modules of virtue. This means that sometimes an individual's behavioral dispositions may be domain-specific. As Adams puts it, 'a person will often acquire and exercise a disposition to act in a certain way in one domain without being disposed to act similarly in somewhat different domains'.[30] These modules can be combined so as to form a more complete disposition which can be thought of as a virtue.

An athlete may develop a module of self-control in the context of sport, but not possess it in other realms. However, she may begin to see the value of self-control in her life as an athlete, and then come to realize that it is desirable to have this trait in those other realms. She may then set about acquiring the trait of self-control in those domains as well. When this is done successfully, these different modules can be combined and taken together to be a single virtue.

It is plausible to think that the more domains across which one is able to develop modules of any particular virtue, the more likely it will be that one will be able to acquire still more modules of that virtue until it can be said that she has the general virtue itself. We have seen that humility, prudence, courage, self-control, and a form of justice can be developed in the context of sport. This, then, gives us good reason to think that sport can play a role, and for many people a significant role, in the cultivation of an excellent character.

But why does participation in sport often fail to contribute to the formation of excellent human beings as much as we would like, or perhaps even expect? There are a variety of answers to this, but one that is relevant here has to do with intentionality and character formation. Many athletes genuinely intend to achieve a level of excellence in their sport and order their lives accordingly. However, many of them do not carry that same intention into other domains of life where other modules of particular virtues come into play. They

---

[30] Robert Adams, *A Theory of Virtue* (New York: Oxford University Press, 2006), 125.

may seek and display courage on the field or self-control in training, but not in other contexts. They may not be motivated to form and carry out such an intention, or they may simply need to be encouraged to apply the lessons learned in sport to other realms of life. If they do form such an intention, including both a specific goal and a means for implementing it, then the chances for success are significant.[31]

With this in mind, athletes, coaches, parents, and others involved in sport need to seek to foster moral growth by explicitly encouraging the formation of such intentions outside of the context of sport. As Aristotle would argue, athletes need moral exemplars to imitate. But they also need these exemplars to be experienced practitioners who from the beginning of their athletic careers initiate them into the forms of athletic and moral excellence present in their sport.[32]

Sometimes, an athlete may simply need to be challenged to pursue a vision of human excellence that has a wider scope than his sport. For example, consider a story Thomas Morris tells about his days as a philosophy professor at the University of Notre Dame.[33] One semester Morris walked into an auditorium of three hundred first year students taking an introductory philosophy course. Surveying the class, he was struck by the number of large bodies in the lecture hall, and after investigating Morris discovered that there were fifty-five varsity athletes in the course, five times more than the usual. The department that advises athletes encourages them to take classes from professors who have won teaching awards as a way to encourage their academic interest, and Morris had recently won such an award. Twenty-nine of those students were freshman American football players, and twenty-six of them failed the first exam. Because of this, Professor Morris held a meeting with these students, saying

> To play a game as complex as football at the level at which you play it takes a great amount of natural intelligence....You've mastered a tremendous complexity of subtle skills. That shows me you're not only intelligent, you're teachable. These three qualities – intelligence, teachability, and self-discipline – are transferable qualities. They can be applied in any endeavor. They are all you need to do well in the classroom. I am confident that you will

---

[31]   For empirical evidence in support of this claim, see Peter Gollwitzer, 'Implementation Intentions: Strong Effects of Simple Plans', *American Psychologist* **54** (1999), 493–503.

[32]   Op. cit. note 6, 49–50.

[33]   Thomas V. Morris, *Making Sense of it All* (Grand Rapids, MI: Eerdmans, 1992), 40–41.

not fail in philosophy. I am confident that you will use these important qualities to succeed at this task just as you have succeeded at others before.[34]

And according to Morris, they did. This anecdote reveals an important truth about sport and moral development. The virtues (what Morris calls qualities) are transferable from one context to another. In this case, the relevant moral and intellectual virtues which these athletes had developed in the context of their sport were successfully transferred to the context of university studies. But this only occurred after they were explicitly encouraged to intentionally apply the modules of teachability and self-discipline which they had developed as athletes to their academic pursuits. An emphasis on the transfer of virtues developed in the context of sport to other contexts should become a deeper part of the culture of sport.

6. Practical Implications

Whether or not sport builds character is in large measure up to those of us who in some capacity love sport. Approaching sport as a moral practice carries numerous practical implications. Here, I will briefly note four.

One of the most important implications of the foregoing, given an Aristotelian approach to ethics and recent work in sport psychology, is that coaches ought to see themselves as and seek to be (at least) good role models, and ideally moral exemplars.[35] This is especially important for coaches at the youth level, given the importance of childhood with respect to moral development. In the *Nicomachean Ethics*, Aristotle claims that childhood is very important with respect to the formation of habits and the development of character, for better or worse.[36] In addition to this, Aristotle argues that we need capable individuals to serve as moral exemplars as we seek to become virtuous. Coaches are well-situated to fulfill this role.

[34] Ibid., 41.
[35] McNamee also makes this point, op. cit. note 2, 80. On the potential impact of coaches, see Brenda Light Bredemeier and David Light Shields, 'Sport and the Development of Character', *Handbook of Research in Applied Sport and Exercise Psychology: International Perspectives*, (eds) Dieter Hackfort, Joan Duda, and Ronnie Lidor (Morgantown, WV: Fitness Information Technology, 2005), 277–294.
[36] Aristotle, *Nicomachean Ethics*, Bk. II.

A second implication is that coaches, athletes, parents, and fans should seek and celebrate excellence in the pursuit of victory, not merely victory in isolation from other goods. Winning matters, as it is generally the best way to determine athletic excellence. But it is not all that matters. Winning should be pursued within the limits of morality. We should not take winning to be the sole criterion for athletic excellence, given the role of such factors as luck and mistakes by officials in determining the outcome of some contests.

Third, athletes must take responsibility for their beliefs about morality and sport as well as their character in the context of sport and the rest of life. If they take sport to be a moral practice, if they are fortunate enough to have moral exemplars to imitate, and if they are intentional about character development via their sport and transferring the lessons and habits acquired to other realms of life, then their involvement in sport will be conducive to their flourishing as human beings.

Finally, consider the following words contained in the Olympic Creed:

> The most important thing in the Olympic Games is not to win but to take part, just as the most important thing in life is not the triumph but the struggle. The essential thing is not to have conquered, but to have fought well.[37]

When we approach sport as a moral practice, we struggle for athletic excellence and victory, but we fit this struggle into a larger and more important human struggle, the struggle for moral excellence.[38]

Eastern Kentucky University
mike.austin@eku.edu

---

[37] http://www.la84foundation.org/6oic/OlympicCurriculum/social-studies5.pdf; accessed 20 October 2011.
[38] I would like to express my appreciation to Heather Reid for helpful comments on an earlier version of this paper.

A Plea for Risk

PHILIP A. EBERT AND SIMON ROBERTSON

Mountaineering is a dangerous activity. For many mountaineers, part of its very attraction is the risk, the thrill of danger. Yet mountaineers are often regarded as reckless or even irresponsible for risking their lives. In this paper, we offer a defence of risk-taking in mountaineering. Our discussion is organised around the fact that mountaineers and non-mountaineers often disagree about how risky mountaineering really is. We hope to cast some light on the nature of this disagreement – and to argue that mountaineering may actually be worthwhile *because of* the risks it involves. Section 1 introduces the disagreement and, in doing so, separates out several different notions of risk. Sections 2–4 then consider some explanations of the disagreement, showing how a variety of phenomena can skew people's risk judgements. Section 5 then surveys some recent statistics, to see whether these illuminate how risky mountaineering is. In light of these considerations, however, we suggest that the disagreement is best framed not simply in terms of *how risky* mountaineering is but whether the risks it does involve are *justified*. The remainder of the paper, sections 6–9, argues that risk-taking in mountaineering often *is* justified – and, moreover, that mountaineering can itself be justified (in part) *by* and *because of* the risks it involves.

1. Disagreement about risk

It is common for mountaineers to find themselves in disagreement with non-mountaineers about the degree and nature of risk involved in mountaineering. On the one hand, many non-mountaineers have a certain image of a mountaineer in mind, one often 'informed' by stereotypes of a risk-seeking climber. On the other hand, while mountaineers usually acknowledge that there are risks, they tend to regard these as 'acceptable' and suggest that non-mountaineers often overestimate them. After all, they urge that competence and experience reduce the risks – and the remaining risks are worth taking: it is such things as the spirit of adventure, the beauty of remote places, the aesthetic of movement, and the comradeship of

doi:10.1017/S1358246113000271   ©The Royal Institute of Philosophy and the contributors 2013

Royal Institute of Philosophy Supplement **73** 2013

Philip A. Ebert & Simon Robertson

the rope, say, that not only motivate their risk-taking but also make the risks worth it.[1]

Let us dwell on this disagreement a bit. There are two common ways to resolve a disagreement. One is to show that (at least) one party is mistaken. The other is to *dissolve* the disagreement by showing that the different parties are not actually disagreeing; in the present context, for instance, one could demonstrate that they are actually employing different notions of 'risk' and are therefore talking past one another. We will discuss the second option first.

It is common to distinguish different aspects of risk. One aspect concerns the *likelihood* that a certain event occurs. There is also a *loss* aspect: an event is risky if its occurrence would bring a significant loss. Most often, risk is viewed as a combination of these: something's being risky depends on both the likelihood of its occurring *and* the seriousness of the loss were it to occur. Lastly, there is also a more *psychologistic* notion of risk: risk is often associated with feeling out of control. People don't always clearly distinguish these different aspects.[2] Thus, there could be occasions when disagreements between mountaineers and non-mountaineers are explained by the fact that they are deploying different notions of risk and hence are talking past each other. However, we doubt that all such disagreements can be explained away like that. When they cannot be so explained, further work is required to resolve the disagreement.

In the following, we treat *risk* as a combination of the likelihood of an accident occurring and the significance of the resulting loss. Then, it seems, the disagreement about risk in mountaineering will be due to conflicting judgements about at least one of these two ingredients. Before turning to the likelihood aspect, we'll briefly consider the loss component.

One possible thought here is that many mountaineers may actually judge the prospect of injury (or even death) more acceptable than

[1]   In *Motivations for Mountain Climbing: The Role of Risk* (University of Sussex, U.K., PhD-Thesis, 2011), Nina Lockwood shows via a number studies that although risk is one important part of a mountaineers' motivation, risk *per se* is not the key motivating factor. See also E. Brymer, *Extreme Dude: A Phenomenological Perspective on the Extreme Sports Experience* (University of Wollongong, Australia., PhD-Thesis 2005), which highlights various 'spiritual' elements informing the motivations of many mountaineers.

[2]   For a useful survey of different notions of risk and risk perception, see Wibecke Brun, 'Risk Perception: Main Issues, Approaches and Findings', in G. Wright and P. Ayton (eds), *Subjective Probability* (Chichester: John Wiley and Sons, 1994): 395–420.

many non-mountaineers do. For one thing, mountaineers may hear about climbing-related injuries and simply come to regard these as 'part of the game' they love. Importantly, though, they also hear of fellow climbers recovering from serious injuries and returning to the sport. This may in turn 'desensitise' mountaineers in ways that make commonplace losses appear less serious. Thus, the thought goes, conflicting risk verdicts might sometimes be explained by differing views about *how bad* bad outcomes actually are. However, we think that there are also likely to be other, more relevant explanations for the disagreement. We'll now turn to the likelihood aspect.

2. Heuristics and biases when judging mountaineering risks

Given that relatively few people (mountaineers or not) actually study statistics about the relation between mountaineering and risk, when making judgements about those risks it seems that we naturally rely on certain 'heuristics': useful shortcuts that help us reach conclusions efficiently, including (for our purposes) conclusions about the likelihood of an event occurring. Although these shortcuts may yield adequate judgements in many cases, they can sometimes result in inaccurate judgements or biases.

Psychologists have identified a number of such heuristics. The first we'll look at is the so-called *availability heuristic*.[3] The idea, roughly, is that when people face difficult questions about the frequency of a category – numbers of dangerous plants, divorces among couples over 60, or, more relevantly, deaths while mountaineering – people often think of relevant instances of this category by retrieving them from memory. In cases where the retrieval is easy and straightforward, people tend to think the category has many such instances. In cases where instances aren't so easily obtained, people tend to think there will be fewer instances. However, the easiness of recalling such instances might not always be a very good guide to judging frequencies. In the present context, given that mountaineering disasters make for good newspaper headlines and are often widely publicised (even made into movies), it becomes fairly easy to recall instances

---

[3]   First introduced in Daniel Kahneman & Amos Tversky, 'Judgement under Uncertainty: Heuristics and Biases', *Science* **185** (1974), 1124–31. Kahneman's excellent *Thinking, Fast and Slow* (London: Penguin Books, 2011) discusses many other heuristics and biases; see also C.F. Chabris & D.J. Simons, *The Invisible Gorilla: How Our Intuitions Deceive Us* (New York: Broadway Publishers, 2011).

that exhibit the dangers of mountaineering. And since non-mountaineers can readily retrieve such disasters from memory, this might lead them to overestimate the risks in mountaineering. This is not to say that they definitely do overestimate the risk (we will look at some statistics later) but rather a warning that the intuitive mechanism people use to judge those risks might be less reliable than they realise.

Another relevant factor is *imaginability*. In their original article, Kahneman and Tversky mention the following case:

> Imaginability plays an important role in the evaluation of probabilities in real-life situations. The risk involved in an adventurous expedition, for example, is evaluated by imagining contingencies with which the expedition is not equipped to cope. If many such difficulties are vividly portrayed, the expedition can be made to appear exceedingly dangerous, although the ease with which disasters are imagined need not reflect their actual likelihood.[4]

Such considerations could help explain why people tend to overestimate the likelihood of accidents in mountaineering, though they will not explain why mountaineers and non-mountaineers differ in their judgements. However, a further heuristic, the so-called *affect heuristic,* expands on the imaginability idea and may help to explain this disagreement. According to the affect heuristic, it is not only the ease with which climbing disasters come to mind that affects our risk judgement, but also our emotional reactions to those disasters. Death in mountaineering conjures up frightening images of long falls leading to horrid injuries, or of long and painful suffering before dying. In short, to die in mountaineering is to die a gruesome and often lonely death; and such thoughts can exacerbate fear. The *affect heuristic* describes how our risk judgements are influenced by such emotional reactions. We here have a case where the difficult question about the actual risk in mountaineering is substituted by the easier question of how one feels about the activity (especially in light of the bad outcomes one might conjure up). What the affect heuristic implies is that the disagreement with respect to mountaineering risks might not merely be a disagreement about the presumed likelihood of a bad outcome but that it also involves an important emotional dimension. Non-mountaineers, who have no positive emotional attachment to the activity and who might recall only emotionally distressing outcomes, are likely to judge the risks higher

---

[4]   Kahneman & Tversky, op. cit. note 3, 1128.

than mountaineers.[5] Hence, the affect heuristic may explain why mountaineers and non-mountaineers differ when judging the risks.

3. Media bias and risk

In addition to the above heuristics, there are further elements that may help explain the disagreement. There is, in particular, an important element of media bias. Due to widespread media-coverage, many non-mountaineers are aware of numerous mountaineering fatalities. To name but a few: Mallory's ill-fated 1924 Everest expedition; the 1996 disaster on Everest when eight mountaineers died; and the 2012 tragedies on both Everest and Mont Blanc (four mountaineers died on Everest, nine from a single avalanche on Mont Blanc). It is fair to say that most mountaineering related news a non-mountaineer receives concerns the dangers it involves. Yet comparatively few mountaineering successes (or even *great* achievements) are mentioned in national media. For example, the *Piolet d'Or* – the most prestigious award for outstanding mountaineering achievement, given on a yearly basis – hasn't been covered by the BBC news website.[6] Typically, we only hear about successful mountaineering endeavours when a new 'record' is set (the youngest or oldest or fastest alpinist to ascend a well-known peak, say) or when the first 3G phone-call is made from Everest's summit. Mountaineers, though, are more likely to hear about a wide range of impressive achievements (through specific climbing media, friends, and so on).[7] Given another feature of our cognitive life, namely that humans have a tendency to regard the evidence they have as all the evidence there is,[8] this media-bias may explain why non-mountaineers judge the activity very risky.

In addition, as Nick Colton[9] nicely observes, there is a further side to mountaineering that rarely makes it into current media and that many non-mountaineers are unaware of. Colton distinguishes two 'models' of a mountaineer. There is a *conqueror-model*, on which mountaineers are goal-oriented conquerors – very much the type of figure that might make it into the news and sustain common stereotypes. But there is

---

[5] See Kahneman op. cit. note 3, chs.12 & 13.

[6] At least it returns no search results on their website.

[7] Granted, as mountaineers we also hear more about talented mountaineers who die but who don't make it into mainstream news.

[8] Labelled by Kahneman (op. cit. note 3) the '*what you see is all there is*' (WYSIATI) principle.

[9] Nick Colton, 'Conquerors or Connoisseurs?' *On the Edge* **115** (2005), 64–65.

also a *connoisseur-model*. Here, the mountaineer is less goal-oriented and is not climbing at the limit of her ability; she instead climbs less risky routes and is motivated largely by aesthetic considerations (of movement, or beautiful surroundings, say). While non-mountaineers often know little about the *connoisseur-model*, most mountaineers move from one model to the other and thus have a more informed, indeed balanced view of their activity. As a result, mountaineers are likely to judge mountaineering *as a whole* less risky than someone who is exposed only to popular media conceptions of it.

4. Risk, uncertainty, competence

The final aspect we'll consider when it comes to explaining disagreements about the degree of risk concerns mountaineers' *competence*. By climbing regularly, mountaineers become more 'in tune' with the risks involved, developing the skills to identify, assess and manage them. When a non-mountaineer looks at a rock face and thinks it crazy for anyone to climb, a competent climber might see an established and well-protected route on immaculate rock and rightly judge it not very risky. What for a non-mountaineer will seem an unquantifiable uncertainty, and hence be judged too risky, may to a mountaineer's eye present a more specifiable and indeed lower risk. Hence, competence plays an important role in making informed judgements about mountaineering dangers.[10]

So far we have offered different ways to explain how the disagreement about risk in mountaineering can arise. These explanations combine nicely to offer a multifaceted picture of the possible sources of disagreement. However, we haven't settled yet who is correct in their risk judgement. It is now time to have a look at some recent statistics and to discuss how they might help adjudicate whether non-mountaineers overestimate the risks or whether mountaineers underestimate them.

5. Accident statistics

Statistics available from European Alpine Clubs usually only provide the number of accidents (including deaths) that occur in mountains. To properly evaluate the risks involved, however, this isn't enough.

---

[10] We return to the role of competence in section 8.

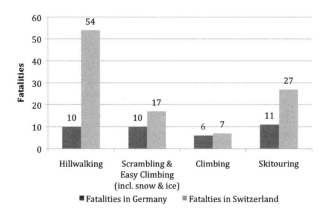

Table 1.

To see why, let us look at the fatalities involved in the following activities in Germany and Switzerland in 2010:[11]

What is surprising is that hillwalking results in more fatal accidents in Switzerland than the other activities listed here combined (in that year)! However, the total number of accidents is not a good indication for how dangerous the activity is, unless we have some indication of how many people are engaged in it. Even then, there are further difficulties. We cannot straightforwardly use the population of Swiss hillwalkers as a base class, since many people who hillwalk in Switzerland come from other countries. Moreover, finding out how many people go hillwalking in Switzerland is not enough: some may go hillwalking every week, others once a month, and so on. So, to more accurately quantify the dangers across these activities we would need to know how many fatal accidents occur per day (or even hour) spent doing them.[12] Unfortunately, there are very few

---

[11] The data is drawn from official accident statistics issued by the German and the Swiss Alpine Clubs, available on their respective websites. We here focus on fatality rate, though similar considerations apply to injury rate and severity.

[12] Most statistics do not use exposure time but rather go by mountaineer, climb or summiteer (the latter two thereby excluding those who turned back without summiting because of the risks involved). This makes a comparison to other activities difficult; see: http://www.medicine.ox.ac.uk/bandolier/booth/risk/sports.html. We here make the simplifying assumption that the dangers are quantified by fatality rate only. Ideally, we would also need to know the injury rate and seriousness of those injuries. There is, however, little information available on this. See also fn 21.

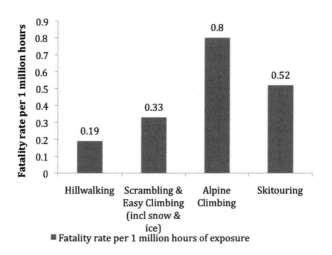

Fatality rate per 1 million hours of exposure

Table 2.

such statistics. Nonetheless, the following was published by the German Alpine Club:[13]

It is important to note that, although Table 1 suggests that hillwalking (in Switzerland) has surprisingly many deaths in comparison to the other activities listed, when normalised to *hours spent* (as in Table 2) alpine climbing has a considerably higher fatality rate (amongst members of the German Alpine Club). Now there may be a temptation, when assessing the risks of the activities listed under Table 2, to compare these with the fatality rates (per hours of exposure) for other (non-mountainous) activities. And doing so may appear to deliver some surprising results: cycling (~0.46)[14], motorcycling (~3.42–8,5)[15], competitive marathon running (~1.5)[16], swimming in

---

[13]   Peter Randelzhofer, 'Wie riskant is Bergsport?', *Panorama* **2** (2010) 68–70 (not a peer-reviewed journal). The statistics are based on accidents by members of the German Alpine Club (800,000 members), with the exposure time calculated on the basis of 7,900 returned questionnaires.

[14]   Based on transport statistics for Great Britain 1979–89, accessed from http://ec.europa.eu/transport/road_safety/specialist/knowledge/ped-estrians/crash_characteristics_where_and_how/data_considerations.htm

[15]   Based on the transport statistics for Great Britain 1979–89 (lower number) and the National Highway Traffic Safety Administration USA (http://www-nrd.nhtsa.dot.gov/Pubs/811639.pdf) for 2010 using the average speed of 35mph to calculate exposure time.

[16]   Calculated on the basis of Simon Matthews, 'Mortality Among Marathon Runners in the United States, 2000–2009', *Am J Sports Med*

New South Wales (Australia) (2.5)[17]. This certainly looks surprising: alpine climbing and mountaineering aren't as dangerous as these other (supposedly more mundane) activities! However, much care has to be taken before reading too much into such comparisons. Here are some reasons why: Firstly, the statistic is based on members of the German Alpine Club, who have easy access to affordable outdoor education and training. So we may assume that the sample is biased towards more informed, better trained mountaineers.[18] Secondly, the statistic is based on German Alpine Club members, who, we may assume, pursue their activities mainly in and around Germany; yet most of the higher and more dangerous alpine ranges lie outside Germany. So, we surmise, the above statistic may underestimate the risks of mountaineering in general and might not yet provide a solid basis for comparison with non-mountaineering activities.

Furthermore, it would be wrong to conclude from this that mountaineering isn't dangerous. For one thing, there are 'many games climbers play':[19] high-altitude climbing, fast and light alpine climbing, big wall climbing, ice climbing, ski-mountaineering, sport climbing, soloing, and more. And there are different *ways* to play these games – as connoisseurs or conquerors, for instance. These different games and ways to play them have very different associated risks. On the one hand, for instance, the fatality rate for climbing Denali (6196m) is roughly 6.3 fatalities per 1 million hours exposure time;[20] and the results for some other high-altitude routes will likely

---

40 (2012), 1495–500. Note that this is based on competitive races, rather than training (which is usually associated with lower fatality risk).

[17] Damian Morgan, 'Estimates of Drowning Morbidity and Mortality Adjusted for Exposure to Risk', *Injury Prevention*, **17** (2011), 359–359. For a much higher number, see R.J. Mitchell, A.M. Williamson & J. Olivier, 'Estimates of Drowning Morbidity and Mortality Adjusted for Exposure to Risk', *Injury Prevention*, **16** (2010), 261–266.

[18] Many accidents are likely due to incompetence and lack of experience; and so this selection bias could make for a lower than average fatality rate.

[19] See Lito Tejada-Flores, 'Games Climbers Play', in *The Games Climbers Play* (London: Diadem Book, 1978).

[20] Based on S.E. McIntosh, A.D. Campbell, J. Dow, et al., 'Mountaineering Fatalities on Denali', *High Alt Med Biol* **9** (2008): 89–95. It is worth noting that the fatality rate at Denali is slowly decreasing. However, other statistics suggest that the high-altitude game is very dangerous; see J.S. Windsor, P.G. Firth, M.P. Grocott, G.W. Rodway, & H.E. Montgomery, 'Mountain Mortality: A Review of Deaths that Occur

be even worse. Yet on the other hand, other climbing activities – like sports climbing and indoor climbing, which often involve quite long falls – have a low risk of injury and death.[21] So, what can we take from this and how can it inform the above disagreement?

While the German study may suggest that mountaineering considered as a general activity (encompassing all different sub-disciplines, including alpine climbing and skitouring) are not as high-risk as often thought, there is no denying that some specific mountaineering games are (statistically speaking) very dangerous.[22]

During Recreational Activities in the Mountains', *Postgraduate Medical Journal*, **85** (2009), 316–321.

[21] L.C. Schussmann, L.J. Lutz, R.R. Shaw, et al., 'The Epidemiology of Mountaineering and Rock Climbing Accidents', *Wilderness Environ Med* **1** (1990), 235–48, suggests that rock climbing has a lower injury risk than football or horse riding. A. Neuhof, F. F. Hennig, I. Schöffl, & V. Schöffl, 'Injury Risk Evaluation in Sport Climbing', *International Journal of Sports Medicine* **32** (2011), 794–800 and V. Schöffl, A. Morrison, U. Schwarz, I. Schoffl, & T. Küpper, 'Evaluation of Injury and Fatality Risk in Rock and Ice Climbing', *Sports Medicine* **40** (2010), 657–679, comes to a similar conclusion: sport climbing and indoor climbing have a lower injury rate than activities like rugby, football (soccer) and basketball.

[22] So, for example, in a recent movie Steve House, a professional high-altitude mountaineer who pioneered light and fast alpine approaches in greater mountain ranges, noted that he has shared his rope with 19 climbers who have since died (https://vimeo.com/40379197). Similarly, Will Gadd, a leading ice climber, writes: 'I often hear friends make statistically insane comments such as, "You can die on the way to the mountains just as easily as you can die in the mountains". That statement, for the record, is a stinking pile of self-delusional excrement that does not smell any less foul with repeated exposure', noting that 27 of his friends have so far died in the mountains (http://explore-mag.com/2831/adventure/the-grand-delusion). Gadd is right that certain mountaineering sub-disciplines are extremely risky; and, given that he is a leading exponent in several of these sub-disciplines, he will be exposed to many more fatalities than the average mountaineer. Note, however, that this is compatible with our main claim: that certain forms of climbing are extremely dangerous while, on the whole, the general activity (encompassing all age groups and many different forms of mountaineering) is not. As well as these theoretical concerns, there is a practical reason not to infer from general statistics too much about a particular situation when more pertinent information is available: just as there is little comfort in reminding yourself that shark attacks are very unlikely when you are swimming in the open sea surrounded by a great white, there is little point in reminding yourself of the climbing stats when you're totally pumped facing a potential ground fall.

Could this observation be used to explain the disagreement between mountaineers and non-mountaineers?

Maybe there is a story that can be told here that would dissolve the disagreement: perhaps mountaineers are correct with respect to the overall activity, whereas non-mountaineers are correct with respect to some quite specific mountaineering games. Hence, they are not really disagreeing because they are making judgements about different things. But even so, there may be a way for non-mountaineers to maintain that mountaineering as a general activity is too risky, even assuming that accident rates are fairly low. The thought is this: Whether mountaineering is too risky doesn't depend merely on the fatality or injury rate, but is rather a matter of whether the kinds of risks mountaineers willingly take on are *justified*. Hence, the judgment that mountaineering is 'too risky' is best explained as a *normative* judgement (*justification* being a normative notion). This, we suspect, may be what really underlies the disagreement.[23]

To motivate this concern consider, by way of contrast, the case of marathon running: here most fatalities are caused by cardiac arrest, due most likely to an underlying genetic disposition. Such deaths are not foreseeable or 'to be expected'; and a competent runner wouldn't ordinarily be to blame for putting herself at such a risk.[24] Yet, so the charge might go, mountaineers knowingly put themselves into a risky situation: there is always the possibility of a minor slip, a little stumble that 'so easily happens' (yet, statistically speaking, rarely does) but that can kill you. There are also objective dangers when crossing glaciers, traversing underneath seracs, or climbing a rock face. Of course, these can be minimised by experience, competence, good equipment, paying attention to reliable weather forecasts, and so on. Nonetheless, there are always residual risks and taking these on is, to put it crudely, no different than taking part in a lottery – in which most people 'get away with it' but those who don't lose their lives on a gamble. Of course, such tragedies rarely happen, and the risk might be minimal in many cases (even though

---

[23] Indeed, one can easily imagine a situation in which a mountaineer and non-mountaineer are equally informed and sensitive to both the distorting effects of the heuristics, media bias, etc., considered in sections 2–4 and the available statistical data – yet still disagree over whether mountaineering is 'too' risky. Here, it looks plausible to say that, their disagreement is really a normative one.

[24] Fatalities in hillwalking are also often due to cardiac arrest (roughly 50% according to the German accident statistic; it is dramatically less in the case of alpine climbing).

they are easily imagined and there are many stories involving 'close-calls'). Still, perhaps, we should *expect* them to happen. Given this, taking on the risks in mountaineering isn't justified; and a climber is ultimately reckless for risking her life on a gamble.

6. Risky, Despite and Because: three claims about risk and justification

The suggestion, then, is that the disagreement between mountaineers and (informed) non-mountaineers may not be simply about *how* risky mountaineering is, but whether the risks it does involve are *justified*. Assuming so, let's characterise the objection to mountaineering as follows:

> **[Risky]** Mountaineering is not a justifiable activity; and that is because of the risks it involves.

In the rest of the paper, we takes issue with [Risky] and argue that mountaineering can be (i.e. sometimes is) justified. If our arguments are plausible, this will help resolve the disagreement about mountaineering risks in favour of mountaineers.

Now one way to oppose [Risky] is to claim that mountaineering is justified *despite* the risks it involves, since the disvalue of those risks is counterbalanced by various other goods mountaineering offers. We'll call this '[Despite]':

> **[Despite]** Mountaineering endeavours can be justified; when they are justified, they are justified (a) *despite* the risks they involve, and (b) by the further goods (distinct from risk) they bring (not by the risks themselves).

[Despite] appears to have become something of an orthodoxy in the few academic discussions on this topic.[25] However, we think that

---

[25]   There are various versions of [Despite]. According to some, mountaineering is justified because it cultivates virtues of character (like courage, self-resilience, discipline, humility, even compassion) which in turn makes us better people. See for example the essays by Charlton, Treanor and Sailors in S.E. Schmidt (ed.), *Climbing: Because It's There* (Oxford: Wiley-Blackwell, 2010) – and, for criticism, Dudley Knowles, 'Review of *Climbing: Because It's There*', *Philosophical Quarterly* **61** (2001), 887–90. For a rather different approach, which we consider below, see Kevin Krein, 'Nature and Risk in Adventure Sports', in M. McNamee (ed.), *Philosophy, Risk and Adventure Sports* (Oxon: Routledge, 2007).

[Despite], even though it gets to the (correct) conclusion that mountaineering is justifiable, gives the wrong explanation for this. In what follows, we'll therefore challenge orthodoxy by arguing that risk is one of the things that actually *gives* mountaineering its value, whereby mountaineering has the value it does in part *because of* the risks it involves. We'll argue for this in Sections 7 and 8. Section 9 then uses this to get to the following conclusion:

> **[Because]**: Mountaineering endeavours can be justified – (in part) *because* of the value that engaging with mountaineering risks has.[26]

Our arguments for [Because], if defensible, will in turn undermine [Risky]. In defending [Because], our claim is that it is partly in virtue of the *residual* risks associated with the possibility of injury or death – due to falling, getting lost on a big face, or failing to overcome the physical challenges – that mountaineering is valuable and sometimes justified.

7. The role of risk

We'll begin our case by noting four assumptions. First, mountaineering does involve some risk. Second, mountaineers know this, yet knowingly and intentionally put themselves into risk situations by mountaineering. Nonetheless, and third, they typically put themselves into situations in which they believe the risks are 'acceptable' – situations in which they believe they can (and will) reduce or otherwise control the risk to (what they judge is) an 'acceptable level'.[27] Fourth, good mountaineers are generally competent at assessing the risks of the climbs they undertake. These points are important. They allow us to say that, although mountaineers intentionally put themselves into risk situations, insofar as they are competent at judging whether the risks are acceptable they need not be the foolhardy risk-seekers commonly portrayed by popular media.

To help motivate our views about the value of risk, we'll contrast them to a line of thought recently pushed by a proponent of [Despite]. Kevin Krein argues that mountaineering can be worth

---

[26]   Although [Despite] seems the orthodoxy within academic circles, in our discussions with mountaineers something more like [Because] is commonly accepted.

[27]   This is a repeated theme throughout mountaineering literature. See also the interviews in N. O'Connell, *Beyond Risk: Conversations with Climbers* (London: Diadem Books, 1995).

doing, despite the risks, given the value of various other goods it realizes.[28] Such goods include, on the one hand, interacting with nature, the opportunity to challenge oneself, freedom from certain rule-governed aspects of social life,[29] and, on the other hand, certain 'experiential goods' like pleasure and exhilaration, and attending senses of personal fulfilment.[30] Realizing such goods may require taking certain risks. Nonetheless, Krein believes, risk-taking is only a *means* to these other (independently specifiable) goods and has no real value aside from that. Hence we get a version of [Despite]: the value of mountaineering consists in a range of goods that are distinct from (specifiable independently of) risk and that do not depend for their value on risk itself having any (non-instrumental) value.

Now we agree that mountaineering can be valuable in virtue of the various goods Krein recognises. However, we doubt that the experiential goods he mentions, when they come from mountaineering, can be so easily separated from the risks involved in mountaineering. To see why, it will be useful to outline a central part of Krein's argument for [Despite]. Krein supposes that what motivates mountaineers to climb gives a good indication of what is valuable about mountaineering. Mountaineers are often motivated by experiential goods like exhilaration. However, he believes, it is not the risk as such that motivates, because there are much easier ways to get the kinds of experiences to which risk-taking in mountaineering gives rise.[31] And thus, since one could get these experiential goods without mountaineering, the value of mountaineering must lie in something other than the risks it involves – for instance, the experiential goods it brings. Hence we get to a version of [Despite].

However, we think it highly questionable whether mountaineers could experience sufficiently similar *kinds* of exhilaration and fulfilment in ways other than mountaineering. For the *kinds* of exhilarating and fulfilment mountaineers get from (facing and overcoming the residual risks involved in) mountaineering are typically quite *specific* to *mountaineering*: surmounting technically difficult, exposed, or unprotected climbs; being isolated or committed on a big mountain face; the experience of prolonged physical adversity; and so on.

---

[28]   Krein, op. cit. note 25. Krein's arguments are more nuanced than we can do justice to here; we examine them in greater detail in 'Mountaineering and the Value of Risk' (unpublished manuscript).

[29]   Op. cit. note 25, 87–91.

[30]   Op. cit. note 25, 82–3.

[31]   Op. cit. note 25, 84. Krein mentions driving fast and Russian roulette.

Take all these elements away and whatever experiences of exhilaration or fulfilment one might get will be *qualitatively* rather different from the experience of risk *in a mountaineering situation*. So, sure, you can get exhilaration from many activities besides mountaineering. But the *kind* of exhilaration and fulfilment involved in mountaineering is very different from that generated by these other activities – and cannot be replicated by them.[32]

Nevertheless, we can learn from Krein's argument. One of the things we think problematic about it is its underlying assumption that the risks involved in mountaineering are merely *means* to other, independently specifiable goods – but somewhat unfortunate or undesirable means, whereby mountaineers would eliminate the risks more or less entirely if only they could.[33] We've implicitly been suggesting an alternative view: risk-taking is *constitutively* bound up with mountaineering – with both the very activity and the experiential goods like exhilaration it brings. More precisely, risk is not just a *means* to these other goods but a constitutive and ineliminable *part* of them; the character of these goods, when realized through mountaineering, is shaped by the risks which can bring them about and that are quite specific to mountaineering. Crucially, then, insofar as mountaineers cannot experience the same kind of exhilaration (say) from other activities, a constitutive ingredient in these forms of exhilaration and fulfilment is the fact that they involve overcoming the risks involved in mountaineering. These 'constitutive' theses will be central to our positive account of the value of risk, to which we now turn.

8. The value of risk

We've so far talked rather loosely about the 'value of (engaging with) risk'. This section clarifies what we mean: first by clarifying what is involved in *engaging* with risk, second by outlining what it is *about* engaging with risk that has value, third by explaining what *kind* of value

---

[32] Some mountaineers are drawn to these other activities. However, they often say that they do them for a different (sometimes a comparatively safe) kind of exhilaration. Moreover, they often report, they don't find these other activities as fulfilling. For a particularly poignant example, see Lionel Terray, *Conquistadors of the Useless* (London: Bâton-Wicks, 2008), 296–8 – where Terray records how his friend Louis Lachenal, no longer able to climb seriously given the frostbite he incurred on the first ascent of Annapurna, unsuccessfully sought a surrogate by driving dangerously.

[33] Krein, op. cit. note 25, 83, 86, 88.

this is. We'll then be in a position to state our thesis that risk is one of the things that gives mountaineering its value and makes it justified.

First, then, risk is something mountaineers 'engage with'; and it is this engagement that we'll argue can contribute to the value mountaineering has. But what do we mean by 'engaging with risk'? One thing it involves is *taking* a risk. However, risk-taking can go very wrong. For that reason, we are *not* committing to the claim that risk-taking is *always* or in *all* circumstances valuable or justified. Rather, the value of engaging with risk comes from both *taking and overcoming* risk. However, that's not quite adequate either: someone might by sheer luck overcome a risk that it is exceptionally reckless to take. The central case in which engaging with mountaineering risks has value, we therefore suggest, is when the risk is *taken and overcome competently*. There are several things such competence involves; we'll mention two. First, the risk-taker must be warranted in believing, given the evidence available to her, that the risk is not unacceptable (where that evidence includes evidence about both the intended route and her own abilities) – i.e. is something she has the skill to overcome.[34] Second, the process of taking and overcoming the risk must be executed with a sufficient degree of mountaineering skill. For short we'll call this 'competent risk-engagement'. Risk-taking is of course an essential component of competent risk-engagement. And, we want to say, risk-taking itself can have value. Its value, however, typically depends on the risks being overcome competently.

Second, if risk-taking in mountaineering has value that is because of the role it plays in relation to various other features of mountaineering which themselves have value. What features do we have in mind?

On the one hand, they include quite general goods to which mountaineering gives expression – goods commonly associated with impressive and admirable human achievements: adventure and exploration, overcoming challenges few are capable of meeting, the telling of incredible skill and determination, and so on.

On the other hand, risk-taking is good in relation to the value of (what we'll continue to label, subject to some provisos to follow) certain 'experiential' goods. Two are particularly notable. One is that risk-taking can make one 'feel alive' and 'in the zone'. This may take multifarious forms. It can involve a supercharged adrenaline rush; but it can also have a more serene, meditative and

---

[34]   One might be warranted in believing that *p*, even though not-*p*; so 'warrant' here is not factive. For a fuller account, see Simon Robertson, 'Epistemic Constraints on Practical Normativity', *Synthese* **181** Supp.1 (2011): 81–106.

sublime exhilarative quality. In either case, the experience often involves a heightened focus upon and appreciation of both yourself and your surroundings, in which salient features of your situation take on an intensified quality – yet a kind of 'wholeness' in which you are not only vividly aware of both yourself and your surroundings, but feel 'at one' with all around you. These quite intense experiences of utter exhilaration often extend long after the real danger is over and can give rise to a sense of personal fulfilment.[35] A second value – one that particularly to attends overcoming mountaineering risks *competently* – concerns the ways mountaineers experience themselves as agents. Again this has numerous dimensions. It can involve quite simply experiencing yourself as an *effective agent*: in general terms, you achieve the things you set out to achieve by competently overcoming the risks constitutive of the challenges you set yourself; at a more specific level, the experience of moving competently (fluently, in control) through the medium in which you are climbing gives rise to a deeply gratifying experience of effective agency. Furthermore, it can involve expressing, through the activity of climbing, something about who you really are and what is deeply important to you; indeed, many mountaineers talk about how climbing is something they need to do in order to be who they really are. This, plausibly, is why they get a deep sense of exhilaration and fulfilment from mountaineering.[36]

---

[35] Importantly, facing and overcoming risk often has a positive effect on the ways we view and value aspects of more day-to-day life. To quote extreme skier Eric Pehota from the ski movie *Steep*: 'It's the ultimate paradox. The closer you come to dying, the more alive you feel: [...] if you just sit around on a couch and watch TV, how can you appreciate that cold beer or that nice, big, hearty steak? But you eat soup, and live in a cold, icy environment for two, three weeks, and, man, you get back, and that's the best burger you've ever had in your life and [...] that beer could be piss warm, and it'll be the nicest beer you've had in your life'.

[36] Capturing a number of these ideas, in the 1984 film of his ski descent of the East Face of Aiguille Blanche du Peuterey, Stefano de Benedetti says, 'This is my mode of expressing myself. This is my mode of speaking to the others of freedom'. And in the movie *Steep* he says: 'In the perfect moment, I was so concentrated, there was no space for other thoughts. [...] When you are in a situation where if you fall you die, everything changes. [...] You act like a different person. You act with all yourself. You are making a completely different experience, and in some way you are discovering yourself. This is the magic of the mountain. [...] But to live so close to the possibility of dying, you understand what is really important and what [is] not. [...] It's

Two further points about the value of these experiential goods. First, we want to say, in the context of risk it is not just the experience (of exhilaration, say) that is valuable but the experience that is produced by *actually* taking and overcoming risks. Second, these valuable experiences can in turn be constituents of more general abstract goods, like wellbeing and fulfilment: a person may be more fulfilled in virtue of the experiences yielded by competently engaging risk.

So far we have shown that competently overcoming risk in mountaineering is related to a variety of values involved in mountaineering: engaging in adventurous activities, overcoming challenges, expressing one's agency, exhilaration, fulfilment, and so on. These are general goods that almost everyone agrees have value. All this is compatible with [Despite], however. But there are two additional and crucial claims that distinguish our view from [Despite]: First, risk is a constitutive and ineliminable element of mountaineering and the character of the experiences it brings (we argued for this earlier). This implies that, if the risk were completely absent, the activity engaged in wouldn't really be a form of mountaineering and the experiences produced would not be experiences *of mountaineering*. So, since the value of mountaineering depends in part on the character of the experiences it brings, the value of mountaineering depends (in part) on the risks it involves. We thus arrive at our second crucial claim: mountaineering and the goods it brings have the particular type of value they do (in part) because of the risks they involve. This is distinct from [Despite], since risk is not a mere (causal) *means* to the various mountaineering goods we've identified. Rather, risk is a *constitutive* and ineliminable *part* of the goods themselves: the character and content of these values, as realised through mountaineering, is essentially shaped by the mountaineering risks they involve. It is in this sense that mountaineering has the value it does (in part) because of the risk it involves.[37]

---

probably the highest moment of my life. Because in the perfect moment, I was, or I felt to be, a little superman'.

[37] To put it in more technical jargon, risk is 'constitutively valuable': a constitutive feature, not just of mountaineering, but of the values mountaineering expresses and the valuable experiences it brings. It may be useful to here distinguish our view from some other axiological theses. In particular, we are *not* saying (1) that risk-taking is *unconditionally* valuable or good in all circumstances (though we remain non-committal as to whether competent risk-engagement is); (2) that competent risk-engagement is *intrinsically* valuable (if that implies non-relationally valuable); or (3) that risk is merely

To summarise our argument so far, then: risk is valuable (in part) because of the goods it realizes – goods that need not be specific to mountaineering, but that are widely recognised as good by non-mountaineers too. But these goods, when realized in the context of mountaineering, have the particular value they do only because they involve competently engaging mountaineering risks. Thus, risk is one of the things that *gives* mountaineering its value, whereby mountaineering has the value it does in part *because* of the risks it involves.

9. Because it is risky

If defensible, this undermines [Risky]. [Risky] claims that, because of the risks involved, mountaineering is not justified. But we've argued that risk is one of the things that gives mountaineering its value; and it is hard to see how something which gives mountaineering its value could also serve to render it unjustified, especially when the risk is overcome competently and the mountaineering goods it is constitutively bound up with are widely acknowledged (by both mountaineers and non-mountaineers) to be valuable. So, [Risky] as a general thesis looks false. Note, though, that we have argued against [Risky] without recourse to the orthodox approach embodied by [Despite]. Indeed, given that risk is a constitutive and inseparable part of mountaineering and the goods it brings, [Despite] is wrong to suggest that the value of these goods is independent of risk.

It may be objected that our arguments (assuming they are successful) do not get us to [Because], however. For one thing, although these arguments may show that mountaineering is not unjustified, they do not show that it is justified; furthermore, the argument of the last section delivered claims about the *value* of risk, whereas [Because] is a claim about *justification*. In response, though, we will here repeat the suggestion that competently engaging risk by mountaineering expresses and realizes important human values. Given that, it is then hard to see what the objection might be to the claim that mountaineering is justified (in part) because of the risks it

---

instrumentally valuable (only a means to other goods). There are several other ways risk could be valuable – *finally* valuable (as an end there is reason to pursue for its own sake), *symbolically* valuable (symbolic of something else of value), and more – but even if risk is valuable in such respects, these do not get to the nub of its value.

Philip A. Ebert & Simon Robertson

involves. For why could mountaineering never be justified, insofar as (a) it is undertaken and completed competently, and (b) it expresses and realizes deep human values? To sustain the objection against moving from the denial of [Risky] to [Because], one would need to give an adequate answer to that question. Such an answer, we submit, looks unlikely.

Note, in conclusion, that our arguments also place competent mountaineers in rather a strong position when it comes to the disagreement with non-mountaineers about the risks the activity involves. On the one hand, if the disagreement concerns *how* risky mountaineering as a general activity is, what evidence there is suggests that it is less extreme or high-risk than many people believe. While, on the other hand, if the disagreement ultimately concerns whether or not the risk-taking is *justified*, we've argued that it can be. One worry was that the kinds of risk mountaineering involves render it an unjustified *gamble*. However, we argued that competence reduces the odds of the gamble, and, more importantly, that the kinds of risks the gamble involves are valuable because constitutively bound up with various other goods that everyone recognises. In short, and putting these two points together, risks are sometimes worth taking. We should emphasise here that we are *not* saying that everyone *ought* to take mountaineering risks, nor even that competently overcoming such risks will *always* bring about the kinds of goods we've identified. Rather, sometimes risk-taking in mountaineering is justified. Finally, we've also implicitly provided an answer to the question mountaineers perennially face: 'Why mountaineer, given the risks it involves?'. Answer: 'Because it's risky – and sometimes it's good to take risks'.[38]

University of Stirling
p.a.ebert@stir.ac.uk

Cardiff University
robertsons3@cf.ac.uk

[38] A version of this paper was presented as one of the London Lectures on Sport hosted by the Royal Institute of Philosophy. Many thanks to Anthony O'Hear for inviting us, and to both he and the Lecture's audience for extremely engaging discussion. Additional thanks to an audience at the University of Stirling for feedback on an earlier draft. We dedicate the paper to the many climbing friends with whom we've shared both a rope and some of the 'best beers ever'. This work was supported by a grant from the Arts and Humanities Research Council AH/J00233X/1 held by Philip Ebert.

Not a Matter of Life and Death?

ANTHONY O'HEAR

'Come on, it's not a matter of life and death', said some Job-like comforter, following a defeat in a football match. 'No', replied Bill Shankly, the granite-like Scot who was manager of Liverpool FC during their days of pre-eminence, whose team had just lost, 'it is more important than that'.

Another scene from the same era. July 13th 1967, at around 3.00 p.m. in the afternoon, on the upper slopes of Mont Ventoux, and Shankly's black humour, if such it was, might not have seemed so clever. Tom Simpson, the world champion cyclist and BBC Sports Personality of the Year of 1965, is lying dead on the road-side. Fuelled by drugs and alcohol, in a desperate effort to force the pace in the Tour de France's most punishing stage, Simpson had collapsed, overcome by dehydration (riders were rationed in those days to four small bottles of water), the pitiless sun and the several hours of riding already accomplished. 'Put me back on the bike' are supposed to have been his last words, though it seems that what he actually said was 'Go on, go on'.

With a mixture of grittiness and sentimentality (neither ever far away where sport is concerned), thinking of Simpson lying motionless in the dust, one is inevitably reminded of Lorca's lament for another dead hero, the bull-fighter Ignacio Sanchez Mejias, whose body is still in the ring:

> A las cinco de la tarde/ Eran las cinco en punto de la tarde/ Un niño trajo la blanca sábana/ *a la cinco de la tarde.*/ Un espuerta de cal ya prevenida/ *a las cinco de la tarde.*/ Lo demás era muerte y sólo muerte/ *a las cinco de la tarde.*

Tommy Simpson and Ignacio Sanchez Mejias are by no means the only sportspeople who died in the pursuit of their goals. To name a few others, taken at random, Ayrton Senna, Daniel Wheldon, Marco Simoncelli (motor sport, and many others before them, of course), Raman Lamba (cricket, of all things, killed by a blow to the head when fielding helmet-less at short leg), Leavander Johnson (boxing), Fran Crippen (swimming), Marc-Vivien Foe and Phil O'Donnell (soccer), Daniel James (rugby), to say nothing of numerous riders, eventers and jockeys (riding being said to be

doi:10.1017/S1358246113000313

the most dangerous sport of all), and of course of climbers, including some of the very best (George Mallory, Toni Kurz, Allison Hargreaves, Peter Boardman and Joe Tasker).

So sport, and not just professional sport, and the extremes of effort and danger involved, leads people to their death. I can actually think of two people known to me who died on the squash court, and of one who died after rowing training in a local gym, the last in his early twenties. Whether or not such deaths are in some objective sense 'acceptable', no one I know has allowed them or knowledge of them to impede their own sporting endeavours.

But it is not just those who play, for fun or (ironically) for a living who allow sport to play a very large role in their lives. Many who follow sport and who talk and write about it treat it as very important indeed. They invest considerable time and money in their pursuit, to say nothing of the emotional investment involved in supporting a team or country or even an individual, often to the extent of engaging in what might seem to the dispassionate to be a collective local or national hysteria. Think of Henmania in tennis, or the way the 2005 Ashes seemed to grip the nation (or at least a large part of it), in this latter case to such an extent that many of those most emotionally involved could not actually bring themselves to watch the final afternoon on television (where, had they actually kept their nerve, they would have seen the South African Kevin Petersen destroying the Australian bowling on this nation's behalf). Many would say that all of this was and is disproportionate. Sport just cannot be that important and grown men (and women) should grow up.

Of course, in some periods of history there have been 'games' that have been seriously matters of life and death, contests such as the Roman gladiatorial contests (or some of them anyway) and the gruesome Aztec spectacles in which losers were viciously butchered and sacrificed to the gods enamoured of D.H. Lawrence. But one way in which the type of sport many of us are interested in is different from these sorts of things is that contestants are not fighting for their lives and, even in disciplines like boxing and wrestling, whose very aim is to inflict physical suffering on one's opponent, losers normally live to fight another day. So our question is whether sport in the sense we are familiar with is something that grown up members of society should spend considerable amounts of time, effort and money in playing and watching.

Is sport important at all? What would be its rightful place in the lives of reasonable people? These are the questions I would like now to consider. To do this, I suggest that we start with a text as old and as foundational as any in our literature, Homer's *Iliad*, and itself in all probability drawing on even older oral tradition, perhaps as early as the eighth or ninth centuries BC. For nearly the whole of Book XXIII is devoted to a description of the games the Achaeans hold to mark the funeral of Patroclus.

Actually, even before the account of the games we are given a clue highly germane to our general theme. Patroclus' shade appears to Achilles, who is organising the games, to remind him that he, Patroclus had first appeared in Achilles' house as a young boy, 'banished for bloody murder', for killing the son of Amphidamas in a quarrel over a dice game. There is, it appears, nothing new about the red mist descending over something so trivial as a game, nor is Patroclus any less upright and decent a character than the Rooneys, Beckhams and Zidanes who have similarly, though less lethally disgraced themselves on the world stage.

As to the games themselves, the Achaeans, taking a break from their more deadly pursuits, are clearly enthralled and wholly engaged by the sport, as over several hundred lines of poetry Homer expects his readers and listeners to be; nor is there any shortage of prizes for the competitors, on-course betting on the part of spectators and tedious 'expert' commentary and advice from ex-players resting on their laurels and pontificating about how it was in the days of their youth. Nothing new in any of this, then; and if some might raise an eyebrow at the trophies in at least two of the events including 'women sashed and lovely', to do so would betray a degree of naivety regarding the post-match activities of some of our top athletes, the main difference between then and now being that what happens on these occasions these days is usually, though, as court cases occasionally reveal not invariably, consensual on all sides.

The first event in the games is the chariot race, which actually reads like an account of a Formula One Grand Prix of today. Of the five competitors, Eumeleus crashes out, attempting too tight a turn, while between two of the others there is what would euphemistically be described to-day as a 'coming together' when the young blood Antilochus pushes the more senior Menelaus off the course as they both make for a narrow gap. There is a furious argument at the end, which is settled only when Antilochus wisely attributes his misdemeanour not, as might be expected in Homer, to the intervention of a god, but to the way in which 'the whims of youth break all the rules'. Quite; some of today's champions clearly anticipated by nearly three thousand years, but in the Homeric case with an apology added. Next, there is the boxing, in which pre-bout, millennia before the self-preening of Mohammed Ali, Epeus, the eventual winner, proclaims himself 'the greatest'. The wrestling, between big Ajax and Odysseus, long since sworn enemies, is clearly what would today be called a needle match, and is saved from a probably lethal outcome only by the intervention of Achilles, in effect stopping the fight: 'Don't kill yourselves in sport'. This injunction is still highly relevant three thousand or so years later. In many sports today, rugby, for example, without an unspoken code setting limits to what might be done, players would be liable to kill each other, which explains why people take such a dim view when these limits are transgressed.

To return to Patroclus' games, In the running (won by Odysseus, Athena's favourite) much merriment and 'banter' (in the Fagles translation) is caused when the lesser Ajax, who was leading at the time is tripped up by Athena, as we are told, slipping in a pile of dung left over from the chariot race. And so it goes on, with fighting with lances, shot-putting, archery and spear-throwing (today's javelin, no doubt).

It could be said that all the disciplines represented in Book XXIII relate pretty closely to battle skills. Further, the sports and games of the ancient world have been described[1] as 'an aristocratic legacy'. But I don't think either of these things mean that what Homer is describing is essentially different from sport in our time. Even if the funeral games are based on battle skills, in the games there are formal rules and set-ups which are not those of battle, and one could easily envisage these developing along their own artificial lines, channelling them into trajectories of their own, ever further removed from the conditions of an actual battle, as they become autonomous activities in their own right. Further, even if the ancient games began with aristocratic pursuits, in the classical world they were never confined to aristocratic entrants (as Lane Fox himself points out); indeed, Baron de Coubertin notwithstanding, the big games of the classical world gradually became the preserve of semi-professional competitors who stood to make fortunes out of successes, just as now, and they clearly attracted audiences from all sections of society.

It is, of course, true that the actual games in the Greek world were all connected to religious festivals, Olympia, for example, being one of the greatest and most important sanctuaries of the Greek world. Much could be said about this aspect of Greek games (as is taken up by Heather Reid in this volume), but I will confine myself here to two small points. For the ancient Greeks, the world was full of gods, in the sense that everything was permeated by an aura of the divine, with no clear distinction between the sacred and the secular, but this did not necessarily mean that there was any specifically religious reference in day to day activities while those activities were being conducted

---

[1]   by Robin Lane Fox, in *The Classical World* (London, Penguin Books, 2007), 43

(perhaps symbolised by the fact that the stadia and race tracks of Olympia were actually *outside* the Altis, the Olympian sanctuary. And (the second point), in Homer's account at least, once the games get going there is no explicit reference at all to the fact that they are part of a memorial to a dead hero, nor do any of the competitors and spectators seem to have any such thought uppermost in their minds as the games go on, or indeed any thought but to play the game.

And that in itself, tells us something about sport. In the main, sporting activities are such that once one is involved in them, even at low levels, what one is doing completely occupies you physically and mentally. At the extreme this intense concentration on something other than oneself, and a feeling that one is taken over by it, is what athletes sometimes refer to by being 'in the zone'. It is as if one is taken over by something outside oneself (and so could easily be interpreted in divine or shamanistic terms if one felt so inclined), sometimes to such an extent that one feels the shot is being played for one, that one is not aware of preparing for it, or how one did it, to take the feeling as it manifests itself in a game like tennis or cricket, but analogous things are perceived in activities as disparate as rock-climbing, distance running and football. It might not be too much to think in this context of what Buddhists speak of as mindfulness or one single pointedness, a degree of attention and concentration so intense that consciousness itself is transcended in a complete bodily and psychic focus on the act itself, to the exclusion of all else, including thinking at an explicit level about what one is doing.

I think that most people who have played any sort of physical game will have got an inkling of this sort of thing on the frustratingly rare occasions when a tennis or golf shot has gone just right without one thinking about it, but even if what I am suggesting here involves a degree of pardonable exaggeration, the following is certainly true. Most sports involve players physically and mentally to such a degree that for the time of playing they necessarily cut themselves off from everything else and from thoughts of everything else. Indeed this self-insulation from the rest of experience can be one of the most refreshing aspects of playing a game. While the game lasts there is no room for doing anything else, worrying about anything else, thinking about anything else. And while one is playing, one has more than enough to think about and to do, to plan, to analyse, to psych out one's opponent(s), etc.

Kendall Walton[2] talks in this context of sport as being a case of 'make belief', that in playing a game of tennis with a friend, for

---

[2]   in 'Sports as Fiction', 2009, available online at http://deepblue.lib. umich.edu

example, during the game I act as if these things really matter, as if I really want to destroy him, as if for the duration of the game everything depends on the outcome. Of course, it doesn't, and as soon as the game is finished, we both come out of the make-belief bubble and have a relaxing drink and a friendly chat. As he puts it 'to participate either as a competitor or as a spectator (of sport) is frequently, if not invariably, to engage in pretense', while fans let themselves be carried away as though genuine and substantial values are at stake.

While there is something right about what Walton says, at least to the extent that for most people playing a game is a self-contained episode, more or less insulated from the rest of their life, I think that to talk of what goes on in a match as make-belief is too weak. Maybe when watching a play or a film or reading a novel, our emotions are in a certain sense 'make-belief' (as Walton famously avers), but when I feel exhilaration at winning a point or anger at messing up (or at my partner messing up), these emotions are real enough, even if transient (as Walton does actually allow). Further in sport, in contrast to fictions of one sort and another, there is always the element not just of unpredictability but rather more of my actions affecting the outcome. What I do, how I play, my focus and motivation – all are vital both to the game and the result. I am wholly involved, whether I like it or not, and even whether I am trying or not. There is nothing make-believe about any of this, all of which points to significant differences between sport and fiction or drama. Nor, if what I am saying is right, are sports fans necessarily wrong to feel that in watching sport genuine and substantial values are in some sense at stake.

It might be said that my perspective on sport is a typically Western one, more specifically a Graeco-Roman one, in that cultures not influenced by Greece and Rome, and maybe latterly by Anglo-Saxon sporting traditions, have not made such a big thing of organised sport. I do not know how true this is, except to say that, for better or worse, sport of the sort described by Homer and of the sort which may have developed on the playing fields of English public schools in the nineteenth century is now truly global, as we see from the well-nigh universal popularity of phenomena such as the Olympic Games and the football World Cup. And in these activities and in the more local competitions and individual games throughout the world, it is possible to see the instantiation of all sorts of genuine values, the sharing of sincere emotions and the exemplification of real and not pretend virtues and vices.

Not a Matter of Life and Death?

In different ways and in different proportions in pretty well all sports you will find examples of application, hard work, effort, perseverance and skill. Indeed without a modicum of all of these you will make no progress at all, and the game is hardly worth playing. Underpinning what we might think of as these executive requirements, there is also the need to practice and to achieve a level of physical fitness at least appropriate to the standard at which one is playing. It is possible that a strict neo-Aristotelian might quibble about whether or not these executive requirements, as I am calling them, are really virtues, given that they may not be aimed at anything intrinsically worthwhile, though such an objection would not be open to Aristotle himself: in the ancient Greek world gymnastic was a key part of human flourishing, and essential to education, recognising indeed our essentially embodied nature and the excellence deriving from a vigorous physicality. There would for the ancient Greeks probably be something slightly shameful about a man, even in jest, proclaiming that his recreations consisted solely in sedentary pursuits; while Homer compounds Thersites' moral shamelessness with a description of him as bandy-legged, his shoulders humped together, curving over a caved-in chest, with a head bobbing above them, his skull warped to a point – at least some of which could, one imagines, have been ameliorated by healthy exercise and an upright posture.

But it is not just hard work, exercise and effort which are necessary to sporting endeavour. In most sports there are plenty of opportunities for the exercise of courage, either moral or physical, and often both. There may well be the conquest of fear, certainly in contact sports, but also in non-contact sports, in facing an intimidating opponent and possible humiliation. There is also learning how to deal with loss and actual humiliation, which happens even to the best and those most unaccustomed to it. In this context Rafael Nadal was impressive on losing the final set of a final (in which he had been leading until mid-way through the second set) to Andy Murray 6-0: 'You don't like to lose 6-0, but it happens.' (Though, one might have thought, not often to Nadal.) 'Andy played fantastic. Accept. That's it.' One could imagine the gritted teeth and mental turmoil behind that 'accept', but he wasn't going to show it, or to begrudge his opponent his day in the sun, and that showed class and grace. I hope that Murray was as gracious in victory, for that is also a virtue sport gives opportunities for.

Of course, to sport's virtues there are also the corresponding vices, to courage and resilience a lack of moral and physical fibre, cowardice even (the player who shirks a tackle), to graciousness in victory and defeat, arrogance on the one hand and moaning and complaining on the other. There are also players who deliberately set out to intimidate (a fine line here between intimidation and what might be called stamping one's authority). There are players, who in the heat of the moment, are unable to control their aggression (again a fine line between unacceptable aggressiveness and the moral and physical force necessary not to be pushed around by one's opponent).

Then there are players who cheat, openly or surreptitiously, and who indulge in what are known as professional fouls. There are those who try to rile their opponents by insulting them, and those who try to influence referees and umpires by constantly complaining, glaring at them, questioning their decisions, and in the case of football particularly feigning injury and pretending to be fouled with the express purpose of being awarded a free kick or penalty. And on the other hand there are players who abide by the rules and the spirit of the game, who show referees and opponents respect, and who refrain what has come to be called 'banter' (i.e. a constant stream of unfunny and often malicious remarks about opponents with the specific purpose of unsettling them).

Given that the vices just listed may well help to sway a result, and are certainly believed to do so, it will take some strength of mind to stay honest, especially as there are coaches – at all levels – who expect their players to manipulate the game in underhand ways. The triumph of injustice is perhaps the hardest thing to deal with in sport, with the temptation to get away with what one can – just so as to even things up – the greater. In the world as it is today, particularly the world of professional sport, is there any point in cultivating personal integrity? Mike Atherton's great innings against South Africa at Trent Bridge in 1998 (98 not out, to win an intensely fought match) was made the more remarkable by the remorseless barrage of hostile bowling he had to face from Allan Donald – when Atherton had actually been caught off Donald early on in his innings. Later on, the unmoved and immovable Atherton gave the glove off which he had been caught, with the red mark of the ball still on it, duly ringed and autographed to Donald to sell at his benefit auction. And whatever the immorality of not walking no one could gainsay Atherton's bravery or his sheer will-power. And yet, for all the dubious behaviour of so many of us when we think we can get away with it, people do on occasion play absolutely straight, and are admired for it, golfers who own up to having inadvertently moved their ball, cricketers who, unlike Atherton, walk before being given out, Arsène Wenger offering Sheffield United a re-match in 1999 after Arsenal had won a cup tie through in effect stealing a goal. But it is not just injustice which arises from human agency that sport teaches us to deal with. Sometimes results are just unjust: chance plays a large role in sport, something else which can be dealt with either with dignity and stoicism, or the opposite.

And finally in this quick and no doubt incomplete review of virtues and vices intrinsic to sport, there are the virtues connected to playing in a team, such as solidarity, co-operation, team spirit and so on. These virtues become particularly impressive when they enable teams which start as underdogs to overcome individually more skilled opponents. They also militate against show-boating arrogance, so prevalent in boxing, for example, which can be distasteful in all sorts of ways.

I would not claim that people who exemplify specific virtues and vices in sport necessarily behave the same way in other areas of their lives. Someone who is mild, articulate and reasonable away from the rugby pitch or the tennis court can exhibit quasi-psychopathic tendencies in the heat of a game. Equally players noted for their stoicism and uprightness on the pitch can be quite weak characters off it. What I would, though, claim is that sporting virtues are virtues and sporting vices vices. As in any other walk of life, sporting virtues require self-control and good judgement, and their opposites lack of these desirable qualities. They are not pretend virtues or make-believe vices, and I would conjecture that there is more overlap here between good character on the field and off it than there is complete disjunction.

And I would say something similar about sporting pressure. However unimportant sport may be, people who feel tense and pressured in sport do feel real pressure, even if it may be short-lived. Keith Miller, the famous Australian cricketer, who had also been an RAAF fighter pilot in the war is supposed to have said when he was asked about the pressure of playing a test match; 'Pressure? Pressure is a Messerschmitt up your arse, not playing cricket.' One can see what Miller, a larger than life swashbuckling character, meant, but what he says is unfair to the likes of Marcus Tresthcothick, a top cricketer who certainly suffered intensely from sporting pressure, to the extent that he had to retire from test matches and undergo serious medical treatment. Trescothick seems thankfully to have recovered, unlike Robert Enke, the German international goalkeeper, who committed suicide in 2009, because of depression and anxiety apparently arising from the pressures of top flight football. Sporting pressure, like sporting virtues and vices, is certainly real enough, and as intense as pressure in other walks of life. The question, though, is whether it is disproportionate, whether it is sensible for people to get so het up about things which (it would be said) don't really matter.

In one sense, they certainly do matter. Mike Atherton could have been seriously injured by Allan Donald, and the same goes for almost anyone preparing for a serious game of rugby, who may well have to cope with potentially lethal assaults, which would certainly attract the interest of the police were they to happen in the street. A golfer stands to win or lose very large sums of money by his performance, as do tennis players, footballers, elite athletes and many others. Even amateur players at much lower levels invest considerable pride in their performances; self-esteem at least is often at stake, even if one pretends to laugh (or drink) it off afterwards. So do spectators, who often follow teams or individuals with anorak like concentration and intense, but ultimately fruitless passion, made all the more poignant because it is a passion which is at bottom passive. And mention of spectators may remind us that sports crowds can be vicious and venomous, an occasion for a licensed display of some of the worst aspects of our nature, a point not lost on George Orwell, who (in 'The Sporting Spirit') wrote of sport being 'an unfailing cause of ill will... leading to orgies of hatred', in which 'savage competitive passions are aroused', with fighting on the field and spectators booing referees and trying to intimidate players. Everything Orwell says is true, and no one should underestimate or overlook the sheer atavistic hatred, mob behaviour and stupidity which can be aroused by sporting contests. But Orwell was a great polemicist, and he tells only half the story, though on the negative side we could add the deformations which have occurred since Orwell's time due to the intertwining of sport and great wealth and also due to the corrupt bureaucracies big-money sports seem unable to avoid spawning. But, as I say, the negative side is only half the story. Sport can also be the occasion for genuine comradeship and magnanimity, between players and spectators alike, as well as friendships which may transcend team affiliations and go far beyond the game itself, and it may (and does on occasion) also help to heal wounds resulting from age-old oppression, prejudice and historical hatreds.

So we come to the question which has been underlying much of the discussion so far. Is anything more than a mild and passing involvement in sport disproportionate, infantile even, a prolongation of what should have tapered off with the transition from childhood? Sport is certainly what Pascal would have called a diversion. It is not just disconnected from other aspects of life, and something done to a greater or less extent for its own sake, but it is a distraction from what really matters. From Pascal's perspective this is certainly true. However, if

Pascal's perspective is implicitly critical of sport, it does not do many other human activities any favours either, including those activities which many would contrast with sport to sport's disadvantage. For Pascal's perspective is that of the four last things, death, judgement, heaven and hell. And it is a besetting human weakness to be unable sit still, as he says, even for a quarter of an hour, in case we should be faced with thought of these ultimate realities. If sport is, in that sense divertissement, a diversion, so is most of what most people do, in a desperate effort to keep their minds occupied with trivia.

The hustle and bustle and busyness with which rulers and magistrates surround themselves, no doubt complaining all the while about being over-worked and under-resourced, is actually what they are seeking, the ostensible ends of their activity a mere rationalisation. They want to do anything but think about themselves, or attend to their parlous condition. Stuck between the infinitely big and the infinitely small, we can cope with neither. We neither understand ourselves, nor can we get a firm footing over the abyss which confronts us, and into which we dare not look, and we hide all this from ourselves by continuous activity. It is perhaps worth recalling at this point that Hume, who shared much of Pascal's philosophical scepticism, in a strange way agreed with Pascal at this point. For Hume the *only* way to avoid the abyss into which his philosophical reflections inexorably led him was to engage in diversion, dining, making merry with his friends and playing backgammon.

'Man's condition: inconstancy, boredom, anxiety.' (*Pensées.* 24/22) From Pascal's point of view it is not just sport which comes off badly. Most of human activity serves the function of diverting us; if we are in business we would not want just to be given the money we work so long and hard to earn; the huntsman likes the six hours of the chase, and would not be at all satisfied with simply being handed the hare or the boar; the magistrate or official is happy only when he has a great number of people pressing on him from all sides from morning to night, so as not to leave a single hour when he could think about his own condition. (See *Pensées* 136/126) Rest is unbearable because of the boredom and worse it engenders; on the other hand, the slightest thing like a billiard cue and a ball can divert us for hours on end.

According to the Stoics, whom Pascal follows in this respect, all those activities which do not contribute in the highest degree to wisdom are equally foolish and vicious, which if hardly a ringing endorsement of sport, may give us some sort of perspective. Tourism, fashion, show-business, gardening, food and drink as hobbies are all, like sport, activities engaged in for their own sakes, but which may well fall far below what Pascal or the Stoics would count as wisdom. No doubt there are also many other activities which may ostensibly serve other ends, but which as Pascal suggests are engaged in for large part for the diversionary potential of the activity itself. Think of the self-important peer waddling in and out of the House of Lords, of the puffed-up local busybody (often a paid councillor) moralising about this or organising protests about that, of the bureaucrat straining every nerve to ensure that he has yet more important tasks to fulfil (public choice theory!), or of the desolation of the retired academic deprived of his adrenaline fix of committees and senates. Sport at least does not on the whole pretend to be more important than it is (even if politicians like to bask in its reflected glory, often to the discomfort of the players so exploited), nor on the playing side at least is it shot through with moralism in the way so much journalism and politics is. Indeed the very fact that in most sports there is a result which everyone has to accept, sooner or later, actually endows sport with more objectivity and backbone than many human pursuits.

The claim against sport is that it too often plays a disproportionate part in people's lives. To this a *tu quoque* argument seems to me to be an appropriate response. Sport is not a matter of transcendent wisdom, nor is it a matter of life and death, even if sometimes people do die because of sport. But then, outside of famines, wars and natural disasters little of what we do is a matter of life and death, and sport is probably no more dangerous statistically than, say, driving or smoking. Nor are most of us capable of spending much time in the icy regions of the spirit inhabited by Pascal or at the intense levels of aesthetic contemplation demanded by Bach or Milton or with the intellectual rigour required by a serious engagement with Plato or Wittgenstein.

If the complaint is that sport is essentially escapism, if what is being escaped from is the drudgery and drabness in which many are compelled to work and live, the colour and excitement and drama of sport may be no bad thing, and in its demands on the attentiveness of the whole person it may actually be a good way of rising above the coils of self-centredness. Further an attractive and often undervalued aspect of much sport is that it is essentially a voluntary activity, an example of the operation of the Burkean 'little platoon' in which people freely and spontaneously form themselves into clubs and societies for playing and watching, and in doing so participate in all the codes and structures such bodies evolve. In this way they contribute mightily to the bonds and orders which a healthy society depends on, but in a bottom-up way, as week after week perhaps millions of people, without any form of compulsion join in local sporting activities, either as players or spectators. This aspect of sport is perhaps hidden by the pre-eminence of such ghastly trans-national bureaucracies as the International Olympic Committee and FIFA and their national counterparts, often virtually arms of the state and even funded by the state. But, for all the noise they make, these are not the norm, at least not in the non-socialist world. Not the least of sport's virtues is that in many countries its very existence is a symptom of a healthy and invigorating freedom, with much to admire socially and educationally in the bodies and organisations such freedoms engender.

University of Buckingham
anthony.ohear@buckingham.ac.uk

Sport and Life

PAUL SNOWDON

I am not (nor, sadly, ever have been) an exponent of any sport at a level above the barely competent, unlike some other writers in this collection. Moreover, I have long since abandoned efforts at engaging in sport and now merely watch it, again with no special powers of analysis or understanding. But one's level of competence and understanding do not, fortunately, determine the importance in one's life of things, and sport has played a large, and I think largely enhancing, role in my life. So I am writing as someone with a lifelong interest in it with the aim of examining this thing, sport, trying to articulate what it is that I have been engaged with, and what it has given me. I am assuming that my own attitudes towards sport are not eccentric or unusual and so these reflections growing out of my own experiences will resonate with others. In effect I am engaging here in what is normally thought of as central philosophical task, that of trying to live an examined life – a life in which one of its components is to reflect hard on the nature and value of some of its other components. It would be, of course, a terrible mistake to think, as some philosophers are supposed to do, that an unexamined life is *not worth living*, an attitude which consigns the vast majority of lives to worthlessness, but we are, probably, committed to thinking that the reflective examination of our lives represents something good.

I want to begin by clarifying, to some extent, the questions, or at least the tasks, that I aim to pursue under my rather portentous title. There is a use of 'life' in, for example, talk of 'work/life' balance in which life contrasts with work and, perhaps, with other things as well. But there is also a very general use of 'life' in which someone's life is what he or she does or endures while alive. In that use, which is mine, one's 'work' is one part or aspect of one's life and cannot be contrasted with it. In this sense of 'life', also, it is not something we can be without and so need to 'get'; all we can get is a *better* life. Clearly, in that general sense of 'life', sport is a part of many people's lives, mine included, in some form or other. But we tend to evaluate elements in lives as making the life good or perhaps bad, or perhaps as simply neutrally filling it. I want to ask, therefore, of what value sport is to our lives? In fact, this question rather hovers over my discussion and re-enters more explicitly near

doi:10.1017/S1358246113000337   ©The Royal Institute of Philosophy and the contributors 2013

Royal Institute of Philosophy Supplement **73** 2013

the end. There is a second and related question; what does engagement with sport offer us? What do we get out of sport? What attracts
us to sport? Or, perhaps, what do we see in sport? The first question
is, as we might portentously put it, a question in value theory; the
second group of questions are high level psychological ones. I
pursue this psychological sort of question most of the time. The
two sorts of questions are not unrelated of course. Part of their
relation is as follows. If one can list what sport gives us, say, P1 to
Pn, then if sport is of value it must presumably be because amongst
those things Pi to Pn there is something that is good for us. The
answers to the psychological question will then contain part of the
answer to the value question. But to nominate something as value-enhancing it must earn that title in some way and what qualifies something as *value-enhancing* is not at all easy to say. I shall not attempt to
say here. I have, though, a third aim. Even if I do not really succeed in
answering my first two questions in a way that strikes people as plausible, I hope that I shall say some true things about sport which will at
least shed some light on what this thing we call 'sport' actually is, and
which, I am assuming, everyone reading this has an interest in.

I should add that I am not interested here in looking at, or thinking
critically about, the current status of sport in popular culture, something that raises many questions. I want, rather, to focus on and
capture what might be called the *basic nature* of sport and what it
offers us.

Since I am at this point engaged in specifying aims, and hence, in a
sense, locating motivations for the inquiry, I want to take a small
swipe at the significant figure of Professor Hans Gumbrecht, the
famous American literary theorist, who has written a fascinating
book on the nature of sport, entitled *In Praise of Athletic Beauty*.[1]
His manifest aim (or part of it) is to provide some sort of defence of
his own life-long passion for sport in the face of the rather weighty
scepticism about it that he senses amongst his academic and intellectual colleagues. I share Gumbrecht's desire to engage with the attitude that he encounters in academics. That attitude is not simply a
lack of interest in sport, on encountering which one can simply say
'Well, I can talk about something else, you know', but of adding,
by insinuation, the thought – and proud of it! The insinuation in
that little coda, that an interest in sport is really a sign of a misspent
life, should not go unchallenged. Gumbrecht's text is one from
which I have learned much and with which I shall engage in the

---

[1]   Gumbrecht (2006). I am very grateful to Professor Annette Richards
(of Cornell University) for bringing Gumbrecht's book to my attention.

course of this talk, but at this point I wish to distance myself from one idea he floats. When Gumbrecht starts his investigation he motivates it by conjecturing that engaging in such an investigation might heighten his enjoyment of sport. As he puts it: 'Would this attraction become more intense if he knew its reason? Perhaps, ... sports do not need this kind of wordy blessing. Still, he would not want to exclude the possibility that trying to understand his fascination may intensify his pleasure...'[2] To understand this passage you need to know that Gumbrecht is, for some reason, writing about himself in the third person. The 'he' is him, Gumbrecht. In response, I am tempted to say that given how intense Gumbrecht's interest in sport has already, by the point where this passage occurs, been conveyed as being it is most unlikely that it *could* become more intense. But more significantly, I suggest, we should not think that philosophical reflections about sport are, or need to be, motivated by the prospect of enhancing our enjoyment of sport; they are, rather, motivated by our shared desire to understand and evaluate ourselves and our lives, doing which is *itself* of intense fascination to us.

1. Sport

I want to begin with the question – what is sport? This is, I believe a rather difficult question. The difficulty is compounded by the evident fact that the word 'sport' is used in different ways. When Lear says that the Gods kill us for their sport, he is using 'sport' simply to mean what they get fun from doing. We need to stipulate that we are using 'sport' in the sense in which rugby and cricket and sports, and where a group of people can engage in or *play* sport. Even here, though, we can start by noting that the word 'sport' has that often encountered ambiguity between mass noun and count noun. We can say that Martin does a lot of sport and David does a little sport. We can also say that Martin enjoys three sports and David only one. Can we say, though, what it is to engage in sport? It is natural to start with the following proposal; to engage in sport is to engage in competitive *games* in which the activities which the games involve are *strongly physical*. According to this proposal the notion of sport grows out of the overlap of the more general notions of competitive games and of strongly physical activity. Giving the talk of sport this focus excludes games which are not strongly physical – such as chess and bridge. It also excludes

---

[2]   Gumbrecht (2006), 16.

strongly physical activities that are not games – such as fell walking, rock climbing, or going to a gym. Now, what makes this proposal attractive is that it fits many prominent examples of what we call sport, examples such as football, cricket, rugby, and the myriad examples of sport engaged in during the Olympic Games. They are undoubtedly physically intense and competitive. This proposal also excludes some examples a definition should exclude. However, it is not a totally precise elucidation and it needs, as we shall see, to be revised. I want to illustrate it and to improve it a bit by considering some difficult cases.

Consider first ancient gladiatorial fighting in the Coliseum. Was that sport? It was, of course, intense physical activity, relying on skill and bravery, and there were, in its context, what we might call 'winners and losers', and, further, watching it (and no doubt taking part in it) would have been terribly exciting, but it was not a game, and so according to the present elucidation, not sport.[3] It was rather a matter of a life and death struggle, a struggle to survive, which spectators enjoyed watching. I think that this implication of the suggested definition is not unacceptable. Gladiatorial fighting should not be counted as sport.

But there are three worries. First, it is not clear that engaging in sport requires that one is taking part in a *competitive game*. One possible example is fox hunting. That is not a competitive game but it is standardly called a sport. However, it may be suggested that in a certain sense there is competition in fox-hunting. It is a case of man versus beast. There is, in a sense, a struggle in that activity between individuals. Normally sport involves a struggle between humans, but sometimes between humans and other animals. Maybe, then, this sort of example does not show that sport need not be competitive. The second difficulty for the proposal concerns the notion of 'intense physical activity'. This is not a clear notion, but further there seem to be what we call sports which do not involve intense physical activity. Examples are darts, snooker, curling, and perhaps golf as played by many people. In fact, there are two sorts of case here. There are sports where the physical effort involved even performing them at the top level is not intense, (such as darts) and there are non-intense ways of doing sport (such as golf played by retired, or even non-retired, academics). These examples seem to show that neither

---

[3]   This case brings to our attention that we talk of winners and losers in contexts where it is not a game, properly speaking, that is going on. Talk of winners and losers relates to success or failure in fulfilment of goals, and the distribution of gains and loses.

feature in the suggested elucidation is strictly necessary for sport. The third difficulty is that the definition fits activities that we would probably *not* call 'sport'. Think of computer games in which participants have to employ intense physical activity, for example, pressing buttons very quickly and moving levers, etc.

In relation to the last point I want to suggest that we can draw a distinction between games where the rules explicitly relate to physical achievements, such a getting a ball into a confined area, and games where the rules are specified in other terms, for example, killing a dragon in a computer game. My suggestion is that even when taking part in the latter games involves physical efforts, they do not count as sports. In contrast, the former do.

Most sports if done well involve intense physical activity, but not all do, and you can engage in sport without being intense at it. An alternative attempt at specifying the type of activity that is necessary in sport is that it is physical activity where there can be degrees of skill and ability. Throwing a dart with accuracy is something at which some people are very skilful, despite its not being in any normal sense intense. So perhaps the physical activity in a sport must be such that one can become skilful at it. Another way of putting this is to require that the physical activity be, in some sense, difficult, hence different skill levels determine outcomes. A second striking fact is the extent to which the activity in sport involves controlling the movement of objects in space. Sometimes the moving objects are the participants themselves, as in a race. At other times they are projectiles, such as darts, arrows, and balls. Sometimes the controlled moving objects are things on which or in which the participant is travelling – as in horse racing or car racing, both of which are counted as sports.

So we end up with the following characterisation of sport in the relevant sense; sport is a *competitive physical activity engaged in as a game* in which the there is a goal *where the achievement of the goal involves physical difficulty in controlling the spatial movement of objects of various kinds.*[4]

2. Sport, Games and Rules

I have done the best that I can, here and now, to elucidate the general notion of sport. What I want to do, though, is to focus my discussion

[4]   The physical intensity of a lot of sport flows from the fact that competition about winning pushes players to participate with intensity, to which other players respond by themselves becoming as, or even more, intense.

on sports which are both competitive games and relatively physically intense. I accept that that is not the whole of what is called 'sport', but this kind of sport forms a large and undoubtedly central case. It is what people tend to think about when the nature and value of sport is discussed. If I can say something about it then it will amount to an account of the bulk of sport.

We do not need at this stage to say anything about the general notion of relatively intense physical action (perhaps involving control of moving objects, including the agent, and potentially gradable in terms of levels of skill). We can simply take those notions for granted. But what of the notion of a (competitive) game? In the previous section I simply relied on a shared understanding of the idea of a game, and of engaging in an activity as a game. But the idea of a game requires some attention. At this point there comes into view one of the most famous sayings in 20th-century Philosophy – Wittgenstein's remark that the concept of a game is a family resemblance concept. This is, I believe, Wittgenstein's main contribution to the philosophy of sport.[5]

So this is a suitable place and time to pause and reflect on Wittgenstein's famous thesis. Wittgenstein's attitude to the concept of a game is two sided. There is a negative side – according to which there is nothing in common to all games. Clearly Wittgenstein means – common to all and only games – he cannot be ruling out that all games have some highly general common feature that maybe all human activity shares. In fact, when Wittgenstein looks for something in common he actually mentions as a candidate being amusing, but being amusing could not represent something that all and only games share, for things other than games are amusing! Despite this being his candidate, Wittgenstein cannot really be looking for such common feature. The positive side is that the notion of a game should be thought of as a family resemblance concept – it gets applied on the basis of a 'complicated network of similarities, overlapping and crisscrossing'.[6]

---

[5]   It might be said that Wittgenstein's remarks about rules could equally well be called a contribution to the philosophy of sport. As a general comment that is true. The chief problem is that it is very hard to say what Wittgenstein is proposing about rules. On one interpretation Wittgenstein is suggesting that rules cannot really tell us what to do. Given the centrality of rules to sport it is to be hoped that Wittgenstein, so interpreted, is not right.

[6]   Wittgenstein (1953) sections 66 and 67.

Now, why does Wittgenstein hold the 'nothing in common' thesis about the term 'game'? We should note this. The nothing-in-common thesis is not equivalent to the thesis that 'game' is indefinable. In the first place, there might be some linguistic formula that could be regarded as equivalent to 'game' but if it, the second expression, worked by picking out its extension without latching onto something in common between all the cases, its existence would not count against the 'nothing-in-common' thesis. For example, though this is not plausible, it may be that all and only games are played; so one could define games as things that people play, but if 'play' itself did not work by picking out a common feature this sort of definability would not refute the 'nothing in common' claim. On the other hand if it were true that 'game' is indefinable that would not mean there was not anything in common to all and only games, it would simply be that 'game' is our term picking that out, and we have no other terms that pick out the common feature. Wittgenstein's reason is that he looks across the set of games and cannot find anything in common between all of them. Now, it is clear that as a procedure, or method, this is not conclusive; failure to find any such thing may simply be an oversight, rather than there being nothing to detect. Further, it is perhaps not entirely clear what Wittgenstein is looking for. What amounts to there being something in common for these purposes? For example, should we say there is something in common to all siblings? Well, we might say; they are all either brothers or sisters. But is that something in common between them all, or is it not something in common but rather two things neither of which is common between all? The answer to that is not clear. There is a further consequence of Wittgenstein's method of argument. It is quite clear that Wittgenstein is happy with the idea of there being something in common between different things, and this means that he cannot be thinking of the idea of family resemblance terms as somehow the solution to the problem of universals, a reading that once had its supporters. He would have to face the question as to what is implied by there being something in common between different objects, and cannot sidestep it.[7] Further, we should not simply accept the idea that the truth of the 'nothing in common' thesis, if it is true, would imply the 'family resemblance' thesis. The relation appears to be more complex than that. For example, it may be that there is nothing in common because we apply the term 'game' to

---

[7] I do not mean to imply that there are important metaphysical implications of that.

two sorts of case, both of which are tightly definable, but which are linked by their sharing a certain feature. This candidate structure would sustain the 'nothing in common' claim but not the 'family resemblance' claim.

So perhaps the jury is still out on Wittgenstein's main thesis in the philosophy of sport.[8] The next step in the debate here would be to propose and test out suggestions about what might be in common to all games. That step will not be taken here.[9]

Now, Wittgenstein's stress on the nothing in common thesis is, for him, linked to the idea that generalisations across the category in question, that of games, cannot be found or given. It maybe we cannot propound much in the way of tight generalisations about games *as a whole*, but we can, I want to suggest advance intelligible generalisations about *sport* as I am understanding it. I want, in order to illustrate this, to engage in a sort of armchair derivation of the character of sport as we know it based on some obvious features of, what I might call, our human condition.

(1) Sports have rules; the rules specify what is permissible in the conduct of the sport, and they specify what counts as winning. These rules in effect define individual sports. There is of course some looseness here, in that the rules of a game can be modified, but it is still treated as the same game. In my lifetime the LBW rule in cricket has been changed, but it remains the game of cricket. Further, and obviously, participants need to know what the rules are. Engagement in sport, therefore, depends, on understanding.

(2) The achievement that counts as winning normally has no significance except as its being treated as winning for that game. Thus, consider football. Managing to get a round ball into a particular area (the goal) has no point or significance in itself. This is what leads some people, critics of sport, to regard

[8]   I am inspired to push against Wittgenstein's dictum by a story that C. B. Martin once told me. He wrote a paper in which he simply repeated Wittgenstein's thesis about games, and sent it to be typed. When they typist handed it back to him she said that Wittgenstein was wrong and she offered a unified characterisation of games which Martin could not fault. Sadly Martin had forgotten the characterisation when he told me the story.
[9]   I regret that the analysis by Bernard Suits of games in his book *The Grasshopper; Games, Life and Utopia* was not known to me when writing this, nor were the very illuminating discussions of games and sport in Hurka (2006) and Tasioulas (2006). I hope to consider their ideas elsewhere.

sport as pointless. They say that there is no point in striving to achieve a pointless goal. This attitude overlooks two obvious things. The first is that these activities derive a significance from being that which counts as winning in relation to the game. And I believe that very few people are blind to competition and its link to motivation. I am relying here on the fact that humans are competitive and understand and can be motivated by the goal of winning. These psychological facts themselves of course need explaining but for the purposes of explaining the role of sport in our lives we can take them as give, as part of the psychological background which can be appealed to in explaining sport. But, second, human motivation does not really respect some general notion of pointfulness. Sir Edmund Hillary plainly wanted to be the first man (or one of the first two) to climb Everest, and no one is really puzzled about that desire and his devoting massive resources to realising it, but one is hard pressed to discern what the point of his being the first man is.[10] It represents a desired and motivating goal that is not mysterious to us, but where no real general point to achieving the goal can be discerned.

(3) The physical processes that the sporting games that we play involve, such things as running very fast, or swimming fast, or kicking a ball, or catching and running with a ball etc., reflect the natural world-involving activities that the human body is capable of, and they are all activities that we can develop skills in. We are creatures who can run and catch and kick and throw and swim, etc. This reflects our shared physical nature and capabilities. Two things follow. First, we do not have sports that involve processes we simply cannot do. Humans cannot fly unaided and so we don't have sports based around that process. Second, we chose activities where there is something approaching a commonly found ability, to put it somewhat roughly. There is no excitement or enjoyment in a sport where only one person can really do it well, say because he or she has some abnormal monstrous throwing arm. And although we organise sporting events where competitors come from all over the earth, *given our shared humanity*, should we encounter physically quite different creatures from

---

[10] I mean by 'pointlessness' that anyone, including Hillary himself, would be hard pressed to say why there is anything better about him being the first man rather than someone else.

outer space there would be no point in having intergalactic Olympic games.[11]

(4) As I have suggested the activities that sport involves or takes up are the ones that reflect our physical nature and potentialities. But the rules reflect our nature in another way. In devising the rules of a sport, the rules of legitimate procedures and the rules about winning, we need to specify them at a level that we as humans can apply them, that is to say with respect to features that we can *detect or observe*. Thus we can tell unaided that a ball has travelled over a line, or that someone is ahead of someone else or that a pass is forward, and so on. So sport is centred on physical activities that we can perform and which are processes that we can observe. Technology influences this, by expanding what is in effect observable. If judges can replay events in slow motion or use time pieces that are very accurate, the performances can be checked in ways previously impossible. The rules of sport, then, reflect our human *perceptual* capacities, as much as our human *actional* capacities.

3. Two Perspectives

The most fundamental point to make about sport is that it figures in our lives in *two* basic ways. We can be participants in sport – play rugby, or cricket or football or baseball – and we can be spectators of sport – we can watch games of rugby or cricket or football or baseball. Now, from a cultural, or as one might say, economic point of view, there is no doubt that sport is primarily something that people observe. Paradoxically, and here I speak about Britain, we are in the grip of both an obesity epidemic, partly because most of us don't participate in sport, and what might be called an obsessive interest in watching intensely physical sport. For most of us, then, the role of sport in our lives is as occurrences to witness. But that comparative sociological truth does not determine for us as theorists about sport which way of relating to sport is more fundamental. I

---

[11]   There is a connexion here with the issue of prosthetic devices in sport, an issue raised by the ambitions of handicapped athletes. It seems evident that if the devices do not give the athlete an enhanced level of performance as compared to how they would perform with a natural limb in place of the prosthetic device then there is no good reason to exclude them from the competition. Determining whether this is so might be difficult, and we cannot demand precision.

want to argue that a proper understanding of sport should start from thinking about it as something we participate in, or 'do'.

I think that the appeal of this approach can be supported by comparing sport and art, in a general sense. I'll take music as my example. I do that for two reasons. The first is that I myself like music and so think about it. But second it has a structure in some ways like sport. Thus, musicians do not create enduring objects – they rather engage in a process of music-making. Sportsmen likewise engage in a process – that of playing the game. The process itself does not create an enduring product. Now, with music there are also the two perspectives that we find with sport. We can be participants in making music, and we can be spectators of music, we can listen to music. It seems to me that unless we regarded the product of musical activity, that is music itself, as something which appealed to us, something that offered us something, there would be little point in participating in its production.[12] So a theoretical understanding of music making has to start from determining the significance for us of the product of musical activity – which is to say music. Along with this goes the following feature of musical activity or participation; the participant needs to check that the product of their activity has the right qualities – their fundamental intention has to be to produce something with the right qualities.

Now, it seems to me that participation in sport is quite different. People do not participate in sport because they regard the activity as producing something that appeals to, or has an interest for, observers or spectators. Further, they do not need to check on whether they are producing something that appeals to the spectator, which gives a point to what they are doing. Rather, the appeal to them of their activity is simply that of engaging in a physically intense competitive game; and what they primarily need to attend is whether they are *winning within the rules*. The precise qualities of what they do and produce is irrelevant. So to understand why we engage in sport we do not need to understand anything about what sport gives spectators.

In contrast to this, it is surely part and parcel of being a sports spectator that one understands what is being observed as a competitive game of the sort it is. Watching involves us understanding (or

---

[12]   It is important not to exaggerate here. We should acknowledge that the appeal to people of making music is multifarious and complex. The claim is that, on the whole, we participate in creating music because of what hearing music gives us.

attempting to understand) the process and that involves understanding the actions of the participants in relation to their goals and the possibilities open to them. This is confirmed by how much better as spectators are those who have played.

The sense then in which the participant point of view is primary is this; people participate because of what they as participants gain from participation; spectators merely get something from observing others who are participating, and that depends on their understanding the observed activities as competitive games.

4. Being a Spectator and Appreciation

I have tried so far to illuminate what sport is, and to argue that we should think of spectators as engaged in watching a sporting activity which itself does not get its point from what it supplies to spectators. How then should we think of what watching sport gives us?

Confronted by this question I am moved to make a few pretty obvious remarks.

(1) It is not to be expected that there is a single answer to this question. Being a spectator at sport is, in this, like being a country walker – engaging in it offers multiple satisfactions. But it is also true that spectators themselves approach the activity of being a spectator in different ways and so it means different things to them. The diversity, then, lies both in the complexity of what is offered and also the diversity of attitudes brought with spectators.

(2) I am going to draw a contrast between two sorts of spectators. I shall call them, perhaps with some linguistic infelicity, the disinterested and the interested, by which I mean spectators who do not care who wins and those who do care, who, as we say, support some competitors. Let me first say a very few simple and obvious things about the disinterested. They witness an evolving time limited struggle, which is played out before them. It is unscripted, and so a context where genuine creativity can be witnessed; you can try to understand the behaviour of the agents; so it engages the analytical intelligence, and presents a strong sense of an evolving drama. But it involves as well overt and intense physical striving aimed at a manifest goal, that of winning. In this it offers what for example watching animals hunting or birds swooping, etc., offer us. It seems to

me that these different things are simply of interest to us as humans – they are the kind of thing that engages our attention, and we get intense satisfaction from witnessing.

(3) Of course the interested spectator has a further dimension of engagement to the proceedings. They have, as it were, an affection, often very strong, for one side or competitor. With that is generated all that extra intensity of watching those we care about. This caring can have many sources but a major one is what people call their sense of identity, your sense of who you are and what you are and where you belong. To be somewhat autobiographical, I am English, and support England, and a Yorkshire man and support Yorkshire cricket, and am tied to Leeds and support Leeds United. These identificatory urges are deep, ineradicable, enhancing and probably beneficially tied to sport.

(4) Another aspect strikes me too. I have been talking about the basis or essence of engagement with sport as a spectator. This is naturally taken as a passive, merely observational role. But that overlooks the active dimension of being a sports spectator. You can be part of a crowd that seethes with emotion and you get caught up in the activities of the crowd, singing, shouting, standing up, publicly reacting. But also you urge your side along and give them advice, an activity that is transparently pointless, (we even give such advice when watching on television), but it is all part of the role of a spectator, a role we play with gusto.

I have been attempting to describe what we might call the 'pay offs' or interests of being a sports spectator. In what I have described there is, I believe, nothing that is hard to understand, and nothing that anyone could regard as objectionable or unacceptable upshots. They are, surely, pay-offs that if they were generated in other contexts (as indeed they are) would not be criticised or scorned.

5. The Aesthetics of Sport

It seems to me that sports lovers have been tempted to search for what one might call higher pay-offs than the ones I have described. More specifically, the idea that strikes many as correct is that what the spectator gains is an aesthetic pay-off. This is, as I understand it, the central theme in Gumbrecht's reflections, which I mentioned earlier. It is evident from the title of his book. And here is a characteristic passage from his book.

> 'If, by drawing on Kant's work, I insist that watching sports does indeed correspond to the most classical definition of aesthetic experience, it is not to give a new aura to noncanonized forms of pleasure. As I have said before, sports do not need that badge of honor – they are already wide open for everybody's potential enjoyment, and this is one of the more positive (and most frequently observed) features of athletics. Furthermore, I would never deny that watching sport has a downside: it can foster stress, aggression, addiction, and poor health habits – you name it. I only hold that these attractions (or attractive nuisances, depending on your point of view) should not distract us from the central and conceptually most obvious explanation for the widespread popularity of sports – their aesthetic appeal.'[13]

The question is whether this 'explanation' is the obviously correct one. I want to generate some scepticism about it in the course of making a few remarks.

(1) If we suppose for the moment that being an aesthetic experience amounts to being an experience of beauty it is clearly true that since beauty is, we think, something that occurs naturally, for example, a natural sunset or a mountain or a plant can strike us as beautiful, we should certainly expect that amongst the multifarious aspects of sporting activity there will be beauty to be found. For example, a perfect off drive executed by Michael Vaughan is a thing of beauty. It would, then, be churlish to deny that sport presents examples of beauty.

(2) The question is, though, about the *centrality or scale* of this aspect of sport since there is no dispute about its presence *in some cases*. One thing to remind ourselves of is that many sports that intensely engage spectators offer, or seem to offer, few examples of beauty. Think of rugby, both league and union, and soccer, boxing, and wrestling, to name but a few. The exclamation 'How beautiful!' will hardly ever spring to the spectator's lips when watching these games. Or so it seems to me. What the spectator witnesses, and what is likely to be expressed in a exclamation, is the skill, the strength, the speed of action and thought, the intelligence, the bravery, and the sheer excitement and intensity of conflict.

[13] Gumbrecht (2006), 39 – 40.

Now, this objection to the centrality of 'beauty' and the aesthetic can be responded to in two main ways. The first would be to contest the claim that such aesthetic features are rarely present. All I can do here is to affirm my own sense of its rarity, and leave the reader to make up his or her mind. The second way of responding is to concede its 'rarity' but to claim that it does not deprive it of its role of what sport centrally and fundamentally gives spectators. One problem with this response is that it deprives a lot of sport of what it locates as the real pay-off of sport. That is unfortunate in both a defence of sport, and in an analysis of its appeal to us. Further, it fails to correspond to how spectators themselves evaluate what they observe. Spectators do evaluate sporting encounters. Now, as far as I can tell, such evaluations do not exclusively attend to the aesthetic; the spectator can regard a contest of exceptional ugliness, say a rugby game in wet and muddy conditions, as a marvellous game, offering them precisely what they were looking for. That makes it unlikely that the desired feature is aesthetic.

(3) Talking of the sensing of beauty also leaves out the whole intensity generated for the sports spectator by supporting someone involved. When I go to a concert to listen to beautiful music I do not think of myself as supporting, or as being behind, the London Symphony Orchestra or Pollini. Equally, I do not exhort them to perform better or try to help them at crucial moments. I do not shout 'Come on the brass section – get involved!'. This whole dimension of being what I called an 'interested' spectator is absent when the central point is the perception of beauty.

(4) It is also relevant to recall the point that engagement in sport, the participant's point of view, is, as I have argued, not aesthetic either. The participant does not aim at beauty or any other aesthetic upshot. That is not the point of their role in proceedings. How odd then if the spectator's point of view, which of course involves his or hers active understanding of the process they are witnessing with such intensity, is primarily and centrally with such *accidental* aesthetic results.

(5) Another reason for thinking that the aesthetic payoffs are not the central ones when watching sport is this; let us suppose that people primarily want an aesthetic payoff from sport, and are simply watching it with that aim, and that they have no understanding of sport as anything else, no understanding that is of the goal of winning, or of tactics or strategy. They simply view the whole thing as an aesthetic performance. How many people

would then be spectators? Try to estimate just how much aesthetic pay-off sport would give them. My own estimate is that very few people would then be sports spectators. If you share this estimate then you should not place aesthetic payoffs as the basic appeal of being a sports spectator.

I hope that these observations seem to have some weight. We can, I want to suggest, think of Gumbrecht's distortion of the point of watching sport as an example of an all too prevalent type of philosophical error. It is an example of what I propose to call Mistaken Assimilations.[14] Gumbrecht, and others, love sport, and they wish to defend or in some way validate that feeling. The temptation is to assimilate what they are defending to something that their critics (or felt critics) do attach importance and value, namely beauty and the aesthetic. Assuming that this is a mistaken assimilation the consequence, or at least one consequence, is to deprive most sport of the pay-off or value that they single out, and so to offer no convincing defence or understanding of it at all. I myself propose that the correct reaction at this point is to simply accept that being a sports spectator offers us the pay-offs that I have described, and not to try to understand it as, fundamentally, an example of some other pay-off.

Mistaken Assimilations also invite an unwanted response by those to whom they are addressed. If the critics of sport who are being addressed start the discussion by acknowledging the value of art and aesthetic experience, then, when they are persuaded that watching sport yields such a pay-off, they can revise their attitude to art, and perhaps limit its value to special cases, or begin to wonder about its value in general. To assimilate sport to art invites a revision of one's attitude to art.

6. Bentham and Mill

I have tried at various stages to bring my discussion of sport into contact with philosophical discussions and the issue we have arrived at, which is what is the relation between sport and art, is

---

[14] Mistaken assimilations are, I suspect, prevalent in thought about many of our basic activities. Amusingly one case involves the understanding of art itself. There is a perennial temptation to think of art as conveying deep and perhaps otherwise inexpressible meaning to us. But this is to assume that the basic point of art must lie in a message we extract from it. In reality, I believe, there are no such messages – and the value of encounters with art should be understood in other ways.

one which has generated important philosophical debate, notably between, of course, Bentham and Mill, and I wish to scrutinise that debate briefly at this point. How did this famous disagreement go? Bentham started it by saying that 'Prejudice apart, the game of push-pin is of equal value with the arts and sciences of music and poetry.'[15] When discussing Bentham later J. S. Mill summarized this opinion as 'Push-pin is as good as poetry'. Bentham's wonderfully provocative remark in effect expresses the claim that there is nothing better to (or about) engaging with art – for example reading poetry and listening to music – than there is to engaging with sport – by playing push-pin, or football. Now, as I read the debate Mill was opposed to Bentham's opinion. Countering Bentham's opinion was part of what Mill was attempting when he proposed the distinction between pleasure of different qualities, those with the so called 'higher quality' being in some way better or more valuable, although when he does this in *Utilitarianism* he does not there use sport as an example of an activity which generates only a lower quality pleasure. However, if Mill intended the higher/lower quality distinction to bear on Bentham's view he would need to classify push-pin as what we might call a 'lower' activity. How should we adjudicate this debate?

Bentham's argument would be that the value of something for someone consists in the pleasure it produces, and clearly push-pin could produce as much pleasure as listening to poetry.[16] This argument is not persuasive *for us* because we do not accept the simple hedonistic conception of value (for an individual) on which it is based.[17] Mill himself was not opposed to the hedonistic framework, but sought to avoid the conclusion, which he thought (or felt) was wrong, by introducing the idea that pleasure itself can have different quality, that with a higher quality being *better* for the individual. No-one can feel that Mill's way of opposing Bentham is satisfactory. In the first place when we grade things in relation to their quality, (as opposed to quantity), which we certainly do with, for example, cloth or wine or grass, we do so (roughly) by envisaging how well

---

[15] Bentham, J, (1830), 206.

[16] I am taking it here that Bentham's claim is about the value for a person, and is not about the communal moral value of these things. Given his framework there is not a great deal of difference between these two issues, of course.

[17] An influential moment in eliminating the hedonistic framework was Nozick's argument based on the idea of the experience machine in *Anarchy, State and Utopia*.

different examples of the general kind would contribute to some end. Thus the higher quality grass grows better and yields a better looking lawn than lower quality grass. But with pleasure there is no function or role that it has in relation to which different cases of pleasure can be compared. So the whole talk of different qualities here lacks application. Further, Mill's proposed test for the higher quality of the pleasure produced by two activities is that people consistently prefer one of them to the other. Amongst many comments that this proposal should attract is that by that standard Mill should either have said that probably push-pin produces a higher quality pleasure than poetry, since people predominantly prefer it, or concede that in fact there are no differences in quality, since no pleasures pass the test for being of the higher quality. Third, when he develops his view Mill's idea is that activities can be divided into the physical and the intellectual and that it is the intellectual activities that produce the higher quality pleasures.[18] But if we take sport, including push-pin, it is obvious that it is intellect involving; as I stressed earlier participants must understand the rules and be able to apply them, which, amongst other things, practically always requires numerical skills. The lower animals cannot participate in this type of activity. Ironically, engagement with art, such as listening to music, or looking at pictures, seems *relatively* unintellectual. We simply savour the sounds and sights and engross ourselves in them. Perhaps lower animals can do that. I am not, of course, seriously downgrading the intellectual requirements of engagement with art, but trying rather to remove any sense of a contrast here between art and sport. For these, and other reasons, Mill's defence of the superiority of art to sport, seems to be a tissue of mistakes.

Now, although Bentham's straightforward, and within his framework relatively cogent, argument cannot be accepted, there is, I believe, some reason to feel sympathy with his conclusion. Consider this; recently I saw that there was an Arts week in Durham, and part of that consisted in brightening up the city by decking it with glowing coloured balls. I assume that will be allowed to be art, and to encounter the lanterns while walking around the city is to encounter art. Now the question that deniers of Bentham's view face is what is more valuable or better for someone in encountering such coloured lights as opposed to encountering and engaging with a cricket game in the same city or playing a game of rugby there. Indeed, what does the encounter with the lights actually give us? Roughly they add interest and charm to our visual experience. To which we can add; so,

---

[18]   See Mill (1861) Ch 2.

amongst other things, does witnessing a cricket game. If we wish to take the case of poetry we need simply to reflect on the experience of listening to Pam Ayers, a popular poet. It is engaging and fun, but so is watching Kevin Peterson.[19]

I cannot here make a serious attempt at uprooting the idea that the experience of art (or, perhaps, Art, with a capital 'A') presents us with some uniquely treasurable features, but reflection on art *in the round* makes that idea difficult to take seriously. I want to suggest though that some such illusion often represents what one might call the reciprocal partner of the error of Mistaken Assimilations. The illusion is that of supposing that the activity to which the one we start with is being mistakenly assimilated is itself one where the pay-offs are *very special and obvious*, whereas in fact it is no clearer in the second case than in the first what the pay offs actually are. I should add that my previous criticism of what I called Mistaken Assimilations in no way depends on the correctness of this briefly developed suggestion.

7. Conclusion

I have talked mostly about witnessing sport and what that gives us. I suggested that we can discern in watching sport pay-offs of a kind that we can all appreciate. This appreciation depends on acceptance of certain psychological claims, for example that we have a taste for excitement and drama, for witnessing skill, for being part of a group and in consequence supporting some of the participants. Above all we should avoid what I call Mistaken Assimilations, in which we think of the point of witnessing sport as being its provision of features which we value *in other areas*.

But I want, finally, to return to the point or points of engaging in, or participating in, sport. One aspect of that is what we get from engaging in competitive games generally. Suffice it to say that they form an immense part of practically all our lives, in some way or other. But I shall not explore games and competition here. The second aspect is that with sport the medium for the game is (usually) intense physical activity. Now, that is something that humans engage in outside sport. People hike and run and climb and exercise. The ubiquity of this kind of activity in our lives suggests that it is part of our nature to engage in it. So participants in sport are, according to this, combining

---

[19] If there is no case for saying that art *per se* is, somehow, better than sport *per se*, it remains open how to compare particular cases.

competition with a fundamental element in our nature. Indeed this element – physical activity – is so much a central part of human life that it merits being labeled a human good. Its enforced absence in lives makes them worse lives. On this conception, which I am proposing but do not here have the space or resources to defend properly, engagement in sport is an instance of a general fundamental human good – bodily activity.[20]

We can, I want to propose, unify and illuminate a number of the themes in this essay by seeing ourselves as having an animal nature, because animals are what we *are*, and sport as we know it can be regarded as an expression of the sort of animal nature – psychological, cognitive and physical – that we, human animals, have.[21]

University College London
p.snowdon@ucl.ac.uk

References

Bentham, J. (1830) *The Rationale of Reward* (London, Robert Heward).

Gumbrecht, H. (2006) *In Praise of Athletic Beauty* (Cambridge, Mass., Belknap Harvard).

Hurka, T. (2006) 'Games and the Good' in *Proceedings of the Aristotelian Society*, Supplementary Volume, Vol **80** (2006) 217–236.

Mill, J.S. (1861), *Utilitarianism*

Tasioulas, J. (2006), 'Games and the Good' in *Proceedings of the Aristotelian Society*, Supplementary Volume, Vol. **80** (2006) 237–264.

Wittgenstein, L. (1953) *Philosophical Investigations* (Oxford, Blackwells).

[20] Because it is philosophers who try to draw up lists of human goods, and their own passion is for more intellectual activities, their lists tend to ignore the very basic physical goods which I am suggesting need acknowledging.

[21] I am very grateful to Anthony O'Hear for the invitation to be part of this series, and to Adam Ferner for his encouragement and help, and to both of them for discussion on sport. I have also benefited from discussions of these issues with Richard Edwards, Ann Higginson, Rory Madden, Brent Madison, Paul Robinson, Katherine Snowdon, Nicholas Snowdon, Victoria Snowdon, and Jo Wolff.

Glory in Sport (and Elsewhere)

TIMOTHY CHAPPELL

> People seek honour both more than they should, and also less
> than they should; therefore, there is a right way to seek honour.
> Aristotle, *Nicomachean Ethics* 1125b20

I

There is a gap between what we think about ethics, and what we think
we think about ethics.[1] This gap appears when elements of our ethical
reflection and our moral theories contradict each other, or otherwise
come into logical tension. It also appears when something that is
important in our ethical reflection is sidelined, or simply ignored, in
our moral theories. The gap appears in both ways with an ethical
idea that I shall label *glory*. This paper's exploration of the idea of
glory, and its place in our ethical reflection, is offered as a case-study
of how far such reflection can diverge from what we might expect, if
we suppose that actual ethical reflection usually or mostly takes the
forms that might be predicted by moral theory. I shall suggest that
this divergence tells against moral theory, and in favour of less con-
stricted and more flexible modes of ethical reflection.

My terms 'ethical reflection' and 'ethical idea' are not meant to be
especially freighted with technical meaning. Ethics as I understand it
is the enterprise of thinking philosophically about the question 'How
should life be lived?', and the further questions that this initial question
generates; 'ethical' is the corresponding adjective. So 'ethical ideas' are
the concepts which we centrally and distinctively deploy in thinking
about these questions; and 'ethical reflection' is just reflection of an
ethical kind.[2] I will often contrast 'ethical reflection' with 'moral

---

[1] Williams 1993, 7, 91.

[2] Hence my 'ethical reflection' is no close relative of Williams 1985
Chapter 9's 'reflection'. That is not a technical term either, but the point
of Williams' usage is that reflection on our own ethical standards can lead
to a corrosive scepticism about them, especially when we think about their
histories. This is not my point here (and anyway, I doubt that Williams' reflection need be as corrosive as he imagines).

Nor do I mean by 'reflection' what many people mean by 'intuition': a

doi:10.1017/S1358246113000283   © The Royal Institute of Philosophy and the contributors 2013
Royal Institute of Philosophy Supplement **73** 2013

theory', by which I mean the project of constructing a deductive or quasi-deductive system for practical choice which, ideally, aims to justify and explain the largest possible number of particular phenomena by reference to the smallest possible number of general principles. My claim will not be that moral theory's characteristic methods and materials can or should *never* be used in ethical reflection. But it will be that ethical reflection at least often takes forms strikingly different from anything that is to be found in typical moral theories, and that one case where this is particularly obvious is the case of glory.

II

The notion of glory may, perhaps, be a neglected one in philosophy partly because of the notion's apparent religious overtones. Be that as it may, to say a little about what glory is is not to introduce a concept that we do not have, but to clarify the content and significance of a concept that we already use (whether or not 'we' are religious). In our society, the idea of glory – though not necessarily the word – is all around us; I doubt I have ever met anyone over the age of two who did not have the concept already. A concern with glory is central to our society's actual, though not always to its officially announced, values. For us glory is typically both an ethical *idea*, a concept that we use, and also an ethical *ideal*, a way of being that we aspire to. I shall have things to say about both the idea and the ideal, and about the connections between them, in this paper.

Glory is something that the sportsmen and sportswomen, the film stars and actors, the pop stars, celebrities, and 'personalities' who dominate our public life and discourse all typically aim at. (Not that they all aim at it all of the time, and under that very description, and wisely and well. Nor that they do not aim at other things also. More on this later.)

If we wanted a single word to show, at least to a first approximation, what is meant by glory, we might coin the word *hurrahability*. The word would be ungainly perhaps, but it would also be usefully ambiguous between three different ways of cashing out the English – *bility* suffix – as making hurrahs *warranted*, as making them *intelligible*, and as making them barely *possible*. The ambiguity is useful

---

quasi-perceptual capacity for 'just seeing' how things are ethically. Whether or not there is such a capacity, the idea that intuition in this sense is the only alternative to moral theory is an obvious straw man.

because assenting to someone else's hurrah-response must mean counting it as warranted, and disagreeing with it must mean counting it as intelligible or possible but not warranted, or else as not even possible.

To use this new word well, we would need to put out of our minds one familiar conception of 'hurrah' now standard in moral theory, on which anything morally positive whatsoever merits a 'hurrah', and anything morally negative whatsoever merits a 'boo'. Obvious facts about our ordinary use of 'hurrah', and about the most usual notions of the morally positive, stand in the way of this equation.[3] It is a remarkable achievement of moral theory to have obscured these obvious facts from our view. The equation nicely illustrates how technical vocabularies are not necessarily more precise just because they are technical, indeed can even be less precise. In real life, when people do their mundane moral duty by, say, paying their taxes or writing their Christmas thank-you letters, our response is not 'hurrah' (not even a bit; not even *sotto voce*). These are morally positive actions, but there isn't even a hint of glory about them. Conversely, there are many things that *do* make us shout 'hurrah', many instances of glory, which are not so much morally negative as never normally evaluated at all (at least not by moral theorists). My discomfort with this anomaly, and with the neglect of the actual meaning of the exclamation 'hurrah' that seemed to lie behind it, was one of the things that got me thinking about glory as an ethical idea in the first place.

Alongside saying that 'glory is hurrahability', and as a way of eluci-dating it a little, we might also say that glory is a kind of *radiance*. There are actions, events, objects, people even, that have a kind of glow or aura about them, that are 'lit up from within' or that 'light things up'; it is this radiance that makes them hurrahable. Obviously to speak of radiance or aura is metaphorical, but it is hard to get beyond the metaphors, which are in any case deeply buried in the English and in many other languages: think of 'brilliant', 'star', 'out-shine', 'splendid', 'luminary', 'lustre', 'illustrious', and the origins of these words where that is not manifest at once. What is glorious is

---

[3] For which perhaps we have originally to thank Hume's notoriously undifferentiated notion of 'the sentiment of approbation' (see Hume 1739, 614). The equation is reinforced in the writings of modern Humeans like Simon Blackburn (1985, 183); another ancestral influence is the basically undifferentiated notions of moral approval and disapproval that Ayer and Hare worked with. Russell (2006) is a modern Humean's defence of Hume's undifferentiated notion.

what is *dazzling*. And when does this dazzle occur? We might put it, with a little formality, like this: glory is – typically – what happens when a spectacularly excellent performance within a worthwhile form of activity meets the admiration that it merits.

As we shall see in section IV of this paper, this formula will not cover everything that might be worth calling glory (hence my word 'typically'). In section VII, we will meet the suggestion that it does not even cover the most central and paradigm case of glory of all. Also, there are glory-*related* phenomena regarding which, though they are certainly excellent and admirable performances occurring within worthwhile practices, it seems too strong to speak of *glory* exactly. Admirable things can be admirably done – can be what Plato and Aristotle called *kalakagatha* – without being admirable enough, or spectacular enough, to count as glorious. Still, such phenomena are on the glory-*spectrum*, even if they are not towards the higher end of it where explicit glory-talk becomes natural, or more natural. And the formula does bring out three different ways of criticising claims that something is glorious. Most obviously, we can question whether a given performance really is spectacularly excellent.[4] But we can also doubt whether that performance, spectacularly excellent though it may be, meets the admiration that it merits. And again we can dispute whether a spectacularly excellent performance happens within a worthwhile form of activity.

This third kind of question is particularly interesting, given that so many of our society's most typical glory-ascriptions happen within forms of activity the worthwhileness of which is at least controversial. Perhaps there can't be glory in push-pin or pinochle, no matter how spectacular my performances in these trivial parlour games. But if we grant that, then maybe we must also dismiss the idea that there can be glory in, say, a cricket match or a rock concert – at least until we can prove the worthwhileness of rock concerts to dismissive classical music lovers, and the worthwhileness of cricket to Americans.

How, in general, are we to prove such worthwhileness claims? Here recall what Alasdair MacIntyre says about his notion of a 'practice' (1981, 193):

> What is distinctive in a practice is in part the way in which con-
> ceptions of the relevant goods and ends which the technical skills
> serve... are transformed and enriched by these extensions of

---

[4] What, for instance, if it fails? There can be glorious failures, no doubt – but presumably theirs is not a glory that anyone sane normally hopes for, and a different kind from the glory of the corresponding successes.

human powers and by that regard for its internal goods which are partially definitive of each particular practice.

It is tempting to think that proving a practice worthwhile must be a matter of showing how it fits antecedently available standards and realises antecedently available goods. But with typical practices – and I think, on MacIntyre's definition,[5] = rock music and cricket *are* typical practices – this is precisely not what is involved. The whole point of the practice is that it creates its *own* standards of worthwhileness and goodness, standards which are internal to the practice and irreducible to any kind of external standards. The practice opens up for its practitioners ways of excelling, and so of flourishing, which would not exist – would not even be describable – without it. That is one reason why it is a mistake to fault practices like cricket, or rock music, or ballet, or the theatre for not feeding the hungry, say, or contributing to the economy. Whether or not such activities do feed anyone, or make any money, that is not what they are distinctively aimed at doing. They are aimed at achieving and exploring their own internal goods, which we have no good reason to think illusory just because they are not the same as some other goods, e.g. welfare and justice (to give two examples that have particularly interested moral theorists). If these activities fail to be worthwhile, it is because they fail to achieve their *own* goods, not because there are some other goods that they do not achieve; or because their own goods are indeed illusory goods – where, however, illusoriness must be more than mere difference from some other set of goods.

III

So glory can attach to spectacular performance within any activity which satisfies the conditions to count as a MacIntyrean practice. (In games which, e.g., lack the complexity to count as practices, perhaps something analogous to glory can still be found: when I dance triumphantly around the room after winning a family game

---

[5] MacIntyre's definition is this (1981, 187): 'By a "practice" I am going to mean any coherent and complex form of socially established cooperative human activity through which goods internal to that form of activity are realised in the course of trying to achieve those standards of excellence which are appropriate to, and partially definitive of, that form of activity, with the result that human powers to achieve excellence, and human conceptions of the ends and goods involved, are systematically extended.'

of pinochle I am joking, but the point of my joke lies in the relation of this 'triumph' to real triumphs.) And appreciating this glory is a matter of appreciating the particular standards of performance that the practice itself generates. To understand why, for example, it could be called a glorious moment when Andrew Flintoff ran out Ricky Ponting in the Fifth Ashes Test in August 2009, you need to see much more than the breathtaking technical mastery involved – the lightning speed and accuracy of Flintoff's field and throw; you also need to know what, in general, a run-out is according to the rules of cricket, and why it matters to achieve one.

You also need to understand why, in particular, *this* was a good moment to achieve a run-out within this specific match. Alongside the aspects of the glory of Flintoff's run-out that are internal to the nature of the game of cricket, there are also narrative aspects, concerning the history of the game. ('Every practice has its own history': MacIntyre 1981, 194.) It matters, for example, that the background is a story about 120 years of cricketing rivalry between England and Australia, and it matters about the importance of this particular match within the 2009 series. (If they had won, Australia would have retained the Ashes.) There are also personal aspects to what happened, concerning the dramatic personae that Ponting and Flintoff had developed within that series as it unfolded: Ponting's alleged uptightness and dourness had made him (unfairly, I think) the bogeyman of the English crowd despite his playing extremely well, whereas the famously laddish and over-relaxed Flintoff was their talisman despite injuries that made him seriously under-perform both as a batsman and as a bowler. Against that background there was a delicious appositeness, what sports-writers like to mark with their favourite adverb 'ironically', in Flintoff's sudden appearance in his very last Test as Ponting's and Australia's nemesis. This element of appositeness, we might almost say of wit, contributed to the glory of the moment too.[6]

This brings out, not only how glory can have an essentially narrative structure, but also how it can be perspectival. English cricket fans

[6] Anthony O'Hear writes (personal communication): 'I was at the Oval, right behind [Flintoff] for that run-out… it was completely out of the blue – it looked an innocuous run until we saw the pick-up and stumps shattered with, as it seemed, one movement. And, we were feeling, not a moment too soon, as the bowling was getting nowhere at that stage, Ponting looking impregnable and in great nick, as indeed was Hussey, who was only got out at the end of the innings. 200 or so runs was looking ominously achievable, and some annoying Australians in front of us kept jumping up shouting "All day, mate!" So the "glory" moment was all the sweeter, particularly to round off a series we didn't really deserve to win.'

like me cannot reasonably expect Australians to find the Ponting run-out quite as glorious as they do; as Australian friends have more or less said to me, the natural reaction for them is something like 'It's your party, mate, so enjoy it' (often with the acid addition 'while it lasts'). Nor would I expect an American (not even one who understood cricket) to see the glory that an English person may see in the moment of the Ponting run-out.

Similar remarks apply to a second and 'less trivial' example of glory, from politics. (Politics is not a game, but it is a MacIntyrean practice: it realises goods both internal and external to itself. If Aristotle could, anachronistically, be brought into this discussion, he would perhaps say that politics is the *arch*-practice, the practice which gives their point and place to all the other practices: *Politics* 1252a1–7.) This second example is Winston Churchill on the balcony of Buckingham Palace on VE Day, May 8 1945:

> The unconditional surrender of our enemies was the signal for the greatest outburst of joy in the history of mankind. The Second World War had indeed been fought to the bitter end in Europe. The vanquished as well as the victors felt inexpressible relief. But for us in Britain and the British Empire, who had alone[7] been in the struggle from the first day to the last and staked our existence on the result, there was a meaning beyond what even our most powerful and most valiant Allies could feel. Weary and worn, impoverished but undaunted and now triumphant, we had a moment that was sublime. (Churchill 1954, 439–40)

Churchill's glory on VE Day was not the glory of a particular performance that he was then engaged in: it was a cumulative or retrospective kind of glory, arising from his courageous and steadfast leadership over five and a half years of a war that Britain had initially looked almost certain to lose, and which it was vital for the Allies to win, not only for their own interests but for the future of the whole world. This is a perspective, and a narrative, that needed to be in place before a spectator in the Mall could fully grasp Churchill's sublime moment. German or Swiss spectators would not and could not have fully shared this perspective. If they knew all the background, they might fully have appreciated *why* the moment was glorious. They would still, in a sense, be seeing that glory from

---

[7] 'Alone'? Polish, Czech, Slovak, and French readers will dispute that. (In Prague I recently saw a memorial 'to the victims of the Second World War, 1938 to 1945'.)

outside – as a proposition about what others were experiencing rather than as an experience of their own.

These points about the perspectival nature of at least some glory might make it seem that glory is essentially a *reaction*, something inside us rather than in the world. Philosophical critics of a certain ir-realist sort will very probably say that what I call glory is simply what happens in our emotions or attitudes when certain phenomena come our way.

Here the irrealist offers the suggestion that glory might be reducible to emotional reactions, as if that might be the full and complete story about what glory is. A realist will typically counter that glory is something entirely observer-independent, that glory-properties have to be out-there-in-the-world if they are to be anywhere at all: will talk, in short, as if he loses the argument if he admits that our emotions and reactions have *any* place in glory.

Both these positions seem, like many other positions that moral philosophers get themselves into, unnecessarily extreme and over-simplified positions. Maybe the truth about glory is that, for the full-blown form of the phenomenon, you need both glory-properties in the world and reactions in spectators – and above all, a *fit* between properties and reactions. But whether you need to be a realist to talk of this contrast between properties and reactions, or of reactions fitting or not fitting the properties in question, is not as obvious as it might seem. Intelligent irrealists about value typically think that they can make these moves too: that their theories allow for the possibilities of correctness-conditions for moral utterance, and of moral experience that is like experience of properties, and would fail as theories if they didn't.

IV

A different aspect of glory that needs to be brought out is glory's capacity to bestow meaning or significance on life – to 'make it all worthwhile'. Some connections between meaningfulness and glory may already be evident in my Churchill example. Perhaps the victorious crowds in front of Buckingham Palace felt inchoately that all the terrible sufferings and loss of the war years could be redeemed, some sense could be made of them, if this moment of glory was where, in the end, they led to.[8] (The converse certainly seems true: a defeated population's emotions are very likely to be dominated by the shame that is the opposite of the sense of glory, and by the confusion that

---

[8]   I am grateful to Joss Walker for discussion of the Churchill example.

is the opposite of the sense of significance.) Nietzsche's famous remark, in the Preface to *The Birth of Tragedy*, that 'only as an aesthetic phenomenon are existence and the world justified', seems to be a related thought; seeing 'existence and the world' as beautiful is surely one way of seeing them as meaningful or worthwhile.

This connection between glory and meaningfulness comes out very clearly in another sporting example, at the end of Garrison Keillor's tale of the day Babe Ruth visited Keillor's fictional mid-west small-town of Lake Wobegon (Keillor 1989, 108):

> A true hero has some power to make us a gift of a larger life... He did something on that one day in our town that made us feel we were on the map of the universe, connected somehow to the stars, a part of the mind of God. The full effect of his mighty blow diminished over time, of course, and now our teams languish, our coaches despair. Defeat comes to seem the natural course of things. Lake Wobegon dresses for a game, they put on their jockstraps, pull on the socks, get into the colours, they start to lose heart and turn pale – fear shrivels them.
>
> Boys, this game may be your only chance to do good, he might tell them. You might screw up everything else in your life and poison the ones who love you, create misery, create such pain and devastation it will be repeated by generations of descendants. Boys, there's plenty of room for tragedy in life, so if you go bad, don't have it be said that you never did anything right. Win this game.

We might almost say that the sense of glory *is* the sense that significance (of one sort) has been achieved, that meaning (of one kind) has been brought into what was previously shapeless and unreconciled.

The greatest work on glory in the history of Western literature is also the first work in that history: Homer's *Iliad*. And there too, alongside a great deal about the glory of war and of sporting prowess[9] (it is pretty

---

[9]   Simone Weil famously argues (Weil 1940) that the central theme of the *Iliad* is the horror with which force transforms its victims – and its perpetrators – into things, mere objects. No doubt that is *a* central theme of the poem. Yet the *Iliad*'s attitude to violence, unlike Weil's, is clearly not simply negative. It might equally be read as *celebrating* murder, mayhem, and mutilation, with a relish that is at least unhealthy and arguably pornographic. If there is something of Wilfred Owen in Homer's heroes, there is something of the Viking in them too. Another of the *Iliad*'s central themes is the honour and glory that can be won by force, whether in the 'artificial' context of sport, or in the overshadowing 'natural' context of the unending war. For Homeric warriors, such as the Trojan Sarpedon at *Iliad* 12.310–28, there is an obligation to fight in return for honour (*timê*), and *kleos* (posthumous

clear that Homer's contemporaries regarded war as a MacIntyrean practice), we find, on Helen's lips, the hope that glory might bring meaning (*Iliad* 6.356–358, my own translation):

> Zeus has laid a bad fate on Paris and me –
> Bitch as I am, blinded and wild as he is –
> That for ages to come we might be the matter of song.

Helen's one consolation too, in the miserable and hopeless position that she and Paris find themselves in, is her hope that some kind of posthumous glory will, as I put it above, 'make it all worthwhile', shed a retrospective glow of significance and beauty on the events surrounding her that somehow validates their horror. She redeems her *kakos moros*, she makes sense of her own and her lover's sordid misdeeds and terrible predicament, by 'foreseeing' the glorious and unforgettable epic – the *Iliad* itself – that they will become part of. And her claim to be unforgettable succeeds, simply by being unforgettable.

By the time we get to this example, our notion of glory no longer quite fits the initial characterisation that I gave in section II: the radiance or aura that typically attaches to a spectacularly excellent performance, within a worthwhile form of activity, when it meets the admiration that it merits. As Homer depicts her, Helen can lay claim to no performance that merits any admiration at all. Being abducted by Paris, thus triggering a bloody and brutal war that lasts ten years, hardly counts as a worthwhile form of activity. The glory that she hopes for is different, though it is not merely fame either; it is the

---

fame) is regularly the one consolation that Homeric heroes have for the imminent prospect of death and Hades: see particularly *Odyssey* Book 11. Again, the deputation of Greeks who go to persuade Achilles to return to the war find him in his tent, singing to the lyre the *klea andrôn* (*Iliad* 9.189), 'the famous deeds of men' – just what Homer was doing himself in reporting it. (Thanks to Chris Emlyn-Jones for discussion.)

One particularly notable context where Homer exploits the contrast between the glory of sport and the glory of war is the final duel between Hector and Achilles, where Hector turns and runs for his life, and Achilles chases him as if they are athletes in a race. But no ordinary race (*Iliad* 22.158–161, my own translation):

> A good man ran before, a great man after;
> And desperate fast, for their race had as prize
> No bull-hide relic such as athletes win:
> The prize they sprinted for was Hector's life.

glory – the radiance and aura – of being *herself*, Helen, 'the face that launched a thousand ships'. Yet as W.B. Yeats understood, that too can be glory:

> That the topless towers be burnt
> And men recall that face,
> Move most gently if move you must
> In this lonely place.
> She thinks, part woman, three parts a child,
> That nobody looks; her feet
> Practise a tinker shuffle
> Picked up on a street.
> *Like a long-legged fly upon the stream*
> *Her mind moves upon silence.*

Sometimes, as with Helen, glory is *just* the radiance or aura I spoke of, without *any* relevantly connected performance. That may make it harder to state the correctness-conditions for ascriptions of glory, but it need not mean that the radiance in question is any less really glory, and it need not mean that glory of this sort is any less able to bestow significance on our lives.

Homer's concern with glory in the agonistic contexts of sport and war, and also beyond those contexts, is echoed throughout the later Greek tradition,[10] and in the other traditions that followed and inherited the Greeks'; including our own. When we think today about glory and shame, *kudos* and *aidôs*, in war or sport or elsewhere, we engage with an evaluative vocabulary that was perfectly intelligible twenty-eight centuries ago at the very beginning of our culture, and is no less intelligible to us now.

Yet even in the ancient world Homer's evaluative vocabulary was not without its critics; he himself seems to have been engaged, *inter alia*, in criticising the values presented in his epics. Of course the *Iliad* takes glory to be a central ethical *idea*, and I have argued that we do too. But there are the further questions whether the *Iliad* also take glory to be a central ethical *ideal* – something to be aimed

---

[10] Herodotus, for example, tells us in the first lines of his *Histories* that one of his reasons for writing is so that the exploits of Greeks and barbarians might not be *aklea*; and Eteocles' prayer, at Aeschylus, *Septem contra Thebas* 683–5, is not that he should avoid disaster, but that if disaster comes on him, it should come without shame (*aiskhynê*). 'The implicit definition of a Greek, as contrasted with a barbarian, becomes – a member of a community entitled to attend the Olympic Games.' (MacIntyre 1981, 138)

at and lived for – and whether we should. Or is it with glory as Falstaff says it is with honour?[11] Perhaps glory should not be an ethical *ideal* for us, something we pursue, because it is a bogus ethical *idea* – a mere word, a delusion, a sham concept? These questions turn our attention to the issue of how glory relates to ethics, and to moral theory. I turn to them now.

V

One argument against taking glory as an ethical ideal, which is already perfectly evident to any attentive reader of Homer, is that glory keeps bad company.[12] Tyrants and maniacs regularly appeal to glory, as Alexander, Napoleon, Hitler, Franco, Stalin, Mao, and Mussolini all famously did, to overwhelm our critical faculties and to justify their misdeeds. Isn't glory the propagandist's stock in trade? And doesn't that make it too debased a currency for any serious purpose?

One response to this first argument is the well-known Latin tag *corruptio optimi pessima*: the better something is, the worse its perversion. Appeals to glory are certainly the propagandist's stock in trade, but there is a reason for that: because appeals to glory, *where genuine and justifiable*, are a potent proof of value. That Goebbels misused the language of glory does not speak against glory, but against Goebbels. After all, Goebbels misused the language of justice too.

For related reasons, it is not a serious criticism of glory as an ethical ideal to point out – truly enough, of course – how ridiculous people can make themselves by pursuing it. Apparently, it is the ideal of glory that drives people to do things like going on reality TV; indisputably, most people who go on reality TV make complete fools of themselves. Sure, but sometimes people who are driven by the

[11] William Shakespeare, *Henry IV Part I*, Act 5 Scene 1, lines 131–140: 'Can honour set to a leg? No. Or an arm? No. Or take away the grief of a wound? No. Honour hath no skill in surgery then? No. What is honour? A word. What is in that word honour? Air – a trim reckoning! Who hath it? He that died a' Wednesday. Doth he feel it? No. Doth he hear it? No. 'Tis insensible then? Yea, to the dead. But will it not live with the living? No. Why? Detraction will not suffer it. Therefore I'll none of it. Honour is a mere scutcheon – and so ends my catechism.'
This is not, incidentally, the only passage where Shakespeare has Falstaff parody Socrates; cp. the Hostess's account of Falstaff's death in *Henry V*, Act 2 Scene 3.
[12] Thanks in particular to Alex Miller for pushing me on the bad-company argument.

ideal of justice make complete fools of themselves too. Another Latin tag applies here: *abusus non tollit usum*, that a thing can be misused does not show that it has no good use.

What about the use of glory-talk to justify misdeeds? *Corruptio optimi pessima* and *abusus non tollit usum* apply to that too. For a different kind of challenge to the notion of glory, recall my initial characterisation of it in section II, as 'what happens when a spectacularly excellent performance within a worthwhile form of activity meets the admiration that it merits'. I pointed out in II how something can fail to be a worthwhile form of activity because it is trivial, like a simple parlour game, or perhaps completely pointless, like the collection of saucers of mud.[13] An activity can also fail to be worthwhile by being, not pointless, but *morally bad*. Spectacularly excellent performance in a wicked activity cannot be glorious, and wicked people, like Mao and Hitler, who claim glory are making a false claim.

But then (it might be argued), if moral goodness, or at any rate permissibility, is a necessary condition of glory, that must mean that assessments of whether something is or is not glorious are not themselves moral assessments, but some different kind of assessments to which moral assessments are only a preliminary. Hence – it could be said – glory, while it may be a value, cannot be counted a *moral* value.

If this argument worked, then so would the following: generosity cannot be a virtue, because I cannot exercise *true* generosity in morally bad ways, e.g. by giving away things which are not mine to give, or by being arbitrarily or capriciously generous. Moral permissibility is only a necessary condition of true generosity; therefore generosity, while no doubt a value, cannot be a *moral* value.

Both arguments fail, because the moral badness of bad generosity or wicked glory consists in some specific kind of immorality – injustice or the like. Hence generosity and glory are not shown to be outside the ethical domain, just because there are other ethical standards besides their own that apply to them. There can be more than one ethical standard, and what succeeds by one ethical standard, e.g. by being glorious, may fail by another, e.g. by being cruel.

Does this make the ethical domain too wide? As I said earlier, the ethical domain as I understand it includes all the questions that we distinctively ask and all the concepts that we distinctively use in inquiring how life should be lived. That certainly makes the ethical domain wider than it is for those who think, as moral theorists very

---

[13]   Unless collecting saucers of mud has now become a peculiarly inscrutable philosophers' game, a little like Mornington Crescent perhaps.

often have, that the ethical has to do with little more than obligation to others, or 'moral principles', or something like that. But, I suggest, this width is a good thing, because without it the ethical, and in particular obligation, is not intelligibly connected to anything else. Until we see our reason 'to be moral' (which in this context usually means: to be just or fair to others, even at the risk of loss to ourselves) in its proper relation to our other reasons, and in particular to those reasons that have to do with the question 'What can make life meaningful?', we will not see it at all. A life in which I simply fulfilled my obligations would be a Sisyphean one – unless fulfilling my obligations was somehow connected, for me, with meaning and significance. But if it is connected with those things, then it will be connected, directly or indirectly, with glory too. It is not for nothing that Rai Gaita concludes his discussion of a famous example of extraordinarily self-sacrificing behaviour in the unspeakably terrifying and sordid conditions of Auschwitz with the words: 'Charles's behaviour showed a goodness *to marvel at*' (Gaita 1991, xvii, my italics).

Thinking about glory can give us other reasons too to widen our conception of the moral. Moral theorists usually work with a dichotomy between moral and prudential reasons. Since glory is an ethical idea that does not seem to fit well on the moral side of this dichotomy, it tends to get put on the prudential side: glory must be a value my pursuit of which serves *my* turn, not anyone else's; and so, a self-interested value.[14] Thus the moral-prudential dichotomy is quickly equated with the altruistic-egoistic dichotomy, and from there it is but a short step to a series of charges that moralists down the centuries have routinely made against glory: that the motivation of glory is essentially *selfish*, that it turns us into rampaging egoists, feeds the wrong parts of our psyches, puffs us up with self-conceit and self-regard, prevents us from acquiring humility or self-knowledge, and so on.

One way to rebut these charges is simply to look at the evidence, from sport or the theatre for example, that glory can be a team achievement at least as easily as an individual one, or that for every

[14]   Adkins' well-known contrast between 'cooperative' and 'competitive' values (1960, 7 ff.) is somewhere in between the normal moral/prudential contrast, and the contrast between obligation-based and glory-based values that I am drawing here. It is not the same as either of the other two contrasts, though it sometimes seems to have seduced Adkins himself into equating all three. For a critique of Adkins's competitive/cooperative distinction see Long 1970, who rightly points out that many of the Homeric Greeks' most characteristic interests are not amenable to this distinction because they are about a glory that is achieved by *teamwork*.

great performer with a bloated ego, there is another whose feeling about her own achievements is something more like amazed gratitude, and a third who cannot stop beating herself up about all the things she *didn't* achieve.

Another and deeper way is to look more closely at the thought that actually motivates those who pursue glory.[15] Often their motivation, what they want when they act, is something like: 'that I should win this glorious victory', 'that I should achieve this spectacular achievement'. Such an agent's motivation essentially mentions him ('that *I* should win'). It is not enough, to fulfil his wish, that *someone* should win the victory or achieve the achievement. But it also essentially mentions the victory or achievement too. It is not enough, to fulfil his wish, that just anything agreeable should happen to him, or even just any victory or achievement: he wants *this* one. Furthermore, it is absolutely familiar that an agent working within some particular MacIntyrean practice should make great sacrifices in his pursuit of excellence in that practice. The more you look at the personal cost that can be involved in becoming, say, a great ballet dancer or novelist, the less it looks at all accurate to say that participation in such practices, since it cannot be classed as morally (and so altruistically) motivated, must be prudentially (and so egoistically) motivated. Perhaps, in most or maybe all MacIntyrean practices, the primary beneficiary is neither the agent nor the spectators, but the practice itself.

Thus the effect of thinking carefully and clearly about glory ought to be to break down the dichotomies between moral and prudential, altruistic and egoistic. It ought to help us to see that a lot of motivation is neither self-interested nor other-directed (which of course is not to say that such motivation cannot be criticisable either prudentially, or morally, or both). But this is not the only dichotomy traditionally observed by moral theorists to which glory suggests counter-examples. Two more familiar dichotomies come into view when we consider two more well-worn criticisms of glory. The first of these is that glory makes us pathologically dependent on the opinions of others. The second is that we should forget about glory and concentrate on what lies within the scope of our deliberate control: as it sometimes folksily put, that we should 'do our best and leave the rest'.

The idea that we should 'do our best and leave the rest' interestingly reflects a particular way of drawing the line between what we

---

[15]   With the argument of this paragraph cp. Bernard Williams' distinction between the egoism/ altruism distinction, and the I-desire/ non-I-desire distinction: Williams 1973.

Timothy Chappell

are and are not responsible for (and indeed between what we are and what we are not). A philosopher is likely to say that the distinction it draws is a recognisably Kantian one, though behind Kant the distinction also has deep roots in the Christian tradition, particularly in its Protestant form.[16] The idea is that what I intentionally do is specially mine, expressive of me; everything else is in truth not really mine, or an expression of me, at all. I can control whether I perform well – or at least, I can control it up to a point. (Our need for this qualification, and our difficulty in exactly identifying the 'point' in question, are both revealing.) But I cannot control how others react to my good performance. Therefore, how others react can be of no moral concern to me. But glory as characterised in section II ('what happens when a spectacularly excellent performance within a worthwhile form of activity *meets the admiration that it merits*') essentially involves others' reactions. Therefore I cannot have a legitimate moral concern with glory.

But this sharp division between what I do and do not intentionally control is not the only possible division that we might make about responsibility. More to the point, it is not even the only actual division: 'we know that in the story of one's life there is an authority exercised by what one has done, and not merely by what one has intentionally done' (Williams 1993, 69). It is not that the intentional/unintentional distinction cannot do *any* work in ethical thinking about responsibility. But it is that that distinction cannot do *all* the work. One striking example of the absurdities that can result if we try to place too much weight on it comes when C.D. Broad is reviewing Ross, and citing Prichard as a further authority for a certainly false view about obligation that all three of them seem, bizarrely enough, to agree on:

> [I]n the strictest sense, a person cannot be under an obligation to produce any change which is not wholly within his power. Now the only change which it is wholly within an agent's power to produce is that mental change which Prichard calls "setting oneself to perform" an action. Whether this will produce the expected overt movements of one's own body depends on conditions which are out of one's power, though they are in fact generally

---

[16]   Though not, interestingly enough, in the Calvinist school of Protestantism. Most Protestants (and a lot of Catholics) follow early/ middle Augustine in making the will absolutely central to their accounts of responsibility and blame. The curious thing about Calvinism is the way in which it makes room for forms of blame and culpability that have to do with the whole shape of one's life pretty well *irrespective* of one's will. In this, no doubt, the Calvinists are rejecting early/middle in favour of late Augustine.

114

fulfilled. And whether these bodily movements, if they take place, will produce the intended changes in the external world depends on conditions which are not only out of the agent's power but also may easily fail to be fulfilled. Hence, strictly speaking, no one is under an obligation to make any particular bodily movement, and *a fortiori* no one is under an obligation to make any particular change in the external world. (Broad 1940, 232)

If this is where a view about the intentional/unintentional boundary leads us to, then something has clearly gone wrong enough to make it worth reassessing the idea that there is any such thing (or at least, any sharp single boundary).

Related doubts about another familiar dichotomy – this time between independence and dependence – emerge when we think about the charge that glory makes our well-being pathologically dependent on the opinions of others. Here, at first sight, the problem seems to be one of misdirection: 'The object of well-directed activities is the things that are good in themselves; but the object of activities aimed at glory is *applause*; and applause is not a good in itself; so activities aimed at glory are not well-directed.' This argument fails, because its second premiss is false. There would indeed be something misdirected, perhaps even pathological, about a pursuit solely of applause. Come to that, there would be something misdirected about a pursuit solely of merited applause. But a pursuit of glory is not the same as either.

Think of the fantastic goal that is scored – but in an empty stadium; or of the marvellous opera that is composed – but never performed; or indeed, somewhat closer to home, of the wonderful philosophy paper that is written – but no one ever reads it. The whole point of writing philosophy papers is that they should be read; the whole point of composing operas is that they should be performed. We can imagine variants of these activities which do not, as they do, constitutively involve the expectation of uptake. But such variants would be precisely that – variants, a different kind of activity. (A kick-a-bout in an empty stadium, however skilful and intricate it may be, remains a different kind of activity from a cup final; a 'philosophy paper' written only for the eyes of REF or tenure assessors or as a try-out to clarify one's own ideas is, arguably, not really a philosophy paper at all.) The kinds of activity in which we seek glory have a reference to an audience – in some cases perhaps only a single person, in other cases necessarily more[17] – constitutively built into them.

---

[17]   As Hallvard Fossheim has helpfully reminded me, glory is constitutively inter-personal, not only in the sense that there are two parties (agent

Timothy Chappell

Doesn't that mean that it's impossible to aim at glory *without* aiming at applause? The only honest answer to that seems to be Yes. But this answer does not mean that, in these cases, aiming at glory necessarily exhibits a pathological dependence on the opinions of others. Here as with section III's question whether the real existence of glory is in reactions or in properties in the world, what we need is a combined account. When I give a philosophy talk, my objective can be two things combined: that I should give a brilliant talk, and that my audience should respond to it as a brilliant talk. Certainly there would be something pathological about me if I aimed only at the audience-response. (Something like this is what goes wrong in the cult of fame and celebrity.) A philosopher who reads out an hour's worth of the phone-book to his seminar audience, and then is *pleased* when they cheer his nonsense to the echo, is a sick man. But surely there would also be something pathological about him if he cared only about the quality of his talk, and was utterly indifferent to the response (if any) of his audience (if any). A philosophy talk is a performance of a particular kind. Essentially, performances of that kind are aimed at audiences. When his audience is absent in body or in spirit, or fully present but gives an inapposite response (either way), something has gone wrong: part of the good he aimed at has not been achieved.

There is an interesting parallel here with some familiar arguments about pleasure. Philosophical hedonists often talk as if all I can be aiming in any activity is the pleasure that it produces, and as if it would be an unnecessary over-complication of theory to think about the activity too; philosophical anti-hedonists often suggest that the only thing I should aim at is the completion of the activity, perhaps even that there is something morally corrupt about me if I am interested in any separable resultant pleasure as well. I suspect that here also both sides of the question are over-simplifying and exaggerating, and that the truth lies in a more moderate and more complex combined account. The point of these activities is *both* that some performance should be completed, *and* that pleasure should be found in that performance. When I go for a walk in the hills, I want to complete the walk. But I also want it to be pleasurable

---

and audience), but also because, at least in many cases, the (proper) audience is irreducibly a plurality of people, and the individuals in this plurality are reacting not only to the agent, but also to each other. There are interesting complexities here, including the complexities about the psychology of crowds that Elias Canetti famously explored.

rather than unpleasant, which is not the same thing (not even an ad-verbial aspect of the same thing; there is nothing adverbial about blis-ters or pulled muscles). There would be something pathological about only wanting the pleasure and not caring about the walk, but there would be something equally pathological about only wanting the walk and not caring about the pleasure. Just likewise with the components of glory, if we take these to be spectacular performance and condign applause: something goes wrong if you only aim at the applause, but something also goes wrong if you only aim at the per-formance. Hence it is also true that aiming at glory need not be self-defeating, provided you aim at both of these constituents; just as (*pace* the 'paradox of hedonism') aiming at pleasure need not be self-defeating, provided pleasure is not all you aim at.

It follows that aiming at glory (like almost everything else we do, in fact) does necessarily involve us both in dependence on others, and in concern with factors which are – 'strictly speaking', if you follow Broad – beyond our intentional control. Composing a splendid opera, running out the Australian cricket captain at the key moment, doing all that is necessary to bring about the hour of victory on the Palace balcony, or scoring a beautiful goal is only part of what I need for glory; amongst other things, I need the reactions of others – the *right* reactions of others – as well. The involvement of the audience in the play or the crowd in the Cup Final constitutes those as different sorts of events from the dress rehearsal or the kickabout in the empty stadium. It is a cliché of sport that the roar of the crowd gets the players' adrenalin going, and a cliché of theatre that the finest perform-ances constitutively involve the audience. It is a cliché about clichés that clichés are clichés for the solid, if rather boring, reason that they are true. Here then we find dependence; but *pathological* dependence? Only if it is pathological for humans to depend on each other at all.

Among the many philosophers and moral theorists who in one way or another have wrongly rejected various sorts of human dependence – one thinks at once of Nietzsche, Augustine, Sartre, Hobbes – it is curious to note Aristotle. How odd that the philosopher who has come closest (though not *that* close) to a positive account of at least one aspect of glory in his discussion of *megaloprepeia* (*Nicomachean Ethics* IV.2, 1122a–b), should also be the philosopher who claims that well-being consists in complete *autarkeia*, freedom from depen-dence (*Nicomachean Ethics* 1097b8).[18] But human life begins and

---

[18]   Aristotle expresses his reservation about the dependence involved in glory most clearly when he writes that honour, *timê*, 'seems to be more in those who honour than in him who is honoured; but our intuition is that

ends in physical dependence, with a great deal of social interdependence in between (MacIntyre 1999), and its goods are necessarily fragile (Nussbaum 1986). How could this possibly be news?

VI

Thinking about glory, and about the objections that those well-versed in moral theory are likely to put to glory, either as an ethical idea or as an ethical ideal, has shown us how glory undermines some of the most characteristic dichotomies of moral theory: moral/prudential, altruistic/egoistic, within/beyond intentional control and obligatory/non-obligatory, independent/dependent. Another objection that might be put to glory suggests another challenge to a dichotomy dear to moral theory. This objection is that glory is *unfair*. Glory is undemocratic, because it makes one person the centre of attention for everyone else in a way that cannot be generalised – or as I almost said, universalised.

True, under most imaginable acceptable organisations of any complex society there will be quite a few different kinds of glory available, so that more people than you might at first expect can get their Warholian fifteen minutes of fame. True, but banal. And more importantly, this response ducks the deeper question why anyone should expect glory to be fair, democratic, universalisable etc. in the first place. Paradigmatically, glory arises when an extraordinarily spectacular performance or action or state or event or result (...), achieved within a worthwhile practice, is greeted with the extreme

---

the good is something of one's own, and not easily taken away' (NE 1095b25–27). Aristotle evidently means that *timê* is easily taken away *because* it is 'more in those than honour than in him who is honoured'. Even if this is true, another point is also true. This is that once I *have been* honoured, that honour is (typically) mine 'for keeps'. As people say to champions and to sporting and other heroes, 'You've done this, and *no one can take it away from you*'.

Aristotle's relation to the idea of glory is interesting, and interestingly different from many other philosophers in the canon because of his non-relation to the Christian tradition (of which he is not even a precursor, not at least in the distinctive way that Plato is: see below). In his ethical thinking glory is closely linked with his very central ideal of *megalopsychia,* nobility – another ethical idea that we too unquestionably think important, whether or not we think we think it important. I hope to write about nobility too some time soon.

enthusiasm that it warrants. In the nature of the case only a minority of things can be extraordinarily spectacular. So in the nature of the case only a minority of things can be glorious. And the closer we approach the paradigm, the smaller this minority is likely to be. The very structure of the concept of glory entails a kind of partiality; and as we know from elsewhere, e.g. the debate about moral demandingness, partiality is something that moral theory has usually struggled with. In the long-running ethical debate over demandingness, ethicists today are – perhaps – getting closer to admitting that one sort of partiality might be a basic given in the moral life. Reflection on the ideal of glory ought, I suggest, to prompt them to admit another sort of partiality as well. As these kinds and instances of partiality multiply, so we will move that bit further away from moral theory's usual picture of a deliberative world organised around a unique, monotonic, and indeed monotone ranking of impartial obligations. And a good thing too.

That was a point about what happens when things go right with glory: when there *is* something extraordinarily spectacular, and it *is* greeted with the extreme enthusiasm that it warrants by the audience that it deserves. A second way of reading 'glory is unfair' is as the objection that things don't go right nearly often enough. As a matter of fact (this objection says), in a world like ours, wonderful performances and achievements are routinely ignored, and hopelessly bad ones routinely lionised. Not just some but most excellence goes unrewarded, most charlatanry unexposed; the brilliant philosophy articles get rejected for stupid reasons, the dull-as-ditchwater articles get published for even stupider reasons. What Hamlet calls 'the insolence of office and the spurns That patient merit of the unworthy takes' are everywhere. And I am not just thinking of Simon Cowell.

On its own this point does not prompt much more of a response than 'Tough'. Could it also, more interestingly, be made a premiss of an argument for rejecting the whole idea of glory, for withdrawing from the whole glory-institution, as intrinsically and ineliminably unfair *in toto*? Perhaps it could; perhaps that is part of what some of glory's extremer critics may have been getting at; Thomas à Kempis is not far away here – and neither is Nietzschean *ressentiment*. But if we go that way, we need to go it open-eyed. Glory is a deeply-rooted human phenomenon, as deeply-rooted as, for example, the promising institution, or the buying-and-selling institution. The twentieth century has shown that it is not impossible to tear out and replace whole areas of our social world in the name of equality or fairness. It has also shown the exorbitant cost of doing that, and how little reason there usually is to prefer the replacements that it leads to.

VII

The dichotomies that we have seen challenged by the idea of glory – moral/prudential, altruistic/egoistic, controlled/uncontrolled, independent/dependent, and lastly impartial/partial – all have a similar ancestry; they all arise in both of the two great traditions of other-worldliness that lie at the foundations of our culture, Platonism and Christianity. Not every Christian or Platonist has been completely hostile to glory. But there are signs of such hostility in the founders of both traditions: Jesus avoids the crowds lest they should make him king (John 6.15), and when Socrates' friend Agathon wins the drama competition, Socrates keeps away from his house for a day 'from fear of the crowd' (*phobêtheis ton okhlon, Symposium* 174a8). And the traditions' convergences on this topic of glory are striking. Both traditions alike tend to say that glory is a false ideal because it makes us self-centred and proud, and prevents us from possessing the Christian virtue of humility or the Socratic virtue of self-depre-cating self-knowledge;[19] glory makes us care about what we cannot control, makes our well-being pathologically dependent on the opinions of others, and makes us unfairly exalt some at the expense of others; above all, glory distracts us from what really matters.

So what does really matter, according to the Platonist or the Christian? Strikingly enough the answer, for both the Platonist and the Christian, itself involves glory – just a different kind of glory:

---

[19]   Notice how close these two virtues are. Too much has been made of the idea that the pagan Greeks had nothing corresponding to the Christian concept of humility. The Christian virtue is basically an ability to see how small one's own place in the universe really is, correcting for our usual ego-centric bias. In the pagan Greek tradition – of which Socrates, in this respect at least, is typical – self-knowledge, *sôphrosynê*, and *aidôs* in the sense of modesty cover much the same conceptual space. Certainly deliberate self-abasement of the kind found e.g. in the *Imitatio Christi* is foreign to pagan Greek ethics; with the striking exception of Plato *Laws* 716a, *tapeinotês*, 'lowliness', is usually condemned even as an attitude to God, e.g. by Plutarch, *Non posse suaviter vivi secundum Epicurum* 1101e. But then plenty of Christian writers have argued that such self-abasement is foreign to Christian ethics too, because pathological, or dishonest, or both. However, humility is a subject for another paper.

Evil can have no place with divinities, so it is bound to haunt this world and mortal nature; hence we must try to fly from this world to the divine world as fast as possible. And that flight is the process of becoming like God as far as we can – "becoming like" meaning becoming just and holy, together with wisdom. (Plato, *Theaetetus* 176a7–b2; my own translation)

If ye then be risen with Christ, seek those things which are above, where Christ sitteth at the right hand of God. Set your affection on things above, not on things on the earth. For ye are dead, and your life is hid with Christ in God. When Christ, who is our life, shall appear, then shall ye also appear with him in glory. (St Paul, *Colossians* 3.1–4, KJB; the word of Paul's which is here translated by "glory" is *doxa*, not the Homeric *kleos*)

St Paul is explicit, and Plato implies,[20] that Christians and Platonists are not *opponents* of glory after all. They just have a different, and radically otherworldly, conception of what glory is from those, such as Homer, whom they criticise. The highest and most pre-eminent example of glory is divinity itself. So, it might seem, glory is something we can only contemplate; there is nothing we can do to achieve it. The thought that it would be a presumptuous tempting of God even to try to achieve glory for ourselves is one that has deep roots in both the Greek and the Judaeo-Christian traditions: 'Not unto us, o Lord, not unto us, but unto thy name's sake give the glory' (Psalm 115.1, KJV).

And yet both Christians and Platonists say that human goodness is ultimately about *homoiôsis theôi*: attaining the likeness of divinity.[21] And by this they do not just mean passively contemplating divine being. They also mean actively engaging in human doings that in one way or another refract and reflect the glory of divine being. For Christian and Platonist alike, what it *is* for human doings to be glorious, is for them in some way to do this reflecting and refracting. As St Paul puts it (*2 Corinthians* 3.18, JB):

---

[20]   For something more explicit from Plato, see his descriptions of the Platonic heaven at *Republic* 514a ff., *Symposium* 210a ff., and *Phaedrus* 246a ff.

[21]   For more on this theme in Plato see Sedley 1999; and in Christianity, see Adams 1999, Chapter 1, Section 3. 'Be imitators (*mimêtai*) of God, therefore, as dearly loved children, and live a life of love, just as Christ loved us and gave himself up for us as a fragrant offering and sacrifice to God' (*Ephesians* 5.1–2, NIV).

> And all of us, with our unveiled faces like mirrors reflecting the
> image (*eikona*) of the Lord's glory (*doxan*), are being transformed
> into the image that we reflect in brighter and brighter glory (*apo
> doxês eis doxan*).

Rather similarly, at *Timaeus* 37d8 Plato famously calls time a moving
image of eternity (*eikô kinêton tina aiônos*); and apparently part of
what he means by the phrase is that the things of time have it in
their nature to imitate the things of eternity – insofar as such imitation
is consistent with their nature as things of time.[22]

Seen in this way, as derivative from the divine glory, the glory that
is attainable in this life can easily become something that, for both
Christians and Platonists, matters intensely. It matters to Plato in
the *Apology* to vindicate Socrates; and vindicating Socrates does
not just mean vindicating him in the abstract, it means vindicating
him *to Plato's contemporaries*. The New Testament insists that,
while what Christians do in this world may not be the most important
thing, it is still important to live in the here and now in a way that not
only manifests the glory of God in some objective sense (whatever
sense that might be), but also does so in a way that those around
the believers *actually recognise* as manifesting God's glory.

Having said that, both for the Christian and for Platonist the contemplation of the divine being always remains our primary route to
glory; any kind of action that we can do will always only be glorious
in a secondary sense. Ultimately, Christian and Platonist will say,
seeing is worth more than doing, and this for an obvious reason:
because the most glorious thing that we could ever do could never
be as glorious as the most glorious thing that we can ever see.

Perhaps the basic thought here is that it does us a great deal of good
to find something good enough to deserve to be worshipped by us – if
only we can. Earlier in the paper I spoke of the danger of having our
critical faculties overwhelmed by blaring propaganda. But perhaps
there can be a danger, too, in *not* having our critical faculties

---

[22] *Timaeus* 37c6-d8: 'When the father who had brought it into being
saw that [the universe] was in motion and alive, and had become the
delight [or 'the statue': *agalma* is ambiguous] of the eternal gods, he was
pleased, and in his delight conceived a plan to make it even more similar
to its paradigm [the world-soul]. So just as the paradigm of the universe is
alive and eternal, so likewise he did as much as he could (*eis dunamin
epekheirêse*) to make this universe (*tode to pan*) of the same nature.
However, the nature of the world soul turns out to be eternal; and this property could not be fitted in full measure (*pantelôs*) to what has come to be. So
his plan was to make it a kind of moving image of the eternal...'

overwhelmed, on those occasions (of course they may be rare) when overwhelmed is just what our critical faculties ought to be: 'Is there not, in reverence for what is better than we, an indestructible sacredness?'[23] You do not need to be a theist – let alone a Christian or a Platonist – to think that there might be situations where it is appropriate to be overwhelmed. Perhaps you only need to be a mountaineer:

> Toward four o'clock in the morning we returned to Glen Etive. Our most sanguine expectations had been met; our eyes feasted and our hearts elated. We had set out in search of adventure; and we had found beauty... What more may we fairly ask of mountains? ...Something in that night cried out to us, not low nor faltering, but clear, true, urgent – that this was not all: that not half the wonder had pierced the clouds of our blindness: that the world was full of a divine splendour, which must be sought within oneself before it could be found without: that our task was to see and to know. (Murray 1947, 226)

VIII

Looking back over the main argument of this paper, some readers might still want to object as follows. 'If all this is right, then perhaps you have shown that not all values can be partitioned between the moral and the prudential, and that glory does not fit this dichotomy (and maybe doesn't fit some other dichotomies either). That still doesn't mean that glory is a moral value. Indeed it means that it *isn't* a moral value.'

This is certainly true, if by 'moral value' the reader means 'value closely tied to the institutions of moral obligation, moral praise, and moral blame', as justice and benevolence usually are. It is quite true that our idea of glory isn't closely linked to those institutions. There is the interesting fact that glory involves (at least rough) analogues of moral praise and blame: think of what we say about an international rugby-player who drops the ball two feet from an undefended try-line. But these are *analogues* of moral praise and blame, not the very same things. (Contrast 'He really shouldn't have dropped that pass' with 'He really shouldn't have punched that spectator'. The first does not license 'He was *wrong* to drop that pass', as the second licenses 'He was wrong to punch the spectator'. The most it licenses is 'It was *bad play* to drop that pass', which is not quite the same thing.)

---

[23]   Carlyle 1838, Book 1, Chapter 2.

It's also true, if by 'moral value' the reader means 'the sort of value that moral theorists have typically talked about'. Glory is obviously not a value that moral theorists have discussed much; that, of course, is one of my reasons for discussing it here. Indeed it is an interesting question whether typical moral theories today even *could* discuss it much without becoming quite atypical.

> For any man brought up in a western democratic society the related concepts of duty and responsibility are the central concepts of ethics; and we are inclined to take it as an unquestionable truth, though there is abundant evidence to the contrary, that the same must be true of all societies. In this respect we are all Kantians now. (Adkins 1960, 2)

Despite the well-known protests of Susan Wolf, Michael Stocker, Bernard Williams, Alasdair MacIntyre, and others, the situation in academic moral theory has not changed fundamentally in the fifty years since Arthur Adkins wrote these words. (More to the point, moral theory keeps reverting back to the criticised form, no matter how often and how thoroughly that form is criticised: an interesting symptom of hidden forces at work.) The keynote of typical moral theory remains the earnest, dowdy, plodding pursuit of unendingly exigent obligations. Whatever else moral theory may offer us, the life of fulfilling our obligations cannot be a *glorious* way to live. Indeed it is hard to see how glory can have much place at all in the moral theorist's picture.

One reason why not is because of what, following Bernard Williams, we might call the purity of morality – a phenomenon I touched on above in section V: 'The purity of morality... expresses an ideal, presented by Kant... in a form that is the most unqualified and also one of the most moving: the ideal that human existence can be ultimately just... it will be no good if moral value is merely a consolation prize you get if you are not in worldly terms happy or talented or good-humoured or loved. It has to be what ultimately matters' (Williams 1985, 195).[24] The one case where we might

---

[24] For Socrates' role in the emergence of this ideal of purity, see Adkins 1960, 155–6: 'Megara says significantly that death is a terrible thing, but to die in a manner which would give her enemies the opportunity to mock would be a greater evil than death [Euripides, *Hercules Furens* 281 ff.]... Until Socrates, no one takes a firm stand and says "Let them mock". It cannot be done: if others' opinion is overtly the standard, and if one's beliefs about the nature of life support that standard, it is both logically and psychologically impossible to set one's own views against it.' For one instance of Aristotle's general rejection of the Socratic/Platonic purity of morality, see Aristotle's brisk words, on the virtue of *megaloprepeia*, at

expect moral theory to allow there to be something like glory is the case of strictly *moral* heroism: the case of a heroic fulfilment of our moral duties. But even there, there is no glory in the sense that I have defined. The only thing that can matter for a moral theorist is just the heroic duty-fulfilment itself. Any applause or approbation that comes the moral hero's way in recognition of his exploits – being beyond his control, something which makes him dependent on others, prudentially valuable, and partial – is a strictly adventitious matter, of no *moral* value whatever. (The applause might of course have prudential value.[25] Indeed given, once more, the exhaustiveness of the moral/prudential dichotomy for typical moral theory, it will have to have prudential value if it has any value at all.) This makes it impossible for typical moral theory to accommodate glory in the sense I have meant, as the good that we get in a *combination* of spectacular performance and due recognition; typical moral theory is bound to split this phenomenon in two. But splitting it in two means not recognising it at all.

This point is aptly illustrated in *The Methods of Ethics*. Much in Henry Sidgwick's writings is a sign of something. His brief and discouraging remarks on fame in the Introduction to the *Methods* are a sign of how readily such an ethical idea as glory can become invisible within modern moral philosophy's characteristic outlook – an outlook which Sidgwick himself of course did much to create.

> Many men sacrifice health, fortune, happiness, to Fame; but no one, so far as I know, has deliberately maintained that Fame is an object which it is reasonable for men to seek for its own sake. It only commends itself to reflective minds either (1) as a source of Happiness to the person who gains it, or (2) a sign of his Excellence, moral or intellectual, or (3) because it attests the achievement by him of some important benefit to society, and at the same time stimulates him and others to further achievements in the future: and the concept of "benefit" would, when examined, lead us again to Happiness

---

Nicomachean Ethics 1122b: 'a poor person could not be *megaloprepês*, and anyone who tries is a fool'.

[25] Or, as Sidgwick suggests in the main-text quotation, it might be morally good instrumentally speaking. The instrumental good/final good distinction is another of moral theory's favourite dichotomies. Like the rest of them, it is rather too simple to fit all that much of real life very accurately, which is no doubt why the dichotomy's originators, Plato and Aristotle, use it fairly sparingly (though in Aristotle's case, arguably not sparingly enough).

or Excellence of human nature, – since a man is commonly thought to benefit others either by making them happier or by making them wiser and more virtuous. (Sidgwick 1907, 9)

In the first place Sidgwick does not talk about glory in the sense I have defined, as something that essentially conjoins outstanding achievement and recognition. He talks here only about the recognition part of glory, which he calls 'Fame'. (Sidgwick's capitalisations are usually a sign of something, too.) Then he identifies just three ways in which 'Fame' might have appeal to (as he says) 'reflective minds', a phrase which it is tempting to interpret as 'minds that share Sidgwick's will to system'. And then (Sidgwick tells us, in a manner which, perhaps deliberately, almost parodies Aristotle's[26]), the third of these ways of appealing turns out to be a rather creaky conjunction of the first two ways, which are the appeals of 'Happiness' and 'Excellence'. It is obvious already what *these* capitalisations stand for: we are moving already towards Sidgwick's famous dualism of practical reason, on which the only fundamental question about anything taken to be a value is whether its value is really 'prudential' (and so self-interested) or 'moral' (and so altruistic). I have been arguing that glory is a distinctive kind of ethical idea in its own right, something that should be understood as itself rather than analysed into some other thing. Sidgwick's own emerging architectonic already forces him to deny this, and to treat someone who ostensibly aims at glory as 'really' aiming confusedly at an amalgam of the self-interested and the altruistic. The diagnosis is unconvincing and contrived, and much redescriptive patching will be needed to keep it afloat. Here as elsewhere, the effect of moral theory's schematisms is not neatness and simplicity but mess, adhockery, and complication.

Whenever the temptation to count glory as a self-interested value returns – and return it unfailingly will, given the way our tradition of moral theory has gone – it is vital to keep reminding ourselves what glory is, and what it is not. At least as I have used the word here, 'glory' means the radiance or aura that typically arises from the achievement of something spectacularly excellent, within the framework of some worthwhile practice, together with the acclaim that that achievement merits from the audience that it deserves. 'Glory' in my sense does not mean the acclaim on its own, or the thirst for that acclaim. Nor does it mean childish attention-seeking, self-regard or conceit, or the obsession with status and recognition-level that

---

[26] Sidgwick 1907, xxii: "So this was the part of my book first written (Book iii, Chaps. i–xi), and a certain imitation of Aristotle's manner was very marked in it at first, and though I have tried to remove it where it seemed to me affected or pedantic, it still remains to some extent."

might lead someone in an idle moment (or is this just *my* dirty little secret?) to google his own name to see how many hits he gets. Such states of character are pathological, certainly. But they have nothing necessarily to do with what I mean by glory.

Thoughtful and focused ethical reflection, reflection on Socrates' great question in what way life ought to be lived (*Republic* 352d), has plenty to tell us about the importance of glory as an idea and an ideal that people can, and often do, make central to their schemes of life, and in particular see as a key source of significance and meaning for their lives. Exploring the content of such reflection brings out some of the ways in which activities and projects that are directed at glory, such as a career in the theatre or in sport, normally seem to us perfectly intelligible parts of the pursuit of human well-being. What is striking about so much academic moral theory today is how little, by contrast, it typically says to make the value of glory intelligible, and how little it *could* say about glory without changing – e.g. by shedding, or at the very least more carefully nuancing, a succession of characteristic dichotomies – into something quite different. I venture to suggest that this change might even be a good thing.[27]

Faculty of Arts, The Open University,
t.chappell@open.ac.uk

References

Adams, Robert (1999) *Finite and Infinite Goods* (Oxford: Clarendon).
Adkins, Arthur (1960) *Merit and Responsibility* (Oxford: Clarendon).
Blackburn, Simon (1985) *Spreading the Word* (Oxford: OUP).
Broad, C. D. (1940) Critical Notice of W. D. Ross *Foundations of Ethics* (Oxford, 1939). *Mind* **49** (April 1940), 228–39.

[27] For helpful discussions of Homer, I am grateful to Chris Emlyn-Jones. For encouragement to get this paper written I am particularly grateful to Valerie Tiberius (no less than eight years ago) and to Liz Ashford and Hallvard Fossheim (more recently). Thanks also for written comments to Angelo Campodonico, Paul Davis, and Naoko Yamagata; and to Darragh Byrne, Gideon Calder, Ken Jones, Alexander Miller, Joe Morrison, Yujin Nagasawa, Anthony O'Hear, Joss Walker, and other members of audiences in the Royal Institute of Philosophy Lecture Series 2010 in Birmingham, and at the British Association for Philosophy of Sport in Cardiff, March 2010. Of course it goes without saying that the resultant paper is nobody's fault but my own.

Timothy Chappell

Canetti, Elias (1981) *Crowds and Power* (London: Penguin). [Originally *Masse und Macht*, Hamburg 1960.]

Carlyle, Thomas (1838) *The French Revolution* (London: Chapman and Hall).

Churchill, Winston (1954) *Triumph and Tragedy* (Volume VI of his *The Second World War*) (London: Cassell).

Gaita, Raimond (1991) *Good and Evil: an absolute conception* (Second edition 2004) (London: Routledge, 1991).

Hume, David (1739) *A Treatise of Human Nature*, (eds) L. Selby-Bigge and P. H. Nidditch (Oxford: Clarendon, 1978).

Keillor, Garrison (1989) *We Are Still Married* (London: Faber and Faber).

Long, A. A. (1970) 'Morals and Values in Homer', *Journal of Hellenic Studies* **90**, 121–130.

MacIntyre, Alasdair (1981) *After Virtue: a Study in Moral Theory* (London: Duckworth).

Alasdair, MacIntyre (1999) *Dependent Rational Animals: why Human Beings need the Virtues* (London: Duckworth).

Murray, W. H. (1947) 'The evidence of things not seen' 222–7 in Murray, *Mountaineering in Scotland* (London: Dent).

Nussbaum, Martha (1986) *The Fragility of Goodness: Luck and Ethics in Greek Tragedy and Philosophy* (Cambridge: CUP).

Russell, Paul (2006) 'Moral sense and virtue in Hume's ethics', 158–170 in T. Chappell (ed.), *Values and Virtues* (Oxford: OUP).

Sedley, David (1999) 'The ideal of godlikeness', in G. Fine (ed.), *Plato 2: Ethics, Politics, Religion, and the Soul* (Oxford: OUP).

Sidgwick, Henry (1907) *The Methods of Ethics [1874]*, Seventh Edition. (London: Macmillan).

Stocker, Michael (1998) 'The Schizophrenia of Modern Ethical Theories', in R. Crisp and M. Slote (eds) *Virtue Ethics* (New York: OUP), 66–78.

Weil, Simone (1940) 'The Iliad, or the Poem of Force', originally published as 'L'Iliade, ou le poème de la force', *Cahiers du Sud* Dec. 1940/ Jan. 1941; reprinted in *Chicago Review*, 18:2 (1965), 5–30, tr. Mary McCarthy.

Williams, Bernard (1973) 'Egoism and altruism', in his *Problems of the Self* (Cambridge: Cambridge UP), 250–265.

Williams, Bernard (1985) *Ethics and the Limits of Philosophy* (London: Penguin).

Williams, Bernard (1993) *Shame and necessity* (Berkeley, California: University of California Press).

Susan, Wolf (1982) 'Moral saints', *The Journal of Philosophy*, August 1982, 419–439.

Conceptual Problems with Performance Enhancing Technology in Sport

EMILY RYALL

The majority of – usually moral – problems inherent in elite sport, such as whether athletes should be able to take particular drugs, wear particular clothing, or utilise particular tools, arguably stem from a conceptual one based on faulty logic and competing values. Sport is a human enterprise that represents a multitude of human compulsions, desires and needs; the urge to be competitive, to co-operate, to excel, to develop, to play, to love and be loved, and to find meaning in one's existence. From the perspective of an amateur athlete, this pluralism is possible. When one is involved in athletics at the lower echelons, the values that one holds in relation to sport are fluid and flexible; they are prioritised according to a myriad of other influences that are contingent to a particular situation. As such, the reasons that the general population participate in athletic activities and the values they consequently ascribe to it are complex and wide-ranging and thus fall into the sociological realm. The philosophical problem with value in sport is found at the highest level, the professional platform, where discordant values are espoused, particularly the value of ever increasing quantifiable performance. The athletic events at the Olympic Games are the archetypal manifestation of this *Citius, Altius, Fortius* (faster, higher, stronger) aphorism and yet when taken to its logical conclusion becomes evidently absurd.

This chapter seeks to lay out some of the contradictions and conceptual problems inherent in elite athletic performance and consider the practical implications that will inevitably occur with likely developments in technology. In particular, it will highlight the flawed logic of quantifiable progress that is intertwined with athletic performance in addition to considering recent controversial developments in technology and their effects on sport. It will conclude with an indication of the types of issues that will be faced in sport as this conceptual problem, inherent in elite sport, comes increasing to the fore.

doi:10.1017/S1358246113000234   © The Royal Institute of Philosophy and the contributors 2013
Royal Institute of Philosophy Supplement **73** 2013

Emily Ryall

The paradox at the centre of elite sport is one which holds both an incessant drive for record breaking performances as well a desire to preserve the integrity of the human. This is exemplified by Ted Butryn in his paper, 'Cyborg Horizons', when he says,

> Gold medals are to be earned by decidedly (and recognisably) human competitors, while the Olympic motto itself drives athletes to become increasingly and unabashedly "post-human", and to ultimately transgress boundaries between animals–humans–machines.[1]

It is a paradox whereby we continually strive to surpass limits and break records and yet at the same time attempt to maintain an image of the natural athlete; the ancient Greek ideal. Yet in this current technological age, when we look closely at this picture of a Greek hero we realise how much of a diminishing illusion it is. The sports technology industry is worth billions of dollars and is driven by the incessant human desire to improve sporting performance and demonstrate sporting superiority. This technology spans footwear and clothing, sophisticated video analysis, nutritional and ergogenic aids as well other innovations in tools, implements and playing surfaces. The paradox is that whilst technology is embraced in aspiration to the Olympic motto of faster, higher, stronger, it is also often rejected for being antithetical to it.

As highlighted in the quote by Butryn, our assessment of what we deem to be acceptable technological use is directly affected by our moral evaluation of what athletics ought to look like. The sporting arena, above all others, holds a unique place in our attempts to try to maintain a delicate balance between a belief that it ought to be a test of the natural human capability and at the same time, an arena whereby we are able to surpass those limits. In it we wish to remain human but at the same time demonstrate super-human performance.

Caution ought to be maintained however, since the term 'post-human' can arguably be misleading. It suggests that there is a human essence, or a set of necessary and sufficient characteristics, that can be identified; yet which has eluded those who have attempted to determine what these might be. What the term does do, however, is indicate our conceptual confusion that arises with technological innovation. Donna Haraway, in *The Cyborg Manifesto,* first argued that we were living in a post-human

---

[1]   Ted Butryn, 'Cyborg Horizons: Sport and the Ethics of Self-Technologization' in A. Miah & S. Eassom (eds) *Sport Technology: History, Philosophy and Policy. Research in Philosophy and Technology,* **21**, (Series Ed: Carl Mitcham) (Oxford: Elsevier Science Ltd, 2002) 117.

age in the late 1970s.[2] She pointed to many aspects of technology which form a necessary part of the modern life, such as, pace-makers, processed foods, intensive care units, artificial hip joints, heart-rate monitors and synthetic clothing. Since the time Haraway made her claims there have been three decades of technological innovation. Today, arguably technology has an even more endemic hold over our lives.

Similarly, Raymond Kurzweil in his 2005 book *The Singularity is Near: When Humans Transcend Biology* has argued that our knowledge of, and our ability to manipulate, the physical environment will reach a tipping point in the next twenty to thirty years.[3] According to Kurzweil, there will be little distinction between human and non-human at the advanced technological level as artificial intelligence will seem (or be) as human as our own – and machines will easily pass the Turing Test – and we will have the ability to correct, alter and transform our biology at will. At this point we will have the knowledge to be able to maintain absolute control over our existence and physical manifestation. If Kurzweil's claim is demonstrated correct, it will have profound implications for sport, particularly the fundamental value of measuring athletic performance, since the notion of 'natural human' will have significantly altered in form. That doesn't necessarily mean that sport won't survive if Kurzweil's prediction becomes reality[4] but it does mean that aspiring to the higher, faster, stronger motto as showcased by the Olympics will become nonsensical.

1. Defining technology

Before considering the value of athletic performance however, I will start with a brief discussion of the term 'technology'. The standard definition is 'the application of scientific knowledge for practical purposes'[5] with most dictionaries giving a more narrow definition focusing upon the human use of material objects, such as tools and

---

[2]   Donna Haraway, 'A Cyborg Manifesto: Science, Technology, and Socialist-Feminism in the Late Twentieth Century' in *Simians, Cyborgs and Women: The Reinvention of Nature.* (New York: Routledge, 1991) 149–181.
[3]   Raymond Kurzweil. *The Singularity is Near* (London: Penguin, 2006)
[4]   This is demonstrated by Bernard Suits (1978) in his conception of utopia which argues game-playing as the ideal of existence.
[5]   'technology' in the *Oxford Dictionary of English*. Edited by Angus Stevenson. Oxford University Press, 2010. *Oxford Reference Online.* Oxford University Press. University of Gloucestershire. 10 July 2012

machines. Broader definitions include methods of organising and the use of systems or techniques. Its etymology stems from the Greek word meaning 'systematic treatment' with 'techne' referring to a skill or craft and 'logia' referring to the discourse or study of.[6] However, the definition that best encompasses the broad scope that technology covers is:

> The whole range of means by which humans act on their environments or seek to transcend the limits of their natural capacities.[7]

This type of definition resonates with Heidegger's 'technological attitude' in that it highlights the uniquely human way that we perceive and categorise the world.[8] The human condition enables a reflection upon the past and a projection into possible futures. We are able to imagine what might have been and what might be. For Heidegger, this attitude enforces our instrumental conception of the world and can be considered as a mode of existence.[9] It is the way that we navigate through the world; overcoming barriers by identifying solutions through manipulating our environment. In essence, it is an approach that conceptualises a problem, for instance, 'how I can hit the ball further?' and then transfers the knowledge we hold about specific aspects of the world, in this case, knowledge about the properties of materials, in order to provide a solution.

This technological attitude can also be seen to provide a basis for Kurzweil's arguments concerning technological advancement.

<http://www.oxfordreference.com/views/ENTRY.html?subview=Main&entry=t140.e0848700>

[6] 'technology' in the *Oxford Dictionary of Word Origins.* by Julia Cresswell. *Oxford Reference Online.* Oxford University Press. University of Gloucestershire. 5 October 2010 <http://www.oxfordreference.com/views/ENTRY.html?subview=Main&entry=t292.e4936>

[7] 'technology' in the *Dictionary of the Social Sciences*, Craig Calhoun, (ed.) Oxford University Press, 2002. *Oxford Reference Online.* Oxford University Press. University of Gloucestershire. 5 October 2010 <http://www.oxfordreference.com/views/ENTRY.html?subview=Main&entry=t104.e1667>

[8] Heidegger actually calls the way we conceive and relate to the world 'enframing' but the term 'technological attitude' is a helpful indication of what this means. Martin Heidegger, (trans. & intro. William Lovitt). *The Question Concerning Technology and Other Essays* (New York: Harper Row, 1977) 12.

[9] Martin Heidegger, (translated by J.Glenn Gray and F. Wieck) *What is Called Thinking?* (New York: Harper and Row, 1968) 5.

Kurzweil argues that technology develops at an exponential rate. This is most effectively demonstrated in Moore's Law whereby the number of transistors that can fit on a computer chip doubles every two years. This leads to the exponential growth in computing power and explains why the average mobile phone is now more powerful than the computers that enabled men to reach the moon.[10] This law seems to have held relatively well since the development of transistors in the early twentieth century but Kurzweil goes further in applying it to technological innovation throughout human evolution. Kurzweil argues that the mistake most of us make when considering the development of technology, is to view it in a linear rather than exponential way.

> My models show that we are doubling the paradigm–shift rate every decade. Thus the 20th century was gradually speeding up to the rate of progress at the end of the century; its achievements, therefore, were equivalent to about twenty years of progress at the rate in 2000. We'll make another twenty years of progress in just fourteen years (by 2014), and then do the same again in only seven years. To express this another way, we won't experience one hundred years of technological advancement in the 21st century; we will witness on the order of 20,000 years of progress (again, when measured by the rate of progress in 2000), or about 1,000 times greater than what was achieved in the 20th century.[11]

The question then is, if Kurzweil's thesis is correct and this inductive premise holds true for the near future, how will it affect sport, athletic endeavour and the values we place upon it? Sport is in essence, a technological enterprise. It is an evolution from play and recreation because it imposes arbitrary rules that limit the means to reach an arbitrary end. Bernard Suits' definition of a game-playing, within which sport is contained, is,

> [T]he attempt to achieve a specific state of affairs [prelusory goal], using only means permitted by rules [lusory means], where the rules prohibit use of more efficient in favour of less efficient means [constitutive rules], and where the rules are accepted just because they make possible such activity [lusory attitude].[12]

---

10   M. Kaku, *Physics of the Future: How science will shape human destiny and our daily lives by 2100.* (New York: Doubleday, 2011) 22.
11   Raymond Kurzweil. *The Singularity is Near*, (London: Penguin, 2006) 11.
12   Bernard Suits, *The Grasshopper: Games, Life and Utopia.* (Toronto: University of Toronto Press, 1978) 41.

The goal here might be to reach a finish line (which incidentally might be the same as the starting line), or to put a ball in a net; and the rules and means might dictate that this is done by following a designated track or by passing the ball in a particular way to a team-mate. But above all, it requires a particular attitude that accepts these rules (and the subsequent means) in order to allow the game to exist at all. If one does not hold this lusory attitude then one could quite easily reach the goal more efficiently, i.e. cutting across the infield of a track in athletics, or getting a ladder and carrying the ball up to the net in basketball. This is why sport is so peculiar, and so peculiarly human; we deliberately put obstacles in our way to make an activity more difficult to achieve. To return to our earlier definition of technology, it is the way in which we seek to overcome obstacles and solve problems that are placed in our path, despite the fact that the obstacles are ones of our own making. It is by design an inefficient activity. The paradox concerning technology is that this desire to solve problems is then used to make a necessarily inefficient activity more efficient.

2. Technology and the idea of progress

At an elite level, today even the most prosaic athletic sport – that of running for instance – is a highly technological affair, as Pam Sailor's demonstrates in her paper 'More than a pair of running shoes'.[13] The account given of Paula Radcliffe as she prepares to race is highly reminiscent of Haraway's cyborg:

> The sunglasses Radcliffe wears are to prevent tension that is caused by squinting into the sun. Even the smallest bit of tension in the face could filter down to the lower body. The sunglasses also hide her emotion from competitors and help break the dust kicking up from the street and the wind... Radcliffe also wears a strip on her nose to aid her breathing; she has exercise induced asthma... [A]n elastic titanium necklace... is designed to restore equilibrium and improve blood flow... [She was] one of the first marathoners to wear knee-high compression socks. Hers are skin-coloured and they, too, are designed to increase blood flow. To keep the blood flowing to her fingers, Radcliffe

[13]   Pam Sailors, 'More than a pair of running shoes' *Journal of the Philosophy of Sport* **36** (2009), 207–126.

wears gloves. White gloves. She is, after all, the British aristocrat of the race.[14]

Despite technological innovation, sport is a fairly conservative sphere though increasingly driven by what Robert Nisbet calls the 'great idea of progress'.[15] This is based upon the desire for perfection and the drive to eradicate problems and achieve ultimate control over our environment. Technology allows us both to overcome perceived limitations and difficulties, and (we believe) enables us to measure this progress against previous attempts in an exact and objective way. This is seen none more clearly than in the sport record. In the case of sports measured by time, we are now able to calculate performances to a tenth of a thousand of a second.

This focus on quantifiable performance has been the subject of a detailed critique by philosophers such as Sigmund Loland. Loland argues that the notion of ever-continuing quantifiable performance and the value we place upon it highlights fallacious reasoning. He says,

> The logic of quantifiable progress has in a common-sense manner become a normative ideal in sports. For example, without new records, important events like the Olympic Games and the World Championships are considered failures both by the media and the public. This logic seems also to be an ideal for a series of current developments in sports. Through the quest for standardisation and objectivity, scientific and technological know-how is applied to control the uncontrollable, to eliminate chance, and to measure performance improvement in an increasingly more accurate way.[16]

This application of technological know-how has shaved nearly a tenth off the men's 100m sprint record in less than 100 years. Women have improved by over 20%. In swimming, the progression has been even more marked, with most disciplines showing a 20 – 25% improvement for both men and women, with the women's 100m and 200m freestyle showing a 35% improvement in less than a century. Similar

[14]   Liz Robbins, *A Race Like No Other: 26.2 Miles Through the Streets of New York*. (New York: HarperCollins 2008) 140–141.
[15]   Robert Nisbet, *History of the Idea of Progress* (New Jersey: Transaction, 1994)
[16]   Sigmund Loland, 'The Logic of Progress and the Art of Moderation in Competitive Sports' in *Values in Sport*, C. Tannjo and C. Tamburrini (eds) (London: E & FN Spon, 2000) 42.

progression has been seen in other linearly measured sports of jumping and throwing.

Improvements in technique, skill and athleticism have also been seen in both aesthetic sports and team games. The level of technical difficulty has increased in gymnastics and diving, balls are hit harder in hockey, kicked further in rugby, and with more precision and spin in football. Much of this change has occurred alongside developments in technology. The increased power and speed in hockey has been brought about to a large extent with changes in playing surface (from grass to water based synthetic turf) and lighter, rounder sticks. Gymnasts and divers are able to perfect their moves with improved safety harnesses and assisted by three-dimensional video analysis.

Improvements in these types of aesthetic sports and complex games are not too problematic from a logical perspective. Changes in technology result in changes in the game itself. In most cases, improvements in technology have enabled a greater aesthetic pleasure, particularly for the sporting spectator. The modern game of hockey is very different to the game of the 1970s; no longer are players hacking at balls stuck in a grass divet. However, the logical and conceptual problems that come with our expectation for ever-improving progress, is manifested in linear sports that involve measuring and quantifying progress via the standard measurements of distance, weight and time. In order to demonstrate improvements in quantifiably measurable performance, technology will inevitably begin to make a more marked influence on our physical being. As Loland points out,

> The quest for infinite quantifiable progress will sooner or later lead towards pressing moral dilemmas that challenge our very idea of what a human being is all about. The core problem of this logic is that it builds on the impossible demand for unlimited progress within limited systems. Enough is never enough![17]

3. Genetic technology in sport

For Loland, the real concern is with technologies that have a direct effect on our biological make-up. Perhaps the application of genetic technology is where we will really see, what can be called, the 'post-human' athlete. There are already areas of genetic research which

[17]   Op. cit. note xvi, 43–44.

could have a marked effect upon sporting performance including the ability to increase muscle mass, and the ability to increase oxygen uptake. Experiments conducted on mice and monkeys, for instance, have utilised the follistatin gene to block myostatin, a protein that inhibits muscle growth. The effect of which is that the muscular stature of these animals is significantly increased. This is the case even without high intensity exercise. If these results are replicated in human subjects it would affect how, and how much, athletes developed muscle. One needs to be cautious however, in concluding the effects upon sporting performance. Even in activities that depend primarily on strength, muscle mass needs to be balanced with surrounding tissue, such as ligaments, tendons, cartilage and bones. Simply adding a particular gene that increases muscle mass isn't necessarily going to lead to better performances, and may well have the unintended consequence of reducing performance through more frequent injury.

Another application of genetic technology that might have an equally significant effect upon sport is by affecting the use of oxygen in the blood stream. Athletes that carry a greater amount of red blood cells can use oxygen more efficiently and can work harder for longer. Many athletes already take advantage of high-altitude training or oxygen chambers (or indeed blood doping[18]) in order to 'artificially' force the body to use oxygen more effectively. This process has been replicated through gene transfer, whereby genetically modified mice have shown significantly enhanced endurance capabilities.[19] Again, although this technology could have discernible effects on sporting performance, particularly in long-distance or endurance events, it may result in unintended consequences. As shown in the world of elite cycling in the second half of the twentieth century, increasing the red blood cell count places additional (and excessive) demand on the heart.

Nevertheless, despite these two areas where genetic technologies may have a potential application to sport, speculation needs to be restrained. The concern that we would see genetically modified athletes

---

[18]   This practice entails the blood being removed from the body to be reinserted at a later date once the body has replenished its lost blood cells. The effect is an increased number of red blood cells which then are able to hold an increased amount of oxygen.

[19]   P. Hakimi, J. Yang, G. Casadesus, G. *et al*. 'Overexpression of the Cytosolic Form of Phosphoenolpyruvate Carboxykinase (GTP) in Skeletal Muscle Repatterns Energy Metabolism in the Mouse', *The Journal of Biological Chemistry*, **282** (2007) 32844–32855.

Emily Ryall

first appeared in the late 1990's and early 2000's. This was at the height of publicity on the human genome project when scientists, policy makers and ethicists first met to discuss how to deal with this prospect. The solution, it was decided, was to treat genetic technology as a form of doping, alongside steroid use, THG, amphetamines, and blood doping and therefore it would come under the jurisdiction of the World Anti–Doping Agency (WADA).[20] Despite fears that genetically modified ('Frankenstein'[21]) athletes would be competing at the Sydney, Greece, and Beijing Olympics, there is no evidence to suggest that this has yet become a reality and speculation about these types of athletes seems to have died down.

4. Prosthetic technology in sport

The more pressing and likely technology to affect linear-type sports such as athletics is the development of synthetic technologies, particularly in the area of prosthetics. Oscar Pistorius, the South African 'blade runner', is currently the best known amputee athlete who has competed in able-bodied events. Pistorius's disputes with athletics authorities over his eligibility to compete in able-bodied competitions highlights the conceptual problems about the value and meaning of athletic performance, and focuses particularly on notions of 'fairness' and 'performance enhancement'. The question surrounding Pistorius is whether his specially designed prosthetic legs ('Cheetahs') provide him with an unfair advantage over other athletes. The notion of unfair advantage is a difficult one to assess but in this case, the authorities wished to establish whether these prosthetic limbs were akin to wearing jet-powered roller skates, for example. Since the 200m running race is a test of the competitors' ability to run, the conceptual problem is concerned with the definition of 'running'; and moreover whether this includes the use of prosthesis.

In order to answer this question, Pistorius was subjected to tests that measured a range of movements that were deemed inherent to running, including forces, energy consumption and wind resistance. The IAAF's (International Association of Athletics Federations)

[20] WADA Press Release. 'Wada Conference Sheds Light On The Potential Of Gene Doping' 1005 Lausanne, Switzerland, 20th March 2002.
[21] The fears manifested in such language are explored more in Emily Ryall 'The language of genetic technology: metaphor and media representation', *Continuum*, **22** (3) (2008). 363–373.

initial conclusion was that Pistorius's prosthetic limbs did constitute an unfair advantage over abled-bodied competitors for the reason that the biomechanical differences meant that his 'Cheetahs' produced more recoil spring and less drag than 'natural human' legs, so the wearer expends less energy than an athlete with 'natural' legs. Since the IAAF's rules of running at the time had nothing to say about prosthetic limbs, they were amended to prohibit, 'any technical device that incorporates springs, wheels or any other element that provides a user with an advantage over another athlete not using such a device', a category which subsequently included Pistorius's prosthetics.[22] This judgement was subsequently overturned by the Court of Arbitration for Sport (CAS) on the grounds that insufficient variables had been tested. Indeed, the CAS questioned the validity of the testing procedure since,

> [T]he IAAF's officials must have known that, by excluding the start and the acceleration phase, the results would create a distorted view of Mr Pistorius' advantages and/or disadvantages by not considering the effect of the device on the performance of Mr Pistorius over the entire race.[23]

It was concluded that although the recoil spring from his prosthetics gave him an advantage over latter stages of the race this was offset by the fact that Pistorius was required to expend more energy in the initial acceleration stages and when running a bend.

As noted by the CAS, the fact that 'at least some IAAF officials had determined that they did not want Mr Pistorius to be acknowledged as eligible to compete in international IAAF-sanctioned events, regardless of the results that properly conducted scientific studies might demonstrate'[24] indicates the strong resistance the authorities have towards the use of prosthetic technology and the impact it might have upon sport. Despite the ban being overturned, the IAAF continued to press South Africa not to select Pistorius for the 4×400 relay but this time changed their argument from one of fairness to one of harm. They maintained that it could risk the

---

[22] IAAF ruling 144.2 It has since been further amended to 'the use of any technology or appliance that provides the user with an advantage which he would not have obtained using the equipment specified in the Rules.'

[23] Arbitration CAS 2008/A/1480 Pistorius v/ IAAF, award of 16 May 2008. 7. <www.jurisprudence.tas-cas.org/sites/CaseLaw/.../1480.pdf> July 2012.

[24] Op. cit. note xxiii. 8

safety of both Oscar and other athletes if he ran in the main pack since his running style differed to other athletes and his prosthetics could cause an accident. Subsequently, Pistorius was initially prevented from running in the 2011 World Championships, despite being selected for the relay team, due to health and safety concerns. Again, the IAAF later rescinded their view and Pistorius was allowed to compete in the London 2012 Olympics.

As has been considered in greater detail by authors such as Jones,[25] Van Hilvoorde & Landeweerd,[26] Edwards[27] and Lenk,[28] there are several arguments that are raised here from both ethical and conceptual standpoints. That the IAAF has appealed to many of these arguments is indication of their conservative attitude and their desire to preserve a particular purist conception of athletics which hides problematic cases such as Oscar Pistorius and Caster Semenya.[29] Arguably if a competitor doesn't fit the conception of the 'normal, natural' human athlete (and for Semenya, this must be a 'natural feminine' athlete) then they are accused of possessing an unfair advantage. In the case of Pistorius, this was his prosthetic blades, with Semenya, it was her masculine appearance.

It is not in dispute that prosthetic technologies are performance enhancing, since they allow the athlete to compete at all. This highlights the problem with assessing what constitutes *unfair* performance enhancement and raises different questions about the value of sport and what we really wish to test. If we value equality of opportunity then, to use a sporting metaphor, how much should we 'level the playing field'? Do we compensate for inequalities in physical

---

[25] Carwyn Jones and Cassie Wilson 'Defining advantage and athletic performance: The case of Oscar Pistorius', *European Journal of Sports Science* **9**(2) 2009. 125–131.

Carwyn Jones 'Oscar Pistorius, the Paralympics and issues of fair competition' in D. Lampman & S. Spickard Prettyman (eds), *Learning culture through sport* (Lanham, MD: Rowman & Littlefield Education 2011)

[26] I. Van Hilvoorde and L. Landeweerd 'Disability or extraordinary talent: Francesco Lentini (three legs) versus Oscar Pistorius (no legs)', *Sport, Ethics and Philosophy*, **2** (2008) 97–111.

[27] S. D. Edwards 'Should Oscar Pistorius be excluded from the 2008 Olympic Games?' *Sport, Ethics and Philosophy*, **2** (2008) 112–114.

[28] C. Lenk, 'Is enhancement in sport really unfair? Arguments on the concept of competition and equality of opportunities' *Sport, Ethics and Philosophy*, **1** 2007. 218–228.

[29] S. M. Crincoli, 'You Can Only Race if You Can't Win? The Curious Cases of Oscar Pistorius & Caster Semenya' *Texas Review of Entertainment and Sports Law* **12** (2) (2011) 133–188.

ability? If Pistorius should be compensated for the misfortune he received as a child in suffering dual amputation of the legs then should others too be compensated for poor rolls of the dice of life, such as having 'poor' genes, being born in an impoverished country, having no access to facilities or coaches, or being generally uncoordinated, ill-motivated and unambitious?

5. Therapy, enhancement and societal norms

The problems faced by the sporting authorities regarding fairness in performance enhancement will undoubtedly increase if Kurzweil's prediction is correct and as technology is further embedded into our daily lives and our physical being. It may be that it becomes the norm in society to replace biological parts with more reliable synthetic ones, and not simply for therapeutic reasons. Indeed, these cases illustrate how the distinction between therapy and enhancement is conceptually problematic. For instance, baseball pitchers have received elbow surgery to replace damaged tendons and in some cases this has resulted in a stronger throwing action than was the case prior to the injury. This has led other athletes (and often parents of aspiring athletes) to request the surgery without any medical necessity.[30] Similarly, the cost and effectiveness of laser eye surgery has become affordable to much of the general population and many top sports players have reportedly received it, with the most high profile example, professional golfer, Tiger Woods. As these technological enhancements become a societal norm, it raises difficult questions for the sporting authorities as to which performance enhancements are acceptable and which are not. Furthermore, it will be more difficult to prohibit technology that becomes an intrinsic part of the body than technology that is external to the body which can be easily removed or separated, such as the LZR swimming costume. It is not clear how the authorities will deal with cases such as an archer or shooter who has had her eyesight enhanced through surgery. They will need to assess whether it constitutes an unfair advantage over other competitors who have not received such surgery. If the authorities, as in the parallel case of testosterone levels in female athletes, determine that the eyesight is beyond that of 'normal' human levels, and ban these athletes from competing, then this will undoubtedly prove controversial. Moreover, the authorities

[30] Whether the faster pitching action is a result of the surgery itself or attention to a reconditioning programme and other factors is disputed.

might find that they are increasingly re-evaluating these levels as this technology becomes more endemic in society. This difficulty in assessing what is within the range for the abilities of a 'normal' human might become increasingly pronounced if access to technology is not equitable (as is currently the case) and the gap between the 'normal' athlete of the richer nations and the 'normal' athlete of the poorer ones continues to grow.

Ultimately, the concern over performance enhancing technologies stems from questions about the value of sporting performance. There is a real desire to test the athlete not the sport scientist, engineer or pharmacist. Yet, this begs the question as to what *is* the athlete that we wish to test, and how is it possible to separate the 'natural human' from the technology. As Haraway noted decades previously, technology is so deeply embedded into our very being it has become conceptually impossible to set it apart from the modern man. Performance enhancement in sport cannot wholly be rejected since it runs alongside the notion of progress. Arguably, it is our tendency to hold a technological attitude which forms the basis for our tacit expectation that progress is both valuable and inevitable. In sport, one of the clearest measurements of this progress is through quantifiable and measurable performance exemplified in linear sports that are based upon time, weight and distance.

However, an analysis of the effect of particular technologies upon sport demonstrates that sports governing bodies will be faced, and with an increasingly greater frequency, with questions about the fundamental values of athletic performance, particularly at the elite level. If we accept a definition of sport as the 'voluntary attempt to overcome unnecessary obstacles through physical skill'[31] it is apparent that it must contain inefficiency at its core. Therefore, the inherent paradox is that it ultimately runs against the technological attitude and the notion of progress.

6. Conclusion

So one might ask, what should sport be about if it is incongruent with a technological drive? Suits' definition of game-playing perhaps provides us with an indication of the answer; this being his notion of lusory attitude. This attitude is one that accepts that sport is an

---

[31]   Suits maintained that sport was a sub-set of game-playing but with the additional criteria of physical skill and stability (to set it apart from 'fads' or 'crazes' such as hula-hoop).

arbitrary enterprise that enables us to enhance our lives in a much broader way and is encompassed by the values set out in the Olympic charter such as respect, courage, friendship, determination, excellence, equality and inspiration. In contrast, the values of the Olympic motto of *citius, altius, fortius* pursued by many of those involved in elite sport renders the lusory attitude unnecessary.

In conclusion, which technology is and isn't accepted in sport on the grounds of fairness will undoubtedly change as it has done throughout sporting history. One can point to many examples of historical shifts in perception, one of the most notable being the notion of organised and structured training. In the late 19th and early 20th century, serious and dedicated training and practicing before a competition was seen as bad sportsmanship, whereas today the development of professional sport means that those who do not train are now considered uncommitted, lazy, foolish or arrogant. The same could also be said with the use of coaches, nutritionalists, and psychologists. All these performance aids are an accepted part of modern sport. Similarly, altitude chambers, nutritional supplements, video and biomechanical analysis, breathable and cooling clothing materials, and asthma inhalers are all accepted technologies. And, for the time being, prosthetic technologies are too despite the IAAF's unease. Generally, decisions made about the acceptability of performance enhancing aids are reflective of the complex power and political relations between the athletics governing bodies, corporate and commercial company interests, the press and the public. But what is clear is the contradictory logic behind elite athletic performance will become more prominent and more problematic as technology progresses, particularly with innovations in prosthetic, bionic and genetic technology. The value of those linear sports that are considered the principal Olympic events, such as the men's 100m sprint, will increasingly be called into question as further inequities develop and it becomes evident that the notion of the 'natural human' athlete no longer makes sense. But that does not consequently mean that sport *qua* sport will become obsolete – indeed we will see new sports develop and flourish through the use of technological advancements. The sports that are likely to remain most intact with on-going developments in technology are the ones that are least affected by technological changes; sports that maintain those values that ultimately determine our humanness; sports that require traits such as creativity, inspiration, self-affirmation, and the lusory attitude.

University of Gloucestershire
eryall@glos.ac.uk

Is Mountaineering a Sport?

PHILIP BARTLETT

Amusement, diversion, fun. This was the definition of sport offered by the first dictionary I consulted in preparation for this lecture, and if we accept it then there is at least a sporting chance that we will all be able to agree: mountaineering is a sport. But it is not a definition that sits easily with much of what sport is currently thought to be. This talk is part of a series on Philosophy and Sport timed to mark the London Olympics, and amusement and fun are probably not the first words to spring to mind there, certainly not for the competitors. They may be a part of it, but I don't think it unreasonable to think more immediately of commerce, competition, achievement. So this evening I need to consider mountaineering within that context. I also want to make clear at the outset that I shall take mountaineering to mean not just the climbing of high snow-covered peaks, but mountain travel and exploration, and simply recreational mountain walking. There doesn't need to be anything technical involved. At the same time, I must include rock-climbing within my brief, and for at least two reasons. One is that rock-climbing and mountaineering are closely connected historically. In it's early years, alpine climbing often led to rock climbing, the latter being seen as geographically convenient training for 'the real thing' – namely, the annual alpine holiday. When I was a teenager in the 1970s the influence went the other way: I began with rock-climbing in the Lake District, and proceeded to alpine climbing. And secondly, rock-climbing and mountaineering are administratively and politically connected. I suspect that the former, which in Britain as often as not doesn't take place in mountains at all, now absorbs the major part of the public funds devoted to these matters. And it is predominantly on the British experience that I want to draw.

I'd like to start with some history and what one might call the traditional mountaineering outlook with which it is associated. Strictly speaking, mountaineering has no definable beginning. There must always have been farmers who found they had to climb some wretched hill, taking time they could ill afford to rescue a recalcitrant sheep; military men who were ordered to reach some strategic high point and spy out the land; Himalayan traders who found themselves delving ever deeper into mountain country to drum up business; and

doi:10.1017/S1358246113000295

so on. This is not to say that these people didn't find in the mountains unexpected rewards; rewards that we would entirely understand. It is not even to say they went unwillingly. But broadly speaking we can say that they were driven by necessity, whereas mountaineers in the usual sense of the word are not; they do not have to climb, explore, sit in snowdrifts, admire the view. They choose to do these things. Immediately then, one has the characteristic of choice, and that means privilege. If one adds to that the fact that mountaineering is demanding of time or money – one generally needs one or the other, and both are welcome – then it is not surprising that mountaineering as we understand it today grew out of increasing affluence in the West and was for a long time dominated by a social elite.

For how long was this the case? From it's beginnings in the late eighteenth century until well into the twentieth. Alpine climbing began as the playground of an economically comfortable and culturally sophisticated group, which is part of the reason the British played a leading role despite having no alpine-sized mountains of their own. It was pushed forward by, among others, clerics and schoolmasters, because of the disposable time these groups enjoyed.

That of course leaves unexplained why they should have chosen mountains. They might have chosen basketball, or the discus, or salmon fishing, or ocean sailing. It's not hard to see the odd ones out here. Mountaineering, fishing and sailing certainly have things in common, and one very important thing: all of them are the expression of a belief in the inherent good of the outdoors, the worth of communing with an unsullied nature. And no doubt some of those who might have become mountaineers in Whymper's day did indeed take up fishing or sailing. And some did all three. All this springs from and mixes with wider movements in thought and belief: with Wordsworth and romantic poetry, with muscular Christianity and the University reading party, not least with the requirements of an empire which throughout the nineteenth century needed recruits who were excited by the prospect of adventure in remote mountain country. My thesis, then, would be that we can identify a set of values and beliefs to associate with this period which are those of privilege and a degree of sophistication. We could reasonably expect that if we put the question 'Is mountaineering a sport?' to one of its protagonists, he would not merely deny it, but deny it vociferously. Mountaineering, he might say – and it probably would be a he – is more than mere 'sport'. It is more important. Not in the sense of filthy lucre, or that embarrassing tendency to gush that one's interest is not in fact merely an interest, but 'a way of life', but in the sense of subtler, deeper.

Now, quite apart from generalisation, for which I want to apologise now to those in the audience who have an expert knowledge of these things, we have with all this the usual problems of historiography. It's hard to know quite how accurate this view of mountaineering history really is. But it's not a complete fiction. We have the evidence of the written word. In club journals, newsletters, and books we can trace a literary achievement whose characteristics are distinctly those of an educated and privileged class. It is often claimed – by mountaineers needless to say – that mountaineering has a more distinguished literature than any other sport or pastime. This may be correct. Certainly, the best of what is written in the major journals stands comparison with the best essay writing in the English language. Mountaineering has produced a huge library of books, and a significant number of them are of lasting importance. In addition, I am old enough to have seen something of the 'grand old men' of traditional mountaineering at first hand. I remember meeting people like John Hunt, leader of the first ascent of Everest, David Cox, the eminence gris of Oxford mountaineering when I was a student, and Charlie Houston, the leader of the tragic and heroic 1953 American expedition to the world's second highest mountain, K2.

Figures such as these always put me in mind of the immortal remark of Maurice Herzog, leader of the French expedition that in 1950 put himself and Louis Lachenal on the summit of the first of the world's 8000 metre peaks to be climbed: 'there are other Annapurnas in the lives of men'. So much so that it is tempting to suppose that the traditional mountaineer had a civilising sense of proportion that is lost on his modern counterparts. Tempting, but perilous, I think. Less perilous, I hope, to suggest that a sense of proportion is characteristic of the best, or perhaps I should say the most admirable, mountaineers of every epoch.

So: if we grant at least some truth to this image of the 'traditional' mountaineer and 'traditional' mountaineering, is there a distinctly different, 'modern', outlook with which to compare it? Well, I'm not sure how distinct it is, but I think in contemporary approaches we can sense differences. In Britain, one way to do this might be to compare past issues of, say, The Alpine Journal, published continuously in London since 1863, with contemporary issues of 'Summit', the house magazine of the British Mountaineering Council. The BMC is not the governing body of British mountaineering because there is no governing body, but it is as close to one as exists, a government sponsored bureaucracy which does valuable work representing mountaineers' and rock-climbers' interests, in particular over the ever-present problems of open access to rock climbing venues and wild country. Thirty years ago the head of the BMC was the general secretary; he or she is now called the chief executive officer, which may or may not be significant. The umbrella organisation of such national bodies is the International Mountaineering and Climbing Federation, whose website informs us that it belongs to, I quote, 'the group of International Federations who agree to be guided by the Olympic Charter and who recognise the authority of the International Olympic Committee', something which you may or may not find disturbing. Like most house magazines, the BMC's is image conscious and slick. It is full of how-to adverts; not just how-to climb, but how not-to kill yourself in the process, how to rescue yourself from a crevasse if you fall in, how to read clouds and come up with a weather forecast, how to make yourself as comfortable as possible during a bivouac, how to plan your activities, how to train for them, how to up your standard. All the sorts of things that my generation, or at least my social milieu, didn't know about 30 years ago, still doesn't know about, and no doubt should. Though in defence, the traditionalist might argue that there are so many things one should know that if one insisted on waiting until one knew them all, one would never actually get around to going climbing. The traditional mountaineer is an amateur and the modern a professional, and in at least two senses. As I have implied, the traditional mountaineer was assumed either to have a 'proper' job, often in education, or to have a private income; and in any event there was little market for the professional, except in exceptional cases such as Everest. That has changed. The huge increase in outdoor leisure in recent decades has created an audience, and there is now a cadre of professional mountaineers to satisfy it. But when all is said and done, only a small proportion of mountaineers, even today, earn a living from it. A more widespread aspect of professionalism is something hard to define, but perhaps connected to a greater sense that time is limited and must be used efficiently. It involves an increased focus on planning, including training, and being generally well organised. And if all this preparedness backfires and starts to blunt the excitement that all mountaineers crave, then in Summit magazine the modern will find further courses advertised that are likely to be of interest to today's multi-activity outdoor enthusiast-paragliding, kayaking, deep-sea diving, horse riding, sailing. Though interestingly, no salmon-fishing so far as I can see.

To caricature outrageously, we have on the one hand the slightly unworldly traditionalist, badly dressed, with a copy of Horace in the rucksack, a bumbling enthusiasm, and an unspoken assumption that finding himself here, in this previously unexplored corner of the Himalaya, with a few other chaps, some jolly keen Sherpas and a couple of months to conquer everything in sight, is really no more than the natural order of things; and on the other the 'modern', resplendent in day-glo lycra, topo guide to hand, with a planned and steely competence and complete focus on one very particular 30 foot cliff of white limestone, where the next chapter in the history books is about to be written.

Some caveats are necessary at this point. I have talked about the 'traditional' and the 'modern', but these are convenient designations, which cannot be tied too closely to historical eras. Perhaps Bonington was one of the first of the moderns, but then what about a figure like Frank Smythe, already writing books of his adventures with a wider public in mind in the 1930s, or Captain John Noel, filming on Everest long before the modern circus arrived? And it works the other way round too – the contemporary climber who is really a throwback. What of a figure like Stephen Venables, extant in this audience and so presumably a modern in the flesh, and certainly a modern in that he earns his living from mountaineering, and yet in character and culture so reminiscent of the great Presidents of the Alpine Club of London in the nineteenth century? Or Julian Attwood, in all essentials an imperial explorer on the borders of British India in the days of the Great Game?

But most importantly, I am not in this lecture trying to make a judgement of whether the traditionalist or the modern is 'better'. I am interested in discussing what 'is', and perhaps what is going to be, not what ought to be. And that for the very simple reason that I am unclear what criteria one would use to decide on right and wrong, ought and ought not. It seems to me that even the incomparable Kant became unconvincing here. I hope any professional moral philosophers in the audience will forgive me, but I am not clear of the possible objective basis for these things beyond two – and two which, typically it seems, offer very different perspectives. If you believe in God, then God decrees right and wrong, ought and ought not; that is a part of his purpose. You follow his law, and there is no more to be said. Or, like me, you are a Darwinian, in which case you might be led to conflate an 'is' with an 'ought', to believe that the way things are becomes in itself their justification. This position is generally regarded as fallacious, and I shall agree. Having thereby rejected two possible sources of a moral system, I am left with sophistry, the belief that right and wrong, ought and ought not are based, if not purely on fashion, then very largely on the everyday practicalities of a society and it's convenience. What we are used to, what we have imbibed from those around us, becomes the basis of our moral system. Works like *The End of History* or John Rawls's *A Theory of Justice* could only have been written by contemporary liberal intellectuals; in them, the values of contemporary liberal intellectuals emerge, against all statistical probability, as the objectively 'best' values by which a society can live. But that they are perilously close to being no more than statements of fashion is not the problem; the problem is that their authors would like to think otherwise. Again, the difference between naturalism and sophistry as I understand the terms is that the former is in the camp of those who believe that the moral truth exists in some absolute space, rather like a mathematical axiom, if only it can be found; whereas sophistry, so easily criticised as a resignation of moral courage, a degeneration into mere laissez-faire, is asserting that the very notion of an absolute moral system is intellectually incoherent; that morality must, of its nature, relate to life as we find it.

So, returning from this rather presumptuous foray into serious philosophy, it is perfectly true, and spectacularly unsurprising, that I have my own prejudices about how mountaineering should be practised, and perfectly true that these conform, as one would expect, and to a laughably high degree of accuracy, with the ideas and values of my own formative years – that is, British mountaineering circa 1970 to 1980. This much is natural I think, and not a problem. It would only become a problem if I assumed my imbibed attitudes were somehow 'right'. I hope I have made this clear. I am attracted, for a variety of reasons, to a particular way of doing things. I have no evidence, or even belief, that my own preferences are really 'better' than others.

Or have I?

Mountains deliver certain experiences to us, including some that we might find difficult to experience elsewhere. If we can show that a certain way of doing things, certain attitudes, deliver these experiences more fully or more reliably than other ways, then we might argue that this is the 'right' way. So what are these experiences?

Some of you will know that I have a theory about this, and I want now to summarise it, though I accept that any theory has disadvantages. It can be accused of being too analytical, if not reductionist. As I have indicated, mountain literature contains plenty of successful attempts to convey the experience of mountaineering, and without theorising. Amongst contemporary authors, Al Alvarez produced such an evocation in his book *Feeding the Rat*, the rat, who is male incidentally, even when inhabiting the body of a woman, being some vague amalgam of all those frustrated, craving, bored, freedom-loving aspects of the human psyche that want to throw off convention and safety and indulge in a little hair-raising adventure from time to time. The rat may have a fast or a slow metabolism – I am tempted to say it gets slower as one gets older – but sooner or later he will demand a meal. To my mind, this is an arresting and effective image. So I am not trying to suggest that in the attempt to explain mountaineering an analysis is superior to a literary approach. Rather that the two are complimentary.

In any event, the theory. Human beings are complex animals, with desires and sources of meaning in their lives which if not downright contradictory are sometimes very close to it. Two of these I believe form the essence of mountaineering; but more that that, mountains give us the opportunity to experience both of them simultaneously. And it is in that simultaneous as opposed to sequential experience that we can find our highest degree of contentment, satisfaction, or exhilaration.

One of them, which I will call 'the return to the primitive', flows from the arena that is mountain country. That is, we operate in places which inevitably take us back to a more archaic way of living and thinking, and this seems to satisfy a deep seated need – not in everyone I hasten to add, but in many of us. Dr Johnston, not simply on the basis of prejudice but even after travelling to the Scottish Highlands with Boswell, seems to have been quite clear that he preferred London, and he's not alone. Nevertheless, if we believe in the influence of the past, not just culturally but genetically, then it is plausible that wild and remote country feeds into us in a profound way. We might regard much of this as a spiritual experience. In mountains we are returned to fundamental things in terms of what we do – getting comfortable, trying to stay safe, relying on each other, making camp, these things often being repeated day after day in the same way, hence attaining the flavour of ritual. But also we are reminded of philosophical truths – or simply truths. The mountains are big and don't care about us. Once, in past centuries, we might have anthropomorphised them, or filled them with dragons, as indeed was the case in the European Alps pretty much until mountaineering began, and in this sense we cannot, today, relive the mental lives of our ancestors. But so far as reminding ourselves of our insignificance is concerned, we can. There is a change in perspective, a change in the value of things, which soaks into us in wild country. By just being there and undertaking the tasks which need to be done, we engage in what the darling of British mountaineering in the 1970s, Pete Boardman, called 'serious play' – a good phrase, because mountaineering is serious, that is profound, in a way which a theme park is not. But it is also, for us, all play. We visit a more archaic world on a temporary basis, with the knowledge that we can return to our western lifestyle at any time we wish. What we are doing is drawing the benefits of a more natural way of living, but in general without paying the price that the true primitive pays. So there is nothing in the philosophy I am propounding that requires us to idealise or sentimentalise the rural poor, or the primitive, or to rail against western materialism. We are not required to follow Rousseau and arrive at the flawed concept of the noble savage, or even more disastrously to sail with Margaret Mead to the south seas and fantasise over Samoa. We can remain with our feet on the ground and admit that this is all fantasy, yet still claim that wild country, and being forced to operate in it, satisfies us. And even those who do not want to claim that much can at least agree that it's all one hell of a contrast. There are so many fewer people out there than in Oxford street. The sounds of man are less, even if the sound of the wind is greater. There is less to do, but more time to do it properly. In fact there is altogether less confusion-assuming a refusal to countenance satellite phones, lap-tops and other such impertinent paraphernalia. There is suffering, but arguably less anguish. There is in some senses less freedom, but thereby less stress. You do not decide what to do – you do what has to be done. You decided days or months ago what you were going to do – climb this peak, cross that pass. All you have to do now is get on with it. And most of that is already defined – put on your boots, get moving, put up the tent, make supper. And in the unlikely event there is any time left, you can always read all those dauntingly long Russian novels you've always intended to get around to.

All of this amounts in large degree to a lesson in humility, an encouragement to downgrade the importance of one's own ego. But shadowing it in mountaineering is the complete reverse – the celebration of the ego, the explicit goal of giving it free rein. Mountaineering is an egocentric pursuit, an opportunity for the individual to assert him or herself not only against nature but against other people. The image of the mountain climber, ice axe raised, standing in triumph on top of some conquered snowy summit, is accurate. He has proved he can 'do', that determination leads to results, that he has climbed higher and further than the competition. If the humility of the Taoist ideal leads to peace, it is equally true that exercising the muscles of the ego, the sense of being a big cheese, leads to exhilaration.

It is an obvious thought to connect return to the primitive to what I have called the 'traditional' approach, and the egocentricity of individual achievement with the 'modern' – but the merest consideration of history shows us that this is false. The great climbers and explorers of the golden age-these people were as egocentric as Messner, or Bonington, or any of the teenage superstars of today. And I know of no evidence to support the notion that today's climbers are any less appreciative of wild country and of a return to the primitive in general than their predecessors were. In fact, as you listen to this lecture you may be beginning to feel, as I do, that a historical division into traditional and modern is looking distinctly tenuous. A neat division into categories is always a pitfall for intellectuals, and perhaps that's the case here. Furthermore, I think there is something in the role of commentator, as opposed to participant, that encourages one to overstate change. If as a commentator one considers, say, the number of people involved in climbing, if one looks at the statistics, then yes, the numbers have gone up dramatically. It's true that if you go to Stanage, a gritstone outcrop outside Sheffield, you will find more people there on an average weekday than there used to be on a Bank Holiday Sunday. But as a participant, it feels less dramatic. Many of the mountain crags in the Lake District have fewer visits today than they did in the 1970s. In any case, when you are climbing your world contracts to a few feet; there is you, your companion, and the immediate surroundings. What is happening globally is not part of the experience.

So if an historical progression from traditional to modern is to be rejected, is there nevertheless a change in focus within the experience of each individual? I have argued that a return to the primitive and an expression of egocentricity are both essential to the fullest satisfaction mountains can deliver, and furthermore that our most treasured moments occur when we experience them together. But that does not mean they need be equally important throughout our lives. And in general, I don't think they are. When we are young the satisfaction of ego is more likely to take centre stage. This is the time when we are ambitious, not in that private sense that endures, that sense in which throughout life we take pleasure in our achievements, however modest, but in the public sense, the sense that we want to be recognised. It is this desire for recognition perhaps that weakens with time, though it can be difficult to know if the weakening is really due to age or rather to assuaged hunger. I remember looking up in the seering cold of an Arctic dawn at the first unclimbed mountain I had ever confronted. I was young, and exceedingly motivated to succeed. But was I motivated because I was young, or because this game was new? These days, I still like to bag unclimbed peaks when I get the chance, but I am beginning to wonder about the likelihood of ever quite recapturing the excitement, the exhilaration, the sheer joy, of that first time. Is that because I am older, or because I have been there? How would I feel had I never climbed anything new? Well, the mountaineering world is full of experienced people who have never climbed anything new, and I don't get the impression they are all full of angst at the fact. They are older, and if not necessarily wiser then at least more knowing. In youth, things are seen too much in black and white. So and so climbs some untrodden peak, explores some undiscovered country, and is thereby a few rungs further up the ladder. The more experienced realise it was probably largely a matter of luck anyway. When I read *Summit* magazine, I sometimes catch myself becoming irritated at yet another enviable adventure gleefully recounted by the same person as last month. How do they manage to get so much done, these people? Then I recall that the person in question was in the education business, and that their age has made them one of the blessed generation; public servants who were able to retire years early on a full pension. Luck, you see. Something similar applies to most, if not all, achievement. Did the early Everest climbers really represent the best that Britain could produce – out of several tens of millions of people? Of course not. But when the social, educational and financial criteria that I have alluded to were taken into account, organisations like the Royal Geographical Society and the Alpine Club, organisations that determined who should go on these jollies, really had a remarkably limited pool of people to draw on.

Bearing all this in mind, it is not hard to see why there is a sense in which mountaineers believe that mountaineering should not be taken too seriously, just as there is a different sense in which they insist that it should. It should be taken seriously to the extent that it has the power to satisfy profound human needs. And also because it is dangerous. And yet part of that danger is statistical and unavoidable, a servant of fate, and what might be required here is not so much seriousness as acceptance. Hemingway famously remarked that there were only three sports: bullfighting, motor racing and mountaineering, all the rest being mere games. Part of what he meant I think was that in all three the individual, without having anything like the complete information one would like, must make decisions and then accept the consequences. Consequences which may not be to one's liking, of course. A premature appointment with death, for instance. Jumping the queue, as it were. Well; bad luck! As in history generally, 'stuff happens'. Of course mankind can 'do', of course our effort, courage, expertise, matters; but none of this is in itself decisive. Luck, or the lack of it, remains forever at the heart of events. Mountaineering is profound in what it promises, and at times delivers, and yet we should not take our own part in it too seriously. A certain lightness of touch is appropriate. If the process itself is valuable, the level of achievement to which it leads is empty.

It's hard not to feel that the Olympic outlook on sport is pretty much the complete reverse of this. I find it hard to see that beach volleyball, say, satisfies any profound human needs – unless we include the voyeur-istic desires of men – yet how seriously they all take it! Look down on these ants from windswept heights; some running round and round, others throwing things as far as they can, yet others batting balls back-wards and forwards. The less important it is, the more seriously it is taken. As Einstein once enquired of Charlie Chaplin when he was a new boy to the absurdity of public adulation, 'What does it all mean?' And as Chaplin replied, 'nothing'. And yet, if sport is a surrogate for war, whether people generally realize it or not, then we should be grate-ful. The more sport the better. And in Olympic sport to a greater extent than in war, it is generally clear enough who has won. Mountaineering doesn't so readily oblige. It is not, for example, self-evident that he who has climbed the most mountains deserves the most medals. Perhaps it should be the person who has survived the longest. Or enjoyed it the most. Or most successfully combined their egocentricity with an ac-knowledgement of the wider perspective.

Consider two iconic figures of the last century – the Manchester plumber Don Whillans and the Edinburgh intellectual Dougal Haston, who famously climbed together on the South-West face of Everest, once the last great problem of world mountaineering. Whillans said that if you die in the mountains that wipes out the standing of all your previous achievements. Haston claimed that the experienced – and by implication expert-mountaineer is the one who has been in a lot of dicey situations and been lucky enough to survive them all. Whillans and Haston both, you notice, chose a phil-osophy to suit their life and character – as most of us do. Perhaps only the saint and the madman ever really does otherwise. Whillans died in his sleep, arguably of overweight. Haston died in an avalanche, ski-ing an alpine couloir he knew to be in risky condition. Both moved mountaineering forward with new climbs at home, in the European Alps, and in the greater ranges. So who was the better mountaineer? Well, this is silly. One might as well ask, who was the better philoso-pher? They were both figures of international standing. Why say more? Mountaineering achievement simply cannot be quantified in the way an Olympic outlook would require.

This is intuitively understood I think by all mountaineers, though not necessarily by those in the media, sports administration and so on who have their own interests. I suspect it will come as a surprise to many mountaineers to learn that the intention to give medals for mountaineering goes back to the Olympic congress of 1894 and that medals have indeed been given, if sporadically and with no very clear rationale, ever since. It is perhaps worth mentioning a couple of examples, to indicate the bizarre, the mistaken, or just the plain unfortunate position that this relentless attempt to quantify leads to. The members of the Everest expedition of 1922, the archetypal old school trip if ever there was one, were all awarded medals. The leader of the expedition, Charles Granville Bruce, was a Ghurka officer, a great bull of a man, and apparently worshipped by his men. He went on to become a general, so I suppose he was used to medals. George Mallory, too, one can imagine, might have been pleased. But personally, I would like to know the reaction of Howard Theodore Somervell, doctor and after Everest dedicated medical missionary, also a mountain painter of originality. I would imagine he felt both amusement and bemusement. And then more recently, Reinhold Messner, the first man to climb all 14 of the world's 8,000 metre peaks, and much else besides, was awarded a medal at the 1988 Calgary Winter Olympics. But only a silver. Who made that decision I wonder? As Doug Scott has commented, it does rather beg the question as to what a climber has to do to go for gold. Perhaps climb Olympus Mons, without bottled oxygen. Olympus Mons, as you doubtless know, is 82,000 ft high and situated on Mars.

So much for quantification. But in addition, Olympic sport requires the mirror that is other people to make it meaningful. It is not just that winning the 100 metres is egocentric, but that it's a public form of egocentricity. It needs an audience, and preferably some other athletes. Would you run round an Olympic stadium or throw the discus if you were the only person in the world? I can't envisage it. Might you climb a mountain? Certainly. The Olympics today is inconceivable without public accolade, and without TV coverage, whereas mountaineering is still – in 2012 – uneasy about such things. Bill Tilman, a great explorer of the last century, wrote to the effect that every true mountaineer would be dismayed to see anything about mountaineering in the newspapers; how many latter-day enthusiasts have been secretly relieved when some live outdoor climbing spectacular has had to be cancelled because of bad weather? Though admittedly, this may be no more than an instance of the old Chinese proverb: happy is he who sees his friend fall off a roof.

Contemporary rock climbing throws up a lot of bright young things who shoot to stardom before puberty, only to give up the whole game before they've left school because they are no longer getting any better at it. This is perhaps most true of indoor climbing, and that, I think, is telling. There used to be a wicked joke that Boardman climbed Everest whilst still a virgin; but even if he had- and probably someone *has* by now – one could never imagine him giving up. He had too profound an awareness of what mountaineering gave him for that. Whereas one can easily imagine a well heeled client on a contemporary commercial expedition to the mountain getting to the summit and thereafter not giving the game another thought, particularly if they had just achieved some unrepeatable 'first' of the sort I have just alluded to.

So I would suggest that the answer to our question is something along the following lines. There have been changes to what mountaineering is over the last 200 years or so. It has become bigger, more socially diverse, and standards of performance have progressed astonishingly. But philosophically, in terms of values, the changes have been less than headline news might suggest. The real change takes place within the mind and experience of each individual. And it is there, in private experience, rather than outwardly, in public achievement, that the value of mountaineering ultimately lies. I hope I have now said enough to demonstrate that there is very little ground on which mountaineering as currently understood sits easily with the Olympic movement. There are styles of rock-climbing, specifically indoor climbing, that may soon be taken into the Olympic fold, and why not? These are aspects of gymnastics after all, and are only really connected to the mountaineering debate by default. Otherwise, much depends on whether one wishes to remain true to historical precedent. I have made my own view clear, I assume. But that's all it is; a view, formed of habit as much as rationale. Others must decide for themselves. Nor, incidentally, should anything I have said be construed as an attack on awards *per se*. The Piolets d'Or for example, world mountaineering's premier award for outstanding achievement, seems recently to have refound it's sense of direction. My impression is that this is largely due to it's being controlled by practising, or at least recently retired, mountaineers. The same is true, up to now, of the BMC. So far, it has been controlled and run by committed practitioners, some of them operating at the highest level, rather than by – well, anyone else. It would be hopelessly narrow-minded to predict that all such initiatives, all such organisations, will prove detrimental to mountaineering, even mountaineering in the traditional sense. But one prediction I am confident of is this: that if mountaineering allows itself to become entangled with the Olympic machine, it will be chewed up and spat out in unrecognisable and, to my taste, ill-flavoured pieces. Mountaineering is a sport, yes, but of a different hue to the Olympic variety. As the dictionary wisely suggests: amusement, diversion-fun.

Greenhead College
PBartlett@greenhead.ac.uk

Rivalry in Cricket and Beyond: Healthy or Unhealthy?*

MICHAEL BREARLEY

Introduction

What is the point of sport? For those to whom sport doesn't appeal, it seems futile, pointless. Yet a small child takes pleasure in his or her bodily capacities and adroitness. Gradually the child achieves a measure of physical coordination and mastery. Walking, jumping, dancing, catching, kicking, hitting, climbing, being in water, using an implement as a bat or racquet – all these offer a sense of achievement and satisfaction. Sport it seems to me is an extension of such activities.

This development in coordination is part of the development of a more unified self. Instead of being subject to more or less random movements, we learn to move according to central intentions or trajectories. We begin to know what we are doing and what we are about. The small child celebrates its ability to act in such ways. It begins to find a degree of rhythm and control in its movements. The child hones such skills.

So far, dance and sport are barely distinguishable. Activities that may be the forerunners of either enhance this sense of coordination. Increasing such control implies a pleasure in development, which may perhaps be seen as competing with one's earlier self: one source of pleasure in sport is to surpass one's own earlier achievements.

Sport proper starts to emerge when competition with others begins to play a more central role alongside the simpler delight in physicality. 'I can run faster than you, climb higher, wrestle you to the floor; I score a goal against you, hit the ball when you try to bowl me out, win in some way or other'. Aggression combines with flamboyance. Sport is an area where aggression and the public demonstration of skills and of character are permitted and even encouraged. For many people who are otherwise inclined to be inhibited or self-conscious, sporting arenas offer a unique opportunity for self-expression and for spontaneity. Within a framework of rules and acceptable behavior, they can be whole-hearted. Such people owe sport a lot; here they can feel

---

* A version of this paper was printed in *The Point*, 2010.

doi:10.1017/S1358246113000349 ©The Royal Institute of Philosophy and the contributors 2013

more fully themselves. Here they can begin to find themselves, to become the selves that they have the potential to be.

In this process, the child and the adult have to learn to cope with the emotional ups and downs of victory and defeat, success and failure. They – we – learn to keep going against the odds, to struggle back to form, to recognize the risks of complacency. We have to learn to deal with inner voices telling us we are no good, encouraging us to give up, or inviting us to fail rather than risk gloating. In sport the wish to triumph over one's near relatives, fathers and brothers, say, and their representatives, is often strong; there is a need to deal with such emotions, and we find our own ways of doing so, more or less successfully, more or less defensively. The balance between out-and-out aggression and respect for the other, empathy for the defeated other, identification with the winner when we lose – in sport all these processes have to be negotiated. Arrogance and humiliation have to be struggled with.

Spectators identify imaginatively not only with the skills of sportsmen but also with their characters, their characteristic ways of hanging in, of recovery, of fighting back or giving up. These are the dramas of sport.

Sport calls for a subtle balancing too of planning and spontaneity, of calculation and letting go, of discipline and freedom. Coach and former cricketer Greg Chappell said (personal communication); 'premeditation is the graveyard of batting'. Yet one has to train oneself in the sporting skills, form a reliable technique, and work at it. At the peak of performance one is alert to possible lines of attack by individual and collective opponents, yet able to respond with more or less uncluttered minds to the next play or assault. Like parents with children, we have a complicated job to do in enabling our own selves to find the right balance between self-discipline and free rein. Moments when one is, as a sportsperson, 'in the zone', body and mind at one, in harmony, completely concentrated but completely relaxed, aware of every relevant detail of one's surroundings but not obsessed or hyper-sensitive to any set of them, confident without being over-confident, aware of dangers without being over-cautious – such rare states of mind are akin to being in love. They involve a marriage between the conscious control I mentioned above with the allowing of a more unconscious creativity through the body's knowledge. In such states the role of the conscious mind may primarily be a quiet watching.

I would like to raise three further topics before I move on to a more sustained consideration of competition, which will be the main theme of my talk. One is about what team sport adds over and above whatever is involved in individual sport. The second is: is sport a sublimation of war or fighting? Finally I wish to mention the question: is wanting to win neurotic? (I will return to this later.)

First, then: sport divides into team and individual sports. One of the aims of team sport is to turn a group of individuals from a collection into a team, from a group functioning according to basic assumptions (Bion, 1961) into a team with differentiated roles, with room for individual expression but in a context of the whole team's interest – that is, into a team functioning more as a work group than as a basic assumption group. Team sport thus calls for the balance between self-interest and group interest. The members of the team have at times to constrain themselves in the interests of the team; they also have the benefit of the team's support when things are hard for them individually.

Second, what is the relation of sport to fighting and war? Is sport a sublimation of the wish to kill and triumph at any cost? Murderousness does require sublimation by means of the imposition of limits, whether internalized or purely external and also by the shift from actual death to symbolic death. When the cricket batman is dismissed, he has to leave the arena, thus suffering symbolic death. Sport exists within a boundary, often a physical boundary, but also a time boundary; for so many hours or minutes, or until so many actions have taken place, or until such and such outcomes have occurred, for so long these rules apply, this game continues. Specially designated intervals occur, intervals, close of play, or gaps between innings, in which there is a lull, rest or pause. When the game is over, players shake hands, and may have a beer together. Aggression is constitutive of the game, but there are many limits; not any sort of delivery is permitted; there are penalties for breaking the rules, there are ethical issues beyond the rules themselves on which participants almost universally concur.

Such factors distinguish sport from violence or murder. But what about war? Is sport a sublimation of war? The problem with that theory is that in most war-encounters too there are rules of engagement, whether culturally agreed or laid down more formally in international conventions. Thus there are agreed rules regarding the treatment of prisoners of war, there are rules that require respect for the enemy's dead. There are conventions about the different responsibilities of combatants in relation to non-combatants. War allows killing and maiming, but not any killing or maiming. War is itself violence sublimated.

Moreover if one thinks of the play of young animals, or of playful interactions between the young and their parent, one sees that the

Michael Brearley

limitations on aggression are built-in from the start. It is not that there is a an impulse to kill which has to be civilized; more that the impulse to kill is one thing, functioning in certain contexts, whilst the instinct to play – to wrestle, tickle, fight – is another, limited and controlled from the start. So I'm inclined to think that much of the partly aggressive play in sport is intrinsically different in motivation and outcome from the aggression in fighting or in war.

Third, is the wish to win neurotic or immature? Is the risk-taking in some sport (for example, mountain climbing) neurotic or narcissistic? I would say not (I will come back to this later), or, perhaps, not when the risk is realistically assessed and soberly taken; when nothing is done for show. Rather, unwillingness to win, or to strive to win, is often the more defensive outcome.

1. Competition and Cooperation

Rivalry and competitiveness are central to sport, and cricket is no exception. But cricket has a further feature that many other sports lack – that while all the individual dramatic moments that consecutively and collectively constitute the game are between two individual protagonists, batsman and bowler, each of these takes its place in, and is to some extent influenced by, the overall context of the contest between the two teams. So cricket, like baseball but unlike soccer or golf or tennis, involves individual contests in the context of team competition. Unlike baseball, however, cricket's contests between bat and ball can last for long time periods – days, even – and go through many ups and downs. A weather-vane in the shape of Father Time surveys Lord's Cricket Ground, the 'home of cricket' – symbolizing both the fact that time brings everything to an end and, perhaps, the timelessness of the experience of watching and playing cricket. Cricket is unique in its potential for drawn-out struggles between two people, each with his powerful narcissistic wishes for admiration and fears of humiliation, all within a team context. In every sport much is at stake in terms of bearing the threat of failure (for the batsman, as I've said, symbolic death, evoking the deposition of a king).

If human beings were not combative no one would have invented sport. But if human beings were not also cooperative neither team nor individual games would have found a place in society. For reasons I will come to, rivalry can – and indeed should – be taken close to the limit. But alongside this, cricket also involves the recognition of the unspoken or unprescribed realities of the spirit, respect and generosity of the game. This is not merely a matter of obedience to the laws (or rules) governing the game; it also involves the kinds of ordinary civilities that oil the wheels of relationships and collegial activities, the recognition of limits, the consideration and respect, and the give and take of a kind of dialogic interplay on the field.

2. Healthy Competition

Healthy rivalry between respecting individuals requires and fosters a developmentally necessary differentiation of self from other. In many contexts rivalry is a necessary feature of life. It supports proper ambition; it can help develop a full self, with a fuller growth of one's capacities; and it allows the other, in competitive situations, to strive and express him- or herself freely.

Rivalry does not entail lack of respect for one's opponent, whatever the outcome of the match or series. Test cricket – the highest level of the game, international matches played over 5 days – is, like many other forms of sport, rightly a tough business. But there is another side of these tough contests which can too easily be forgotten, and that is the playfulness and consideration between hard, high-powered competitors. When at Edgbaston in 2005 England won a Test against Australia by the tiny margin of two runs, England's hero Andrew Flintoff left the team huddle at the moment of victory and put his arm round his defeated opponent Brett Lee. He was not only commiserating with the pain of defeat, a boot which could so easily have been on the other foot. He also I think acknowledges the kinship between the rivals. For we not only want to defeat our opponents, we also depend on them and their skill, courage and hostility in order to prove and improve our own skills, to earn and merit our pride. There is a unity of shared striving, as well as a duality of opposition. The eleven players on each team form bonds through their shared skills and teamwork that are sometimes hard to replicate in the less dramatic intensities of everyday life. (Similarly after WW1 the closeness felt with their fellow soldiers could make domestic ties for the discharged survivors feel unreal and pallid by comparison). Somewhat similarly, the 22 players in a Test match go through it together, in a way that no spectator does. The Latin etymology of both 'rival' and 'compete' reflect this fact: *rivalis* meant 'sharing the same stream', *competens* meant 'striving together with', 'agreeing together', as in 'competent'.

One motive for striving so desperately for success may link with the desire to refute earlier doubters; a 'highly successful [musician] interpreted her whole career as an extended exercise in proving wrong the primary school teacher who had ignored her talents', writes Ed Smith (2008). The writer refers here to a healthy bloody-mindedness in reaction to a snub. This is part of proper pride. Envy and jealousy also play a part in, and are not always easily accommodated within, ordinary rivalry. Dickie Dodds, the Essex opening batsman, was once out without scoring on a pitch that was perfect for batting. Essex went on to dominate the morning session, and by lunch had reached 150 without losing any further batsmen. Having had to watch his team's success from the pavilion, Dodds came up to Doug Insole, one of the 'not out' batsmen, and said, 'Skipper, I hope you haven't been troubled by any bad vibes this morning?' Insole replied, 'Can't say I have, Dickie, been too busy enjoying myself – why do you ask?' 'Because I've been so full of bitterness I've not been wishing you well.' Here is an understandable and very human envy; since there was also frankness, remorse and regret, it did not spoil the relationship.

In 1976–77, I was fortunate enough to play five Tests in India. One of India's formidable quartet of spin bowlers was Eripalli Prasanna. He was a short, somewhat rotund off-spinner, with large, dark, expressive eyes, and a wonderful control of flight. For some reason, he and I would engage in a kind of eye-play. His look would say, 'OK, you played that one all right, but where will the next one land?' And mine would reply, 'Yes, you fooled me a little, but notice I adjusted well enough.' He had that peculiarly Indian, minimal, sideways waggle of the head, which suggests that the vertebrae of the sub-continental neck are more loosely linked than in our stiffer Western ones. The waggle joined with the eyes in saying: 'I acknowledge your qualities, and I know you acknowledge mine.'

I found it easier to enter in to such an engagement with a slow bowler, who might bamboozle me and get me out, but wasn't going to hurt me physically. But I had something similar with some fast bowlers, especially when we were more or less equally likely to come out on top. With such bowlers I could actually enjoy their best ball, pitching on a perfect length in line with off stump and moving away. I also enjoyed the fact that it was too good to graze the edge of my bat. There was the same friendly and humorous rivalry. The spirit of cricket – or more broadly, of sport itself – at its best, I think.

But how much do we really desire to be tested, in life or in sport? If the opposition's best fast bowler treads on the ball before the start of a Test match (as did Glenn McGrath in the match I referred to above) and cannot play, is one relieved or disappointed? There is no escaping the relief. We all want an easier ride. And it would be easy to be hypocritical, falsely high-minded, and say insincerely that we regret that the opposition team is thus hampered. But at the same time there is also a wish – in the participants as well as among spectators – for the contest to be fought with each side at its best, not depleted, so that no one can cavil at victory or make excuses for defeat; similarly, one might take more pleasure in scoring fifty against the great Australian bowlers Dennis Lillee and Jeff Thomson than in making a big hundred against lesser bowling.

There are many inevitable differences between spectators and participants: one is that the spectator wants to see the very best pitted against each other; part of the pleasure of watching a big innings by a great batsman depends on its being played against the best bowlers around, perhaps in conditions that help them. Spectators (except for the most partisan) enjoy evenly balanced matches, with both sides playing at their best, as well as being at full strength. Again, the players' feelings will be mixed. We all hope our opponents have an off-day, and that we win by a large margin. But the players also have another strand within them, one that values the close contest and relishes the battle. They cannot fully hope for it, as a neutral spectator can, but they can enjoy it and feel most fully alive through it.

Opponents challenge us. If we are up to it, they stretch us, call forth our courage, skill, cunning and resourcefulness; they force us to develop our techniques, or lag behind. Sometimes they compel an honesty about our limitations. In this way, they are like psychoanalysts, helping us to be stronger by revealing our shortcomings. But it is also the case that patients challenge their analysts.

3. Psychoanalysis and Sport

I retired from cricket some time ago; now I work as a psychoanalyst. One patient tells me his relentless denigration of me is for my benefit: it keeps me on my toes and stops me becoming complacent or arrogant as a result of the sycophantic adoration he assumes my other patients give me. This patient's trenchancy has different aims, motives and outcomes. For example, there is in his attitudes and behavior toward me the unconscious aim of letting me know what it is like to be unappreciated. One danger is that the psychoanalyst may get secret masochistic pleasure from such encounters, or may allow himself to become paralyzed. But what this patient says is valid and important in that there may often be something in his critical attitude, which I need to learn from. Moreover, patients need to be able to bring the whole of themselves to the analysis, including that which in ordinary life is often avoided or masked by politeness and insincerity.

This connects psychoanalysis with sport, as well as with art. In all three, within the safe (or safe-ish) boundary that separates each from ordinary or 'real' life, things can be said and done, and emotions expressed, that cannot otherwise be said or shown. For that freedom to be allowed or enabled by the analyst, without his losing his analytic capacities, patients are often deeply grateful. And the analyst too should be grateful for the generosity of the patient in thus risking so much. In parenthesis, there is a further link between sport and psychoanalysis and art, in that whilst nothing in sport, say, matters in comparison with the loss of a single life in, say, Northern Ireland or Afghanistan, it is often only through these safely set-aside areas of play and competition that the range of our qualities can be tried out, expressed and perhaps established as part of a fuller self.

The psychoanalyst Donald Winnicott (1969) addressed this when he spoke of the need for the child, and later the patient, to feel he has hurled the full force of his aggression at the parent or the analyst and yet has not destroyed them (or rendered them weak or ineffectual, unable to function properly in their respective roles). Winnicott argued that such visceral truthfulness is part of the process whereby the child or patient comes to accept the urgency of his own subjectivity while more fully recognizing the subjectivity of the other. It takes courage to risk all in this sort of way, and courage and generosity to accept it without either retreat or revenge. Martial arts like kung fu illustrate and teach this lesson. One has to defend oneself from attack by using the force of the opponent, by stepping back but then stepping forward to deliver a blow that hits home without necessarily being too damaging.

It is in this context that we see most clearly the need we have of wholehearted and skillful opponents. Without rivalry there could be no sport, but rivals also need each other in their cooperative role. They are co-creators of excellence and integrity, in sport as in analysis. As the old Yorkshire and England batsman Maurice Leyland once said: 'Fast bowling keeps you honest.'

4. Fear of Competition

Competition can get out of hand, turning into cheating, vindictiveness and narcissistic destructiveness. Over-valuation of competitiveness can crush and inhibit the growing child. It can spoil relationships, and reduce love to trophy-seeking. I will come back briefly to this in the next section. But it can also be perverted in the opposite direction. Some people refrain from competing wholeheartedly because they are afraid of winning, and even avoid doing so. This may be because of their fear of triumphalism, or because they are over-identified with the pain of the opponent. I knew a young boy who desperately wanted to win the first game with his father, but then equally desperately needed to lose the second, so that neither party would lose face, or have to bear too much disappointment, or have to deal with his own tendency to gloat. One might think, loftily, that the mature attitude to winning in sport is not to mind. The opposite is true. Not minding often means avoiding really trying.

I once played for a spell as a guest player for an English professional side on a short tour involving a number of matches. During the first half of the tour, we had tried our best but lost more than we won. We had been facing good and talented players, in their conditions. The matches were played hard, even though they were not part of any ongoing competitive leagues or series. In the next game, we were led by the newly arrived captain, against a very strong side. This captain preferred to emphasize the entertainment element in the game, this being a supposedly 'friendly' fixture; not wanting to be too serious, he did not use his front-line bowlers, allowing the opposition batsmen to display their most powerful strokes. He thus 'gave' batsmen runs. They scored an even bigger total than they would have without his misguided generosity, bowled flat-out against us, and we limped to a crushing defeat. This gesture of giving runs patronized the other team and robbed each party of the satisfaction of doing their best and striving properly to win. We did not properly lose (though we did lose face and respect). The gilt on our opponents' win was tarnished.

Such dilution or evasion of proper rivalry can also occur out of a wish to look good in someone's eyes. One Test captain, whom I won't name, decided during the afternoon of the last day that his batsmen should play for a draw rather than take further risks in going for a win. He was, however, reluctant to be seen as, and be criticized for being, a defensive captain. This happened to be the first Test for a young batsman in the middle order; he hadn't scored in the first innings, and been given a hard time by the crowd, who wanted its local hero selected in place of the youngster. When he went in to bat the captain gave him the following orders: 'Play for a draw, but don't make it look as if we're playing for a draw.' This was hypocritical and cowardly; the task for the young player was difficult enough without having to act a role. This captain was more interested in how he himself looked than in competing properly or supporting and protecting a young player.

I even have some doubts about what was from one viewpoint a notable example of nobility and generosity. The great Surrey and England batsman, Jack Hobbs, said once that as Surrey had a lot of good batsman, and the Oval pitch was usually easy for batting, when he and Andy Sandham had put on 150 or so for the first wicket, he'd sometimes give his wicket to 'the most deserving professional bowler'. (When the pitch was difficult, or Larwood and Voce were bowling, that was when he really earned his money, he went on). But in making a gift of his wicket, did Hobbs also belittle the recipient of the gift, who had not by his own skill and persistence forced an error? The bowler was treated not man to man, but man to boy. There was, or might have been, an element of the feudal in Hobbs' largesse.

In the great battles of sport, no quarter is given and none expected. These are occasions when observers tremble with awe. When highlights of Test matches in Australia were for the first time broadcast in UK, in 1974, England were blasted by fierce fast bowling from Lillee and Thomson on some bowler-friendly pitches; my Middlesex colleague, Mike Smith, reported pouring himself a large gin and tonic, and hiding behind the sofa to watch.

Many cricket-followers will remember the contest between South African fast bowler Allan Donald and Michael Atherton at Trent Bridge in 1998. A great fast bowler hurled all his aggression, power and skill at a defiant, courageous, gritty, slender English batsman, a battle given an extra tinge of menace by the umpiring mistake as a result of which Atherton had just been given not out when he had gloved Donald to the 'keeper. The most memorable contests are those where the aggression is raw, but contained, perhaps only just, within the bounds of respect for the opposition and for the rules and traditions of the game.

But there is still no need for unpleasant language, for bad-mouthing, for what is known in cricket as 'sledging'. In my experience the great West Indian fast bowlers said nothing to the batsman on the field. One might say: they had no need to – first because of their superlative ability, but second because they were quite able to convey menace by eye contact. It happened that, when I played my first Test match, against the West Indies, in 1976, both teams were staying at the same hotel in Nottingham. I ran into Andy Roberts at breakfast. He gave me a quizzical little look, not crudely unpleasant, but conveying, I felt, something along the lines of 'Shall I be eating you for breakfast or for lunch?' Andy gave these looks on the field too; like Helen of Troy's face, which launched a thousand ships, Andy's conveyed a thousand words.

When England were about to tour India in 1976, some of us who were in the team took the opportunity to ask Len Hutton, one of the greatest batsmen of all time, and a Yorkshireman noted for his dry, enigmatic comments, for advice. Len appeared characteristically guarded. He then uttered a single short sentence: 'don't take pity on them Indian bowlers'.

I am aware, of course, that recreational sport played for fun also has an important role, to do with giving people a chance, sharing the batting and the bowling; of one recreational captain it was said that 'his captaincy had twin aims: to give every player a good game and to beat the opposition as narrowly as possible.' But in sport we have the opportunity, and the license, to assert ourselves as separate and authentic individuals against others who have the same license; and this potential can allow us to find our own unique identity, while respecting that of others. And this is part of a wider growth of the personality, of which one aspect would be the Quaker capacity to 'tell Truth to Power'. One element in telling the truth is being able to say no, to stand firm against powerful and sometimes bullying forces, without becoming a bully oneself. The more strenuous and spirited aspects of competitiveness enhance self-development, courage and sheer exhilaration. They can also be the occasion and source of the development of new methods and techniques. Correlatively, being less than wholehearted is liable to be, though it may not be, a kind of evasion or cowardice.

5. Contempt for the Opponent

However, competition is not always so straightforward or so simple. It is often contaminated by disrespect, contempt, envy and other factors. When such things predominate, competition is corrupted into triumph at any cost, friendly rivalry turns into poisonous scorn, and defeat becomes a humiliation to be averted or reversed at any cost.

There are differences that would be hard to define between appropriate shrewdness in undermining an opponent and boorish expressions of contempt. Cricket is after all not only a physical game; it includes bluff, menace, ploy and counter-ploy. Setting a field is not only a matter of putting someone where the ball is most likely to go, but also of making the batsman wonder what is coming next, or making clear to him that the captain thinks he lacks certain strokes. The aim is that he will be undone by such a 'statement' either into loss of nerve or into reckless attempts to prove the captain wrong. Words may enter into this; a captain might say within a batsman's hearing 'you don't need anyone back there for him' – and I would be inclined to see this as a fair enough nibble at the batsman's state of mind. Viv Richards' swagger at the crease and Shane Warne's slow, mesmerizing nine-step walk which took up most of his so-called 'run-up' allowed each to state unequivocally that this was their stage, and that their opponents had little right to share it with them. All this seems to me to be acceptable, even admirable. But such attitudes can tip over into arrogance, superiority, contempt – even a sort of gang warfare.

Superiority and arrogance may be endemic in a person or a culture. The British Empire was riddled with it. Military and administrative power was identified with cultural superiority. The British had many terms of abuse or disparagement for members of subject races or cultures. Such attitudes, which were often unconscious and automatic, involved stereotyping, projection, and splitting. In the atmosphere of colonial times, these psychological processes allowed white people to represent black players as all spontaneity and exuberance, but lacking in resolution and solidity, technique and discipline. They were said to fall apart in panic more quickly than we whites do, as if children in comparison with us, the adults. Of course this meant that for many years it was out of the question for a black man to captain a national team, for children cannot be adults, and children need mature parental leaders.

If one is treated terribly there are various possible psychological outcomes. Perhaps the most insidious is when a person takes on the identity that is attributed to him and becomes in his own eyes worthless. The racist is internalized, becomes part of one's own self; one begins to treat oneself as an object only. The psychoanalyst Fakhry Davids, for example, describes a young black boy in England who came to see the brownness of his skin as dirty (1996).

But of course traumatic abuse (of which colonial and racist attitudes are an example) can have other outcomes in its victims. One is a countervailing arrogance and even cruelty: the leaders of the French Revolution degenerated within a few years from high principles to self-righteousness and a frenzy of base revenge. Sadism can be exciting. Moreover we defend ourselves against a feeling of inferiority, envy and humiliation by projection, by ridding ourselves of these feelings in ourselves and placing them in others, whether those who are below us in the pecking order or those who previously formed the powerful elite.[1]

One example is of a bowler who regularly expressed contempt for the captain's ideas, provoking sharp and mutually hostile exchanges. It took a long time for the latter to realize that part of the bowler's contempt grew from his own insecurity, that he felt at times humiliated and inferior, and that he tried to deal with such uncomfortable states of mind by inflicting something similar on others and especially on the captain. We are all liable to identify with powerful figures in our attempt to escape from inferiority (whether this inferiority complex is inflicted on us, or becomes part of ourselves, or derives more from our own anxieties), thus trying to reverse the experience of being put down from above.

In other words, the weapon *can* turn into an inverse racism, fueled by hurt and resentment. What is one to say, for example, of one writer's description (whether accurate or not) of Viv Richards batting at Lord's: 'he intimidated, mocked, and perhaps humiliated such gatherings. It was political. The score had to be settled.' Is this an admirable and honorable part of a proper pride in response to centuries of humiliation? Or is it a counter-racism? The writer also stated as part of the player's attitude this sentiment: 'We must not let the brothers down.'

6. Transcending Contempt

Competitiveness can also be a route to, and expression of, proper pride. Cricket was the quintessential game of the British Empire. In the early days, the colonial cricket authorities in most West Indian islands kept blacks (and 'coloreds' according to the designations of the time) out of many clubs and out of representative teams. They sometimes dishonestly based such exclusion on the grounds that black players were professionals, not amateurs. Trinidad was a partial exception in the 1890s,

---

[1] One example is of a bowler in my team who regularly expressed contempt for my ideas, provoking sharp and mutually hostile exchanges. It took a long time for me to realize that part of his contempt grew from his own insecurity, that he felt at times humiliated and inferior, and that he tried to deal with these uncomfortable states of mind by inflicting something similar on others and especially on the captain. We are all liable to identify with powerful figures in our attempt to escape from inferiority (whether this inferiority complex is inflicted on us, or becomes part of ourselves, or derives more from our own anxieties), thus trying to reverse the experience of being put down from above.

Michael Brearley

allowing their fast bowlers, 'Float' Woods and Archie Cumberbatch, and batsman Lebrun Constantine to play in matches against visiting English teams. The same bowlers were not, however, allowed to play in inter-island matches (Seecharan, 2006) Exclusion is a powerful form of splitting. They are not like us; we do not want to play with or against them.

Yet sport can transcend such constructions: it is not easy to keep good players out indefinitely – skill will out. In the West Indies, small integrations led to recognition of the qualities, personal and technical, of the trailblazers, which in turn forced the extension of recognition to other non-white players. Moreover, there were also voices for inclusion amongst the local whites and visiting grandees, just as there were advocates of education, enfranchisement, and human rights. In Jamaica, for example, there was a prominent advocate of Fabian socialism in no less a figure than Sydney Olivier, who was Governor of that island between 1907 and 1913, having previously been its Colonial Secretary. In 1928, the West Indies entered the world stage with a multiracial team captained by a white man. In 1948, George Headley became their first black captain, though his reign lasted for only a single match. And then, finally, after a long campaign led by the Marxist critic C.L.R. James, Frank Worrell was in 1960 appointed the first permanent black captain of the West Indies (see James, 1963). Talent and capability had conquered prejudice.

What is so remarkable about the story of the rise of West Indian cricket – a rise that culminated in an extraordinary period of world dominance during the 1970s and '80s – is that people who had been enslaved and then released into a world of prejudice, arrogance and power, with many of these arrangements extending into cricket, should have been so patient, so keen to learn, so open to values that they found in this colonial game. Self-disparagement is one consequence of racial and other kinds of trauma, yet cricketers like Wood, the Constantines (father and son), Headley and Worrell were able through their exploits and attitudes to build up the self-respect of their fellows, so that the next generation could be stronger, more determined, more in touch with their proper pride. It seems to me that those West Indians were able to be humble (in the sense of knowing they had a lot to learn) without being abject, and proud without being arrogant. They were prepared to celebrate the glass as half full rather than rage against its being half empty. They were willing also to wait. It was thanks to their pride and forbearance that the next generation of West Indians, Richards included, could triumph so memorably in what was able to be, by then, healthy competition between true equals.

7. Conclusion

One central element in sport is competitiveness. I have argued for its value in our development. It is important to have arenas somewhat set aside from ordinary life where such things are permitted and even encouraged, for only in such ways do we give ourselves the chance to challenge our complacency or mediocrity. Our opponents thus become our collaborators in the search for excellence.

British Psychoanalytical Society

References

Bion, W.R. (1961). *Experiences in Groups* (Tavistock: London).
Davids, F. (1996). 'Frantz Fanon: the Struggle for Inner Freedom' in *Free Associations*, Vol **6**: 205–234. (London).
James, CLR. (1963). *Beyond a Boundary*, (Stanley Paul: London).
Seecharan, C. (2006). *Muscular Learning: Cricket and Education in the Making of the British West Indies at the End of the 19th Century*, (Randle: Kingston).
Smith, E. (2008). *What Sport Tells us about Life*, (Viking: New York).
Winnicott, D.W. (1969/1971) 'The Use of an Object', in *Playing and Reality*, (Tavistock: London).

In the Zone

DAVID PAPINEAU

Trent Bridge 2001

Photo 1. Ramprakash's stumping off Warne – 3rd Test at Trent Bridge in 2001. Photograph by Hamish Blair. Courtesy of Getty Images.

On the Friday afternoon of the 3rd test at Trent Bridge in 2001, the series was in the balance. The Australians had won the first two tests easily, but England now found themselves in a position of some strength. They had restricted Australia to a first-innings lead of just 5 runs, and had built a lead of 120 with six wickets in hand. Mark Ramprakash was in and had been batting steadily for well over an hour. Even though this Australian side was as strong as any in cricket history, England had real hopes of getting back into the series.

doi:10.1017/S1358246113000325

David Papineau

This was a crucial time for Ramprakash as well as England. Despite being one of the most accomplished batsmen of the modern era, he had never managed to establish himself in the test team. He'd been in and out of the side for ten years, but had yet to achieve any consistency. As always, his place was in doubt, and he needed a big score.

With nine overs of the day left, Ramprakash did something extraordinary. He danced down the wicket to Shane Warne and was stumped by yards. The shot made no sense in the context of the game. There was no urgency and no reason to attack the bowling. Ramprakash was scoring steadily and simply needed to carry on as he was.

That was pretty much the end of the game and the series. Once Ramprakash was gone, Warne and Gillespie wrapped up the tail and Australia eased to a seven-wicket victory by the middle of the third day. They did lose the fourth test (if that great side had any flaw, it was a tendency to drop games in dead rubbers) but finished with an emphatic innings victory in the final Oval test.

The cricket pundits were nonplussed and unsympathetic. *The Telegraph* referred to Ramprakash's 'moment of weakness' and *The Guardian* to his 'distinct lack of composure'. Jack Bannister was more forthright: 'The red mist descended and he charged down the pitch ... his attempted slog ... would have been unacceptable in village cricket.' David Gower summed up the general perplexity: 'Nobody but Ramps can imagine what was going through his mind when he decided to play that shot at such a crucial time.'

As well as marking the effective finish to the series, this incident also signalled the impending end of Ramprakash's test career. The selectors persevered for a few more matches, and he did score his second and final test century in the losing last test at the Oval. But, after a few more low scores in New Zealand in the winter, the team management finally lost patience, and Ramprakash never played test cricket again. He went on to other successes – he is likely to be the last player ever to score a hundred first-class hundreds, and he gained millions of non-cricketing fans with his stylish and unexpected victory in the BBC's *Strictly Come Dancing* in 2006 – but as a test cricketer he will be remembered as someone whose supreme talent was undermined by mental fragility.

1. Saccading Eyes

This paper will try to understand why skilled sporting performers like Ramprakash will sometimes do the wrong thing in the heat of the moment. By analysing such cases I hope to cast light, not just on sporting psychology, but on the structure of human cognition in general.

At first sight there might seem to be little puzzling here. Didn't Ramprakash simply make a bad decision? When he saw the ball Warne bowled, he decided that he could hit it back over his head, and his dismissal was simply the penalty for his misjudgement.

But the trouble with this story is that there is no room for real-time conscious decisions in batting. Batting is automatic, not under conscious control. There is no time to think once the ball has been released. You can only react.

Let us start with the basic facts of timing. Top-rank bowlers project the ball at a batsman from about 60 ft distant at speeds in the range 50–100 mph. This means that the interval between ball release and bat impact is between 0.8 sec (800 ms) for the slower bowlers and 0.4 sec (400 ms) for the fastest.

These figures are similar for other bat and ball sports. Baseball pitchers project the ball at up to 100 mph from roughly the same distance as cricket bowlers. A tennis serve comes at up to 150 mph from 80 ft away. Squash and table tennis involve similar reaction times.

There is now a striking body of research on how batsmen in cricket cope with these extreme temporal constraints. An initial finding is that the batsman's eyes do not follow the ball throughout its flight. Instead they track it for the first 100–150 ms after release, after which their eyes saccade to the anticipated point at which the ball will hit the ground. The more skilled the batsman, the less time he will track the ball once it is released, and the sooner his gaze will shift to the anticipated bounce point. (Land and McLeod 2000, Müller et al. 2006a, Müller et al. 2009)[1]

To anybody who has played cricket, this will seem surprising, not to say incredible. The first thing that young batsmen are taught is to keep their eye on the ball. And certainly when you are actually batting, your awareness is of the ball moving continuously through the air from the bowler's release until it reaches you. When a

---

[1]   There is also an extensive body of research, across many sports, showing that skilled performers infer much about the ball's trajectory from pre-release information about their opponent's stance, hand and arm position, and so on. (For the evidence in cricket, see Müller et al. 2006b.) It seems that when we speak of the best performers 'having a lot of time' it is because they are especially skilled at using this information. However, while this kind of pre-release anticipation is relevant to my subject, I shall not discuss it further here, but will instead focus on post-release ball observation – which the cricket research shows is certainly no less important to successful batting.

distinguished Australian opening batsmen heard about the eye sac-
cades at a conference, he started his contribution to the discussion
period with – 'I don't believe a word of it'. He was quite sure that
he never took his eye off the ball and that he was aware of it continuously throughout its trajectory.

Perhaps the distinguished Australian was more surprised than he
should have been. It is familiar knowledge in vision science that,
when humans are surveying a scene, their eyes are constantly
jagging around to get different items into central focus. For
example, as you are reading these words right now, your eyes are unconsciously making a series of jerky movements to help you see
different areas of the page with high resolution. Yet our conscious
experience when we view a scene is not of a series of jerky visual frag-
ments. Rather our brain mechanisms build up a representation of a
stable environment containing identifiable features, and that is
what we consciously experience.

No doubt it works the same when you are batting. Your eyes may
be jumping around, but your brain is taking the information it receives from them and figuring out the precise trajectory of the ball.
The best batsmen will say that they can sometimes see the position
of the seam and even which way the ball is rotating, and there is no
reason to doubt them. But this conscious awareness is constructed
post-hoc from different bits of sensory input, and is not a simple
registration of incoming radiation as in a camera.

It is highly controversial exactly which parts of the brain subserve
this integrated conscious awareness, and so uncertain how long it
takes to be constructed. Even so, it seems very likely that the batsman's
conscious awareness of the ball lags behind the cognitive processes that
actually guide the batsman's stroke. If this is right, then the batsman's
movements must be the result of automatic and unconscious mechanisms. The function of the conscious awareness of the ball's trajectory is
then merely to provide a record of what has already occurred.

2. Blurry Lenses

This picture receives strong support from recent work in visual neuroscience. It is now well-established that there are two different visual
pathways with distinct functions that go from the visual cortex to
other parts of the brain. The faster dorsal stream (the 'where
pathway') subserves 'vision-for-action'. It is concerned with the geometrical location of objects and guides our reaching, grasping and
other immediate physical actions. The somewhat slower ventral

stream (the 'what' pathway) subserves 'vision-for-perception'. It is concerned with the classification of objects and informs cognitive processes that depend on such classification. (Milner and Goodale 1995)

Skilled motor behaviour is under the control of the dorsal stream. When we initially learn such actions as tying our shoelaces, driving a car, or executing a cover drive, we use the slower ventral stream to help us coordinate the relevant component movements with the positions of objects we are manipulating. But once the behaviour has become automatic, it comes under the control of the faster dorsal stream. The fine-tuned reaction of an expert batsman to a fast-approaching cricket ball is driven by the dorsal not the ventral stream.

Studies with brain-damaged patients suggest that the dorsal stream operates largely unconsciously. Patients with damage to the ventral stream but with intact dorsal streams report that they lack any visual awareness of the shape or identity of objects, yet are able to manipulate them competently, for example placing cards into angled slots, or adjusting their grip precisely to pick up objects they can't describe verbally. Conversely, patients with intact ventral streams but damaged dorsal streams report no loss of visual consciousness, but display marked delays in motor behaviour such as adjusting their grip to grasp objects.

There is some controversy about the extent to which the immediate control of skilled behaviour is fully unconscious. In normal healthy people there are rich interconnections between the ventral and dorsal streams, which suggests that in normal people at least the conscious processes in the ventral stream could yet have some influence on skilled behaviour.

However, there is further empirical research on the mechanics of batting in cricket which argues that in cricket batting at least it is very unlikely that the ventral stream plays any significant part in guiding the execution.

One difference between the dorsal and ventral streams is that the former has much lower visual acuity. While the ventral stream brings objects into sharp focus, the dorsal stream produces only a relatively blurred representation of the visible surroundings. Accordingly, the Australian sports scientist David Mann has tested the effects of visual blurring on batting performance. (Mann et al. 2010)

He used contact lenses to reduce the visual acuity of expert batsmen from a normal 20/20 to 20/60, 20/120 or 20/180. (These figures indicate the acuity with which you see something 20 ft away compared to the distance required for that acuity in the population in general. So, for example, 20/120 means that at 20 ft things look as blurred to you as they do to most people at 120 ft.)

Mann discovered that for bowling speeds up to 70 mph there was a deterioration in performance *only* with the highest degree of blurring. (That is, only at 20/180 – a level of indistinctness which makes you legally blind.) The 20/60 and 20/120 lenses had no noticeable effect on performance.

Even with bowling speeds in the interval 70-80 mph – which counts as fast-medium even at the highest standards – the 20/120 lenses were needed to affect performance. Blurring at the 20/60 level still had no effect on performance. (Most countries will not give you a driving license if you have 20/60 vision.)

These very striking results argue that batting performance is entirely under the control of the unconscious dorsal stream. The fact that the dorsal stream, unlike the visual stream, does not rely on high-acuity representations offers a natural explanation for why restricting the visual detail available to the batsman made no difference to performance.

Perhaps practising cricketers will continue to find it incredible that their conscious awareness of the ball's flight should make no difference to their shot-selection. After all, this certainly is not how it seems to subjective experience. For those who remain sceptical, I won't belabour the point any further. For present purposes, the important issue is not whether or skilled batting depends on *conscious* awareness. The more basic point is that the kind of actions involved in batting and similar sporting skills happen very *fast* indeed, and certainly too fast for any process worth calling decision-making to intercede between the visual detection of the ball's path and the execution of a stroke.

Maybe – though I very much doubt it – the batsman becomes consciously aware of the ball's path before committing to a stroke. But even so, the time interval is clearly too short for any considered choice of what shot to play. So Ramprakash's rash shot could not have been consciously selected once he had seen what ball Warne had bowled him. Even if there was time for him to become conscious of the ball's trajectory, there certainly wasn't time for him to start thinking about what shot to play.

3. The Yips

Further evidence of the automaticity of skilled sporting behaviour comes from the phenomenon known as the 'yips'. This is what happens if you start thinking explicitly about the bodily movements required for some sporting performance. This can have devastating consequences. Skilled sporting movements *need* to be automatic.

A competitor who starts thinking consciously about the movements they are about to perform will find themselves reduced to the level of the novice who has not yet acquired any automatic routines.

The phenomenon is most familiar from putting in golf. Sufferers from the yips end up jerking and twitching during their putting stroke, with the result that even putts of under two feet are regularly missed. Many famous golfers have succumbed, from Ben Hogan and Sam Snead to Tom Watson and Bernhard Langer. Some recover, often by radically changing their putting style, but others do not. It was said that Sam Snead's putting efforts in his later years were 'difficult to watch'.

It is striking that the yips arise only in connection with those sporting movements that are triggered by the players themselves, as opposed to those that are responses to their competitors' actions. It is specifically when you need to initiate some movement yourself that you are in danger of thinking about the movements you must perform. When somebody else is in control of the timing and direction of an approaching ball or other trigger to your movement, you have no time to think about what you must do – you just do it.

Perhaps the purest form of the yips is 'dartitis'. Darts players don't need to do anything except project their darts at a board just under 8 feet away. Somewhat strangely, there is no time limit on how long you can take for your turn of three throws. Dartitis occurs when you start thinking about what you are doing. It leads to an inability to release the dart or to other throwing-action problems. The career of Eric Bristow, 'The Crafty Cockney', five-times world champion, went into a terminal decline in 1987 after he started having trouble letting go of the darts.

Snooker players can suffer similarly. The fine Irish player Patsy Fagan, UK champion in 1977, had a particular problem with the rest. He would move the cue back and forth dozens of times, to the extent that he became unable to make himself hit the ball when using the rest, an inability that eventually led to his premature retirement from professional snooker.

In cricket and baseball the yips do not affect the batters, but only those who have to throw or bowl, particularly those who are able to do it in their own time. The timing factor seems to be crucial. The New York Mets catcher Mackey Sasser had no trouble throwing out runners trying to steal second, something you have to do instantaneously, but his career fizzled out because he struggled with the mundane and unhurried task of lobbing the ball back to the pitcher between plays. Second basemen in baseball, who often have time to

pause and ponder before throwing out the batter at first base, are notoriously susceptible. The unhelpfully named 'Chuck' Knoblauch of
the Yankees, hitherto one of the most reliable of infielders, had to be
moved to the outfield when he began spraying his throws to first in all
directions.

In baseball all pitchers at risk, as they throw from a standing start,
but in cricket, where the bowlers run in to bowl, it is only the slow
bowlers who suffer. The faster bowlers are running at full speed
when they commence their bowling action, and seem to be protected
for the yips by their bowling being integrated into a sequentially
automatic routine. With slower bowlers, however, who don't really
run in, but simply project the ball after a few slow steps, the yips
are not uncommon. Somewhat mysteriously, *left-arm* slow bowlers
seem disproportionately susceptible: Phil Edmonds went through a
series of bad patches when in the England side, and the Surrey all-
rounder Keith Medlycott had to retire at 26 because he became
unable to let the ball go when bowling.

In general, it seems to be the more cerebral of performers who are
most at risk. Unreflective players who never pause to analyse their
technique need not fear the yips. At most danger are the thinkers
and tinkerers, those who are curious about the nature of their skills.
It is noteworthy that both Patsy Fagan and Keith Medlycott
became prominent coaches after their problems forced them into premature retirement.

The yips should not be confused with 'choking'. The latter term
refers to occasions where competitive sportsmen and women
crumble under pressure and perform well below the level of which
they are capable. In the most striking cases, they will be playing at
their best in the early stages of the match, and collapse only as
victory approaches. (In the Wimbledon final of 1993, Jana Novotna
played a blinder against the great Steffi Graf and was serving at 40-
30 to reach 5-1 in the final set – at which stage she double-faulted
and scarcely won another point. To her eternal credit, she eventually
gained her sole grand slam title by winning the same tournament five
years later.)

The standard theory of choking explains it in the same way as I
have been explaining the yips, namely as a consequence of the
players starting nervously to focus on whether they are performing
the right bodily movements. In my view, this is quite the wrong
explanation for choking. This phenomenon is nothing to do with
the misplaced bodily awareness of the yips, but a quite different
kind of mental infirmity. But I will be better-placed to explain this
when I get to the end of the paper.

4. Changing Strategies

Let us return to the puzzle of Ramprakash's charge down the wicket. It might seem as if I have been ignoring an obvious possible explanation. Might not Ramprakash simply have decided to change his strategy – not while the ball was in flight, but at some earlier point, between balls, or between overs, when he had time to reflect on the situation of the game? Thus he might have formed the view, after appropriate deliberation, that the Australian attack was becoming less penetrating, and that the most pressing danger now was thus not a further loss of wickets, but a failure to turn the temporary advantage into a good lead ... and that therefore the best strategy was therefore to go on the attack, and start lofting Warne back over his head, not necessarily the very next ball, but the next time Warne gave the ball a bit of air.

Well, this was indeed Ramprakash's own story. When interviewed afterwards, he said that he had thought the condition of the game called for aggression on his part. However, I am sceptical of this explanation, and think I can offer a better account.

But that will need to come later. For the moment, let us just note that, even if we do accept Ramprakash's story, there is a sense in which it only pushes the basic puzzle back. We have seen ample reason to think that top-level batting is more like an automatic reflex than any consciously controlled sequence of movements. The basic facts of timing, plus the evidence I have rehearsed in the last three sections, all argue that the execution of a specific shot in response to the bowler's delivery is an automatic reaction honed by thousands of hours of previous practice. But if this is right, how *could* Ramprakash's strategic reflection possibly make a difference to what he did? Wouldn't the grooved channels in the brain continue to do the same automatic thing, quite independently of what Ramprakash deemed to be the best strategy?

Of course, we know that the answer to this question is 'no'. There is no doubt that strategic decisions do often make a difference to batting and similar fast-response sporting performances. Skilled performers can certainly change the way they play by consciously deciding to do so. In saying that this is a puzzle, I am not querying *whether* this happens. The challenge is rather to explain *how* it does, given the automaticity of fast sporting skills.

The extent to which skilled performers can switch strategies is an interesting subject in itself. To stick with cricket, there are cases and cases. Some batsmen are notoriously unable to modulate their approach. Geoffrey Boycott had a reputation as a one-paced batsmen, as did Jacques Kallis early in his career, both sometimes finding it difficult to score faster when the situation demanded it. Neil Fairbrother had the converse problem. He was an extremely accomplished international one-day cricketer, but seemed unable to adjust to the lower-risk technique required for five-day test cricket. Still, these examples are the exception rather than the rule. Cricket is perhaps unique in the way it calls for a range of different playing strategies, with forms of the game varying from a two-hour 20-20 thrash to a five-day test match. Yet most players can perform well in more than one form, even though very different strategies are called for, and some excel in all versions.

Still, the issue at hand is not the precise extent to which conscious decisions affect batting and other fast-response performance. It is clear that they can and often do. The question is rather – *how* can they have this effect? If the execution of a batting stroke is a reflex response to the perceived motion of the ball, then won't it automatically be triggered once the batsman's unconscious dorsal visual stream identifies the ball's trajectory? And won't this mean that the execution of the stroke is insulated from any influence from prior conscious thought?

Note that the kind of influence that we need to understand here is subtler than any simple 'premeditated' shot. Sometimes a batsman in cricket will decide what to do before the bowler delivers the ball. Before seeing the ball, they commit themselves to jumping down the wicket and lofting it, or to stepping towards square leg and clattering it through the off side, or whatever. Such premeditation is generally a bad idea, for obvious reasons, though it can work well in the latter stages of a limited overs match, or if the batsman is confident of the ball the bowler is going to deliver.

But this is not the kind of choice that puzzles me. With a premeditated shot, the batsman has simply opted not to perform a normal pre-honed reflex response to the bowler's delivery, and instead to deliberately play a shot of his own conscious choosing, pretty much independently of what the bowler does. This is no more puzzling than any other deliberate choice to override one's automatic responses and do something deliberate at a preappointed time.

The kind of case I have in mind is different. It is not a matter of overriding your automatic responses. Rather you are still relying on them. You still respond automatically and unthinkingly, within a small fraction of a second, to the specific trajectory of the ball. Yet the way you do this has been altered by your prior conscious reflection. Perhaps you are now responding aggressively, when before you were playing defensively. Still, you have no chosen to play any particular shot, but have simply set yourself to respond automatically.

This is the puzzle I want to address. How can conscious decisions make a difference to automatic batting? Given the speed with which the batsman respond to the ball, there would seem no room for conscious thought to intrude. Yet there is no doubt that a batsmen's earlier conscious choices can make a difference to how they perform.

5. Basic Action Control

In order to resolve this conundrum, we need to think about how human behaviour is generally controlled. In this context, it is helpful to distinguish between a basic system of automatic action control that we share with other animals, and a more sophisticated ability to form long-term intentions, typically as the result of conscious deliberation.

Let me start with the more basic system. While we no doubt have genetic predispositions favouring some behaviours over others, the shaping of most of our automatic behaviour depends on instrumental learning. If doing B in circumstance C has led to a positive result in the past, then we will be the more inclined to do B in circumstance C in the future.

Recent psychological research distinguishes two different forms of such instrumental conditioning: simple stimulus-response (S-R) learning and response-outcome (R-O) learning. (See e.g. Balleine and O'Doherty 2010)

In simple S-R learning, the organism is insensitive to what the behaviour B is good for, so to speak, and will simply tend to perform B whenever it experiences the stimulus of condition C. Provided B has led to rewarding result in the past in condition C, the organism will be disposed to do it again in C in the future.

In R-O learning, by contrast, the organism will form some representation of the positive causal consequences of B – the value of some outcome O – and will only perform behaviour B in circumstances C insofar as it continues to attach a positive value to O. The difference between R-O and S-R learning comes out when the outcome O is 'devalued' – by being associated with some unpleasant experience, say. When the behaviour B is under the control of the R-O system, such devaluation will lead to its non-performance in circumstance C, even though it has been associated with positive outcomes in that circumstance in the past. We can think of the R-O system as leading to the formation of *desires* for the outcomes O, with the behaviour B then depending on the continued existence of such desires.

There is evidence that the basal ganglia are central to both the S-R and R-O systems, and that dopamine release is relevant to both kinds of learning, functioning as a 'prediction error signal' – that is, signalling when rewards are different from what is expected. However, the precise differentiation of the two systems is less clear, as is the way they interact with each other.

In many ways the joint system that results from these two kinds of learning, which I shall call the 'basic action-control system' henceforth, is sophisticated and adaptable. It operates quickly and automatically at any time to select an action suitable to current needs. It has learned from experience which actions are good at ensuring rewards, and reacts accordingly. In effect, it approximates to the economists' picture of a utility-maximizer that at any time selects that action that will maximally generate rewards.

However, there are various respects in which this automatic basic system is less than ideal. For a start, there are circumstances in which ingrained S-R habits will dominate the more sensitive R-O system, and lead the agent to do things which are not conducive to its current desires. Moreover, even when the more sensitive R-O system is in control, it is crucially dependent on which desires happen to be active, and this does not always happen in an optimal way.

This is because desires in the R-O system are to a large extent activated by opportunity as much as need: agents will tend to desire O specifically in circumstances when they have learned they can get O. Past experience may have shown you that chocolate cake is satisfying and so instilled a disposition to want it. But for the most part this disposition will remain latent, and will be activated only by seeing a slice of chocolate cake, or by walking past the bakery which stocks it. (See e.g. Rescorla 1994)

From the perspective of creatures like us, who can plan, and so engineer opportunities to satisfy our desires, this arrangement is a design fault. If O is worth pursuing, it will be as worth pursuing in circumstances where it is not immediately available as those where it is. But we can see why this sub-optimal design would have evolved. For simple creatures, whose choices are always orientated to the here-and-now, the cueing of desires by opportunity will not be significantly dysfunctional. Since there is no *point* to simple creatures desiring Os which are not immediately available, there is no cost to these desires only being activated by opportunity.[2]

---

[2]   The activation of desires by immediate cues can be surreptitious as well as sub-optimal. A series of studies by the psychologist John Bargh has shown that unconscious verbal and physical prompts can unknowingly

6. Intentions

Happily, human beings are not always at the mercy of their less than optimal basic action-control systems. We are also capable of detailed conscious reflection about the best thing to do, all things considered, and of guiding our behaviour accordingly. Sometimes, when time permits, and the issues are both complicated and important, we pause and devote time to working out which of our options is best, and then setting ourselves to execute them.

This then enables us to do rather better than if we were governed by the basic action-control system alone. To the extent that our behaviour is guided by considered reflection, rather than immediate desire-gratification, we can improve on some of the cruder outcomes of the more basic system.

Philosophers discuss this ability under the heading of long-term *intention*-formation. Michael Bratman has been arguing for many years that intentions are a distinct species of cognitive attitudes, not reducible to complex sets of beliefs and desires. (Bratman 1987) And more recently Richard Holton has appealed to the special role that intentions play in our cognitive lives to explain a wide range of phenomena, including weakness of will, addiction, temptation, and will power. (Holton 2009)

In outline, the nature of intention-formation is clear enough. We use all the information at our command, insofar as we can, to identify the benefits and costs of the alternative courses of action open to us. We then weigh up these overall benefits and costs, and on this basis select one course of action. Having done so, we commit ourselves to carrying out this course of action. (Thus, for example, you might be thinking about what to do next Sunday: play in a cricket match, go to the country, or fix the garage roof? You weigh up the pros and cons, pick one of the options, and take steps accordingly.)

There are various advantages to adding the capacity for long-term intention formation to the older system of basic action-control. Most obviously, some choices are both important and complicated, and quick decisions made on the basis of currently active desires are likely to be sub-optimal, as observed above. Moreover, in many cases, we won't have time to pause and reflect when the moment for action arrives. So we will do better to take time for deliberation

---

influence behaviour. Subliminal priming by words like 'friend' leads people to act in a more cooperative way, as does contact with physically warm objects. (Bargh and Chartrand 1999)

David Papineau

earlier, and use the resolution then formed to guide our later behaviour.

There are also advantages of coordination. This covers both coordination between different individuals and also coordination between earlier and later selves within a given individual. Many of our projects depend for their success, not just on our current actions, but on those of other individuals and our later selves. (It's no good now deciding to play in a cricket match if you can't rely on the groundsman to prepare the pitch and on other players to turn up; it's no good now deciding to go to the country if you can't rely on yourself to catch the train on Sunday morning; and so on.) The formation of intentions is a solution to this problem. When people form intentions they bind themselves to certain future actions; this enables themselves and others to be confident of cooperation in complex projects; and this can in turn make commitment to those projects rational when it would not otherwise be.

7. Intentions and Action Control

It is clear enough that humans do form intentions, and that this affects their behaviour, often at some considerably later time. What is not so clear is *how* this works. What is the mechanism by which the formation of intentions has an influence on subsequent behaviour?[3]

One natural hypothesis is that intention-formation affects behaviour by somehow *re-setting* the basic action-control system. This is in line with general evolutionary principles: we should expect a newer system of action control to piggy-back on any already-evolved such system, rather than to involve some new and distinct system for controlling actions.

The idea that intentions re-set the basic action-control system also fits with empirical data on the execution of intentions. Peter Gollwitzer (1999) has shown that merely forming a general intention – for example, to fix the garage roof on Sunday – is not always effective. What makes it more likely you will carry out your plan is that you also form '*implementation* intentions' – for example, to go and buy some nails from the hardware shop once the morning

---

[3] A different question asks about the formation of intentions themselves. What is the mechanism by which deliberation selects a course of action? While this question is relevant to our current concerns, it would take us too far afield to pursue it here.

188

news on the radio is finished, to get the stepladder from the cellar when you get back, and so on.

In effect, implementation intentions determine conditional dispositions to perform behaviour B in circumstance C. It is noteworthy that Gollwitzer's research shows that consciously formed implementation intentions can often be triggered subliminally. For example, you may well find yourself leaving to go and buy the nails even though you have not consciously registered that the morning news is finished. This phenomenon strongly suggests that long-term intentions do their work by adjusting the state of the basic action-control system. The formation of an implementation intention reconfigures this system so that it will trigger behaviour B when circumstance C is next encountered. After that the operation of the basic action-control system can proceed in its normal automatic manner.

So there is good reason to suppose that intention-formation affects behaviour by somehow *re-setting* the basic action-control system. But how exactly it might achieve this is not well-understood. Perhaps the existence of the intention is itself part of the stimulus which triggers the action (because in our experience we have been rewarded for doing B in circumstances where we have an-intention-to-do-B). Or perhaps the intention reconfigures the outcomes we regard as valuable, making us view the performance of B as itself of high positive value. Further hypotheses are also possible.

8. Will Power

Still, whatever the precise mechanism by which long-term intentions reset the basic action control system, we can draw one important moral from the analysis so far. As I am now viewing things, when a long-term intention is formed, it reconfigures the basic action-control system in such a way as to achieve its intended effect. But this then means that the actual execution of the intention will be subject to the vicissitudes of the basic action-control system. As I observed earlier, the basic action-control system is relatively volatile. Current cues and other distractions can influence which desires are active and hence the here-and-now selection of actions. This will apply just as much in the case where the basic action-control system has been reconfigured by long-term intention formation. If the intention-formation does its work by resetting the basic system of action control, and then leaving it to itself, so to speak, then the execution of intentions will itself be subject to current cues and other distractions.

David Papineau

Sometimes this will not matter too much. If you form an intention to fix the garage roof, and so set yourself to go to the hardware store for some nails once the radio news is finished, it won't be of any great consequence if you are absent-mindedly delayed at home for a few minutes by the start of the next programme, or if you get waylaid by the tempting chocolate cake in the bakery on the way there. For many of our plans, precision is not essential. It will be enough if we do roughly what is required, in roughly the right sequence, at roughly the right time.

But sometimes it is important that we adhere closely and precisely to our intended plans. One much-discussed kind of case is where we set ourselves specifically to avoid some temptation. For example, we might have adopted a diet, or given up smoking, or drinking, or some even more destructive habit. In this kind of case it will not work if, once we have formed our intention, we allow ourselves to be seduced by passing temptations, on the grounds that we will be able to catch up later. If we allow ourselves to give in, we will have failed. As experience shows, regimens of abstinence tend quickly to be abandoned once we give in to temptation[4].

Richard Holton thinks of 'weakness of will' as the failure to stick to one's intentions[5]. 'Will power', conversely, is for him what enables us to conform to our intentions. He cites empirical evidence that the exercise of will power in this sense is a real cognitive phenomenon, which causes mental tiredness and cannot be sustained indefinitely.

Holton offers no definite positive account of will power. Here is one suggestion. Will power is simply a matter of holding one's earlier-formed intention in mind. Suppose that when you commit yourself to an intention, this does something to reconfigure the parameters of the basic action-control system so as to perform the intended action. However, if the basic action-control system is then left to itself, happenstance may undo this reconfiguration, not least by allowing some passing fancy to override the earlier resetting. A solution would be to keep on forming the intention, so to speak. To the extent we continue consciously to reaffirm the intention, it will keep resetting the action control system and prevent any happenstantial

---

[4]   It is an interesting question why exactly this should be so. If I fall off the wagon one evening, why shouldn't I be as well-placed to abstain the next day as I was before my lapse? Still, even if this question is hard to answer, it is empirically clear enough that lapses do destroy resolutions.

[5]   Of course it is often sensible to revise intentions when circumstances change. Weakness of will is failure to carry out intentions even when this isn't so sensible.

overriding. (This model of will-power would seem to fit well with the fact that it is tiring to exert it for a sustained period.)

9. Batting Again

Our earlier discussion of fast sporting skills left us with this general puzzle. How can the conscious strategic decisions of a batsman – to play more aggressively, say – make any difference to his performance, given that any physical response to a ball arriving at around 100 mph can only be the expression of an automatic and unthinking reflex? We are now better placed to answer this puzzle.

The first thing to note is that a batsman will have trained himself over many hours to bat in a range of possible modes: defensively, aggressively, keeping the ball on the ground, looking to play it to leg, and so on. We can think of these modes as each involving a raft of conditional dispositions: in defensive mode, leave any pitched-up ball outside the off stump, block any reasonable length ball, etc; in attacking mode, drive the half-volley outside the off-stump; force anything marginally short-pitched, etc; and so on.

At any stage of an innings, a competent batsman will have assessed the situation and formed a view about how to bat – a conscious *intention* to adopt a certain strategy. As with any intention, this will then set the parameters of the basic action-control system. It will direct that system to bat aggressively, say. It will take one raft of conditional dispositions from the batsman's repertoire, and reconfigure the basic control system so that it embodies just those dispositions. (Drive the half volley outside off stump, force the shortish straight ball, etc.) Having been so reset, the basic action-control system will then respond accordingly, without any further intrusion of conscious thought – which is just as well, given the extreme time constraints of batting.

This now answers our general puzzle about the influence of conscious strategic thought on fast automatic responses. We now see that such an influence is just a special case of the way that long-term intention-formation influences behaviour in general. We shouldn't think of conscious deliberation as influencing action directly. Rather, it does so indirectly, by issuing in an intention, which then resets the basic action control system, which does then affect action directly. But the consequent operation of the basic action-control system doesn't depend itself on any further conscious thought.

So with batting. At some stage, when time allows, you consciously reflect and decide, say, to start playing more aggressively. This then directs the basic action control system to switch from defensive mode (from one raft of automatic and extremely fast conditional dispositions) to attacking mode (to a different such raft). The execution of the shot itself is then an automatic and unthinking reflex, but *which* such reflex will be activated in response to that ball will depend on the earlier deliberation and conscious intention-formation.

10. Concentration

The relation between intentions and action control also explains why mental focus is so important in competitive sport.

Recall my earlier point that it is not always enough to form an intention and then leave it to the basic action-control system to carry it out. If there is a gap between intention and execution, the vicissitudes of the action-control system can intrude, and you can end up doing something else at the appointed time.

Now, as we saw, this often doesn't matter. Many intentions are perfectly adequately served if something roughly like the required action is performed at roughly the right time. But sometimes strict adherence is essential. Above I discussed the example of sticking to a regimen of abstinence. Highly skilled sporting performance is another such case. It is not enough to play roughly the right shot when the ball is bowled. Precision is essential in batting and other highly-tuned sporting performances.

There is why concentration, focus, getting your mind right, the inner game, being in the zone – call it what you will – is an essential feature of successful sporting performance. You need to keep your intention in mind to make sure your action-control system does the right thing.

The point applies even at the lower levels of sporting activity. When I play tennis with my friends, it is competitive even if not hugely accomplished. We knock up first. It can be very pleasant in England in the summer. I sometimes think how enjoyable it is to be stroking the ball back and forth with my friend. And then we start playing a match, and suddenly, to my consternation, I notice I am three games down. I have forgotten to switch from knocking-up mode to competitive mode. Instead of stroking it pleasantly back in roughly my friend's direction, I must now punch it as hard as I can to where my friend isn't. This doesn't happen automatically. I have to direct my action-control system to adopt competitive rather than knocking-up mode. And having done so, I have to keep this in mind. If I start day-dreaming about what's for dinner, or worrying about tomorrow's lecture, I will stop playing properly and start throwing away points.

It is interesting that the need to concentrate at tennis only applies to competitive mode. While knocking up you can daydream as much as you like. I think that this is to do with the precision required. The demands of knocking up don't require any great exactitude. You can switch off, so to speak – leave matters to your automatic action-control system and start thinking of other things – and you will still knock up perfectly well. You need only hit the ball roughly in the direction of your opponent. But competitive play does require focus. It is not enough that you return the ball with some stroke or other. You need to maintain a very precise set of conditional dispositions (keep it away from his forehand, mix the slice with the topspin, etc.), and this requires sustained single-mindedness.

I would say that the general point applies even to sporting skills that do not involve complex alternative batteries of conditional dispositions. Not all sports call for switches of strategy. Gymnasts, sprinters and many other sporting performers scarcely need to change what they are trying to do from one competitive context to another. Even so, they still need to focus hard when they are competing. The reason, I would suggest, is that they still need to hold in mind that they are now in competitive mode, to make sure that basic action-control system delivers precisely the right competition responses to stimuli, and not the responses that would be appropriate when they are practising, or when demonstrating something to a novice, or when testing equipment, and so on. Even if only one raft of dispositions is ever in play in competition, there are clearly other rafts that the action-control system can be set to display in the same physical contexts outside competition. If the performer stops concentrating, there will be nothing to stop this system being derailed into some such alternative by happenstantial influences.

11. Choking

I earlier contrasted 'choking' with 'the yips'. While choking is often assimilated to the yips, I think it is a quite distinct phenomenon. The yips are caused, as I explained, by a destructive attention to bodily movements. Choking is rather a failure of concentration.

I have just argued that competitive sporting activity requires performers to hold firmly in mind what they are aiming to do. Of course, this doesn't mean that they should think about which physical movements they need to perform – that would only invite the yips.

But they do need to focus on the results they are trying to achieve. They need to keep thinking about keeping it on the ground, or slicing it deep to the backhand, even if not about the relative positions of their hands and wrists. If their minds start wandering, they are likely to play false shots. They need to keep a tight rein on their action-control system, lest it stray away from the intended course and start working haphazardly.

This is what happens when players choke. Jana Novotna was an excellent tennis player and by the time she first reached the Wimbledon final she was no doubt very used to winning. But she wasn't absolutely in the top rank, and may well have wondered whether she would ever win a grand slam. When you are five points away from lifting the Wimbledon shield, it must be very hard not to start thinking about it. Indeed you would be something of a freak if you didn't. Novotna may have closed out many important victories before, but that's not the same as beating Steffi Graf at Wimbledon to win your first grand slam. It was no doubt the significance of her impending victory that turned her mind away from the game itself – with disastrous results.

It is common enough for players to 'give up' when they are losing. Once it becomes clear that your opponent has the measure of you, it is natural enough to start thinking about your imminent defeat and stop focusing on your strategy. The consequent deterioration in the loser's performance is so familiar as to be scarcely worthy of remark. Choking is pretty much the same thing, except that it is the imminent victory rather than defeat that so distracts the player. You start thinking about how wonderful it will be to receive the applause, and so stop thinking about where to hit the ball – and before you know victory has slipped away.

12. Ramprakash Explained

Finally, let us return to Mark Ramprakash's egregious dismissal. As I said, his own explanation was that he deliberately and quite reasonably decided to go on to the attack, but unfortunately it didn't work out. However, we are now in a position of offer a better explanation. I would suggest that Ramprakash's demise wasn't due to an unsuccessful strategic ploy, but to a fatal failure of concentration.

There is something that I have left out of the Ramprakash story so far. It is widely attested that Shane Warne had been working on Ramprakash for some overs. 'Come on Ramps, you know you want to' he had been saying, putting into Ramprakash's mind the thought of dancing down the wicket and lofting the ball back over Warne's head.

Perhaps we should believe Ramprakash's own story that he had consciously decided to attack, and had re-set his behavioural dispositions accordingly. But it seems to me much more likely that he just lost his focus. For some while he had been firmly maintaining the appropriate test match strategy – keep the ball on the ground, leave the full pitch outside off, ... But Warne's urgings were eating away at his resolve, highlighting the attractions of a lofted drive. (There goes the ball, out of the middle of the bat, straight back over the bowler's head, right into the spectators – believe me, there are few more pleasant experiences in life.)

As long as Ramprakash could keep his mind firmly fixed on his test match repertoire, he was safe. But Warne had planted the seed of temptation. The seductive desire to jump down the wicket and loft the ball was waiting in the wings, poised to grab control of Ramprakash's action-control system. And then Ramprakash nodded. Who knows exactly what went through his mind. But somehow he forgot what he was supposed to be doing, and the result was inevitable.

King's College London
david.papineau@kcl.ac.uk

References

Balleine, B. and O'Doherty, J. (2010) 'Human and rodent homologies in action control: corticostriatal determinants of goal-directed and habitual action' *Neuropsychopharmacology Reviews* **35**: 48–69.

Bargh, J. and Chartrand, T. (1999) 'The unbearable automaticity of being' *American Psychologist* **54**: 462–479.

Bratman, M. 1987. *Intention, Plans, and Practical Reason* Harvard University Press.

Gollwitzer, P. (1999) 'Implementation intentions: strong effects of simple plans' *American Psychologist* **54**: 493–503.

Holton, R. (2009) *Willing, Wanting, Waiting* (Oxford University Press)

Land, M. and McLeod, P. (2000) 'From eye movements to actions: how batsmen hit the ball' *Nature Neuroscience* **3**(12): 1340–1345.

Mann, D., Abernethy, B. and Farrow, D. (2010) 'The resilience of natural interceptive actions to refractive blur' *Human Movement Science* **29**(3): 386–400.

Milner, D. and Goodale, M. (1995) *The Visual Brain in Action* (Oxford University Press).

Müller, S. and Abernethy, B. (2006a) 'Batting with occluded vision: an *in situ* examination of the information pick-up and interceptive skills of high- and low-skilled cricket batsmen' *Journal of Science and Medicine in Sport* **9**(6): 446–458.

Müller, S., Abernethy, B. and Farrow, D. (2006b) 'How do world-class cricket batsmen anticipate a bowler's intention?' *Quarterly Journal of Experimental Psychology: Section A* **59**(12): 2162–2186.

Müller, S., Abernethy, B., Reece, J., Rose, M., Eid, M. and McBean, R. (2009) 'An *in situ* examination of the timing of information pick-up for interception by cricket batsmen of different skills levels' *Psychology of Sport & Exercise* **10**: 644–652.

Rescorla, R. (1994) 'Transfer of instrumental control mediated by a devalued outcome' *Animal Learning and Behaviour* **22**: 27–33.

Olympic Sacrifice: A Modern Look at an Ancient Tradition

HEATHER L. REID

Prologue

The inspiration for this paper came rather unexpectedly. In February 2006, I made the long trip from my home in Sioux City, Iowa, to Torino, Italy in order to witness the Olympic Winter Games. Barely a month later, I found myself in California at the newly-renovated Getty Villa, home to one of the world's great collections of Greco-Roman antiquities. At the Villa I attended a talk about a Roman mosaic depicting a boxing scene from Virgil's *Aeneid*. The tiny tiles showed not only two boxers, but a wobbly looking ox. 'What is wrong with this ox?' asked the docent. 'Why is he there at the match?' The answer, of course, is that he is the prize. And the reason he is wobbly is because the victor has just sacrificed this prize to the gods in thanksgiving, by punching him between the eyes. A light went on in my head; I turned to my husband and whispered, 'Just like Joey Cheek in Torino.' My husband smiled indulgently, but my mind was already racing. I realized that by donating his victory bonus to charity, Cheek had tapped into one of the oldest and most venerable traditions in sport: individual sacrifice for the benefit of the larger community. It is a tradition that derives from the religious function of the ancient Olympic Games and it deserves to be revived the modern world.

Introduction

Modern sport often evokes its ancient Hellenic heritage. The educational link between sport and character, the sociological link between sport and justice, and the political link between sport and peace all derive from the ideals and practice of athletics in ancient Greece.[1] The modern Olympic festival conceives of itself as a

---

[1] For more on these connections, see Heather L. Reid 'Olympic Sport and its Lessons for Peace', *Journal of the Philosophy of Sport* **33**:2 (2006),

doi:10.1017/S135824611300026X   ©The Royal Institute of Philosophy and the contributors 2013

Royal Institute of Philosophy Supplement **73** 2013   197

revival of the ancient Olympic Games and it embraces their history and mythology insofar as they support its mission. One problematic and often overlooked aspect of the Hellenic legacy, however, is the religious character of ancient sport. Whereas common religious belief was foundational to and instrumental in the millennium-long success of the ancient Olympic Games, the modern challenge of uniting a religiously diverse world community has pushed the religious legacy to the sidelines. Given the evidence that religious hegemony was responsible for the demolition of the ancient Olympic Games (they are believed to have been abolished as a pagan festival by the Christian emperor Theodosius), modern attempts to dissociate the Games from religion are certainly understandable. But in jettisoning the Olympics' religious heritage, have we thrown out the proverbial baby with its bathwater? I believe that we may have. The modern Olympic Movement is allowing a commercial paradigm to usurp its higher purpose. In order to ennoble itself, the Olympic Games should redirect its commercial aspirations toward humanitarian goals, thereby reclaiming the ancient connection between Olympic sport and community service.

1. The Ancient Heritage

The connection may not be so distant as it first seems. Even in today's cynical and commercially-driven world of sport-entertainment, athletic champions are often lauded for their 'sacrifice'. Commonly, the word evokes the sweat and toil of training combined with the semi-monastic life supposedly led by athletes. In almost any other endeavor, the effort and lifestyle required would be termed 'professionalism', or perhaps simply 'hard work'. Why in athletics do we call it 'sacrifice'? The obvious answer is an ancient one. Most sport in Greco-Roman antiquity was a form of religious sacrifice. Athletic performance at such festivals was considered an offering to the gods, offered as a service to the community. Extravagant rewards certainly *were* showered upon ancient Olympic athletes,[2] but the

---

205–13, reprinted in 'Olympic Sport and Its Lessons for Peace', *Olympic Truce: Sport as a Platform for Peace,* eds K. Georgiadis and A. Syrigos (Athens: International Olympic Truce Center, 2009) 25–35.

[2] David C. Young, *The Olympic Myth of Greek Amateur Athletics* (Chicago: Ares, 1984) effectively debunks the 'myth' that ancient athletes were amateurs, popular at the time of the modern Olympic revival. Even

religious context of the Games reveals that such rewards were motivated by perceived community benefits rather than commercial economy. The primary function of the ancient festival was not entertainment or product-promotion, but the collective garnering of divine favor in hope of concrete community benefits such as plentiful harvests, release from disease, or victory in war (i.e. food, medicine, and conflict-resolution). Ancient athletes, in the religious context of the games, should be seen foremost as community servants.

Let me illustrate my explanation with the example, I mentioned earlier. Book five of Virgil's ancient Roman epic, *The Aeneid,* describes contests in rowing, running, archery, and boxing. Although the text was written in the last century before the Common Era and the games themselves are supposed to be set in the Bronze Age of Troy, modern sports fans would recognize something familiar in the boxing match. A cocky young Trojan named Dares taunts his would-be challengers by asking permission to take the prize without a contest. Reluctantly, a more experienced local Sicilian named Entellus deigns to fight the Trojan, despite misgivings about his advancing age. The match is a classic duel between the larger, slower, but wiser Entellus, and the younger, quicker, more eager Dares. The nimble Trojan dodges one of Entellus' mighty blows, and the heavier man falls to the ground under his own weight. He returns, however, with a vengeance and rains down such a fury of blows on his opponent that the fight must be stopped to save young Dares' life. Entellus is awarded the prize of an ox, and it is at this point that the narrative takes an unfamiliar turn for modern readers. The mighty boxer strikes the animal flush between the horns, 'bursting the brains out', and the ox falls lifelessly to the ground.[3]

To make sense of Entellus' gesture, we must first understand the religious purpose of ancient Greek sport and, most specifically, the social function of sacrifice. The ancient Olympic Games are believed to have originated sometime around the 8th century BCE, not far from the time that Homer wrote about the Trojan War. Many scholars believe that the games depicted in Homer's *Iliad* depict the athletic contests of his own age, rather than those of the Bronze Age

---

if we can conclude that the financial rewards were great enough to make athletics a lucrative career for some, we should not assume that the reasons they were paid (or otherwise rewarded) are the same as the reasons athletes are compensated today.

[3]   Virgil, *The Aeneid*, trans. W.F. Jackson Knight (London: Penguin, 1956) V.480.

Mycenaeans. By the time Virgil writes his 'sequel' to Homer's epics (almost 700 years later), sport was major force in Greco-Roman culture. Although both authors depict funeral or festival rather than Olympic Games, the religious association is undeniable. The gods Athena and Apollo actively involve themselves in Homer's games, and when Virgil's Entellus kills the ox, he follows it up with a prayer, describing the animal as payment for this victory and for his successful career.[4] The animal sacrifice is at once recompense to the gods and to the community that has supported him.

Greek athletics, perhaps in their origin but certainly in their Olympic manifestation, were a form of religious sacrifice.[5] Long before 776 BCE, Olympia had been a holy place reserved for religious rites and gatherings. The purpose of such sanctuaries and festivals was to mark off a place dedicated to the god, and then to offer gifts to him or her, either in gratitude for fortune gained or in the hope of good fortune to come. Ancient Greeks believed that gods controlled things that they couldn't; things like health, fertility, weather, even love. The relationship between human and divine in this realm was seen as one of exchange.[6] I pray that my ships or army are successful, offering some portion of the benefits if they are. These items (usually a tithe of the booty collected) are left in the sanctuary as payment on my vow (hence 'votives'), and they become the property of the god.[7] During a typical animal sacrifice, one or more prize bulls or lambs is selected, stunned, killed, and butchered on the spot. The thighbones are burnt on the altar along with some fat, the savory smoke a way of attracting the sky-dwelling god to the sanctuary to hear worshippers' prayers. The rest of the meat is roasted and fed to the worshippers in a public banquet.[8]

Somewhere along the line a footrace was added to sacrificial ritual at Olympia.[9] Part of its purpose may have been to entertain

[4]   Op. cit. note 3, V. 482.
[5]   David Sansone, *Greek Athletics and the Genesis of Sport* (Berkeley: University of California Press, 1988) 40.
[6]   Jon D Mikalson, *Ancient Greek Religion* (Malden, MA: Blackwell, 2005) 25.
[7]   Walter Burkert, *Greek Religion*, trans. John Raffan (Cambridge, MA: Harvard University Press, 1985) 68.
[8]   Op. Cit. note 7, 56–7.
[9]   It is clear from archaeological evidence that some cult and sacrifice of some form preceded athlctic activities at Olympia, but just when the games were added is a mater of dispute. For a review of the findings and their implications for cult activity at Olympia, see Alfred Mallawitz, 'Cult and Competition Locations at Olympia' in *The Archaeology of the*

worshippers while the meat was butchered and cooked,[10] but it is easy to interpret the race itself as a kind of sacrifice – another way of attracting the god's attention and favor. The 'track' was originally located within the sacred area and the race was run in a straight line from the far end of the grounds toward the altar upon which the offerings would be made.[11] The Olympic winner (then, as now) did not receive a prize, but in a way, became himself a prize for the god. The tokens of victory: a palm branch, olive wreath, and ribbons tied around his head and limbs, are all associated with sacrificial animals and priests.[12] Also like the sacrificial victim, the winning runner demonstrates his outstanding willingness to come forward to be sacrificed.[13] Given the gods' involvement in the outcome of Homer's funeral games, one may even interpret the Olympic race as a chance for the god to select the victor; to pick his own symbolic sacrifice – the one that pleases him most.

Accurate selection of a pleasing sacrifice was essential since so much was thought to be riding on the favor of the gods. This created a persistent epistemological problem in Greek religion; one important enough to be addressed directly in Plato's dialogue *Euthyphro*. It may be that Olympic-style sport, designed to select single winners from varied pools of contestants, was developed at least partly as a response to this problem.[14] In any case, the victor's status as a symbolic sacrificial offering is vividly evidenced by his being given the honor of lighting the sacrificial flame.[15] Remembering that the purpose of the smoke is to attract the attention of the god, we might speculate that the Games themselves did the same – not just by the skill and prowess displayed, but also by drawing large numbers of pilgrims to the festival. The better the show and the larger the crowd the more likely the deity was to turn

---

Olympics, (ed.) W. Raschke (Madison, WI: University of Wisconsin Press, 1988) 79–109.

[10] Op. cit. note 6, 28.

[11] Panos Valvanis, *Games and Sanctuaries in Ancient Greece*, trans. 'David Hardy (Los Angeles: Getty Publications, 2004) 15, 50.

[12] Op. cit. note 7, 56.

[13] Op. cit. note 7, 56.

[14] This is the thesis of Heather L Reid, 'Olympic Epistemology: The Athletic Roots of Philosophical Reasoning', *Skepsis* **17**:1–2 (2007), 124–132. See also Heather L. Reid, *Athletics and Philosophy in the Ancient World: Contests of Virtue* (London and New York: Routledge, 2011) chapter 2.

[15] Op. cit. note 11, 15.

his or her attention to the festival and therefore to the prayers of the worshipping community. The quantity and value of votive offerings housed at Olympia was renowned in the ancient world and stood as tangible evidence of the festival's practical success. Prayers made to Zeus in association with the Games were apparently being answered, so it makes sense that several other religious festivals followed Olympia's example and added contests of various kinds.

Interpreted in the context of ancient religious sacrifice, then, the athlete's Olympic success not only brings glory to himself and to his family, it also benefits the entire community by attracting the gods' attention to their prayers and bringing concrete goods such as successful harvests and release from disease. The most immediate and tangible example of practical community benefit from worship was, of course, the banquet of meat from the sacrificed animals. In a world without freezers such meat-based meals were rare, and much care was taken in the proper butchering and apportioning of the meat.[16] In addition there were important psychological benefits to witnessing the athlete's success. Since athletic victory was believed to come from a combination of toil (*ponos*), sweat, and divine favor, it inspired onlookers to forge ahead with their day-to-day struggles, called '*agones*' just like the Games themselves. Further, the gathering of diverse (and sometimes warring) peoples on neutral ground to worship a common deity had a bonding effect.[17] It unified and pacified the group, building real community ties as symbolized in the ritual of sharing a common meal at the conclusion of the festival.[18]

So Entellus' killing of the victory ox, in its socio-temporal context, is not a senseless act of violence. Instead, it should be viewed as a religious sacrifice that expresses a venerable athletic tradition. The victorious individual offers his earned glory back to his community, inspiring their hearts, filling their stomachs, and strengthening their bonds: he is an honored and honorable community servant.

2. A Modern Misunderstanding

The modern revivers of the Olympic festival were clearly aware of its religious heritage. As John MacAloon puts it, Pierre de Coubertin

---

[16]   H.W Parke, *Festivals of the Athenians* (Ithaca, NY: Cornell U. Press, 1977), 48.
[17]   Op. cit. note 7, 54.
[18]   For more on this, see Reid 'Olympic Sport and its Lessons for Peace' op. cit. note 1.

'continuously and unambiguously regarded [Olympism] as a religious phenomenon'.[19] But Coubertin did not seek to revive the religious *function* of the Olympic Games – a function I characterize above as one of community service. Rather, he sought to make athletics themselves a kind of religion, a concept he called *religio athletae*. Coubertin described his vision thus:

> The primary, fundamental characteristic of ancient Olympism, and of modern Olympism as well, is that it is a *religion*. By chiseling his body through exercise as a sculptor does a statue, the ancient athlete "honored the gods". In doing likewise, the modern athlete honors his country, his race, and his flag. Therefore I believe I was right to restore, from the very beginning of modern Olympism, a religious sentiment transformed and expanded by the internationalism and democracy that are distinguishing features of our day. Yet this is the same religious sentiment that led the young Hellenes, eager for the victory of their muscles, to the foot of the altars of Zeus.[20]

Undeniably, Olympic symbols, rituals, and ceremonies give the modern Games a religious aura. But the ancient religious function of the games (i.e. to benefit the community) seems to have been lost. In fact, the Olympic symbols have come to be regarded as the source of the Games' commercial rather than spiritual power. The Olympic rings are one of the most widely recognized brand logos in the world and the source of a large portion of the movement's revenue.[21] Has the sport's religious heritage been perverted into crass commercialism?

I think there is at minimum the risk that it has and I think that the culprit, paradoxically, may be 'amateurism'. It was Avery Brundage, a most zealous adherent of the amateur concept, who reluctantly presided over the influx of revenues from sponsorship and television into the Olympic movement. Brundage's commitment to amateurism supposedly derived from a desire to preserve the ancient 'purity' of sport – to keep 'sport for sport's sake' and prevent it from becoming

[19] John J. MacAloon, 'Religious Themes and Structures in the Olympic Movement and the Olympic Games', *Philosophy, Theology and History of Sport and Physical Activity*, eds F. Landray and W. Orban (Quebec: Symposia Specialists, 1978), 161.
[20] Pierre de.Coubertin, *Olympism: Selected Writings*, (ed.) Norbert Muller (Lausanne: IOC, 2000) 580.
[21] R. Barney, S. Wenn, and S. Martyn, *Selling the Five Rings: The International Olympic Committee and the Rise of Olympic Commercialism* (Salt Lake: University of Utah Press, 2004) xii.

a medium for personal promotion or commercial gain.[22] Twisted interpretations of the ancient Olympic Games (for example, as the exclusive province of wealthy elites) were trotted out to support this autotelic athletic illusion, but it was all for the benefit of the benefactors. Amateurism was, as Olympic scholar David Young puts it, 'the ideological means to justify an elitist athletic system that sought to bar the working class from competition.'[23] The early IOC culture was one of modern aristocrats – people who did not work day to day in order to earn their bread, and who often regarded with derision those who did.[24] The 'purity of sport' really meant the purity of the athletes in terms of breeding, class, and often race. Native American champion Jim Thorpe had his medals stripped, ostensibly for having accepted money to play baseball, but many say he was singled out for punishment because of his race and class.[25] Most of us lucky enough to have jobs we love do not regard our salaries as a force of corruption. We might do the work for free, if we were independently wealthy. It is part of who we are; our profession. Olympic amateurism amounted to exclusion based on nobility of class, not nobility of motivation.

Ancient athletes never were amateurs in the modern sense.[26] Lucrative prizes were awarded at countless regional festivals, and Olympic victors were routinely granted immense public honors, including tax exemptions, choice seating at public events, and free meals for life in the municipal dining facilities. Evidence for such rewards can be found in no-less famous a text than Plato's *Apology of Socrates*. Unfortunately, pleasant fantasies about ancient aristocracies kept people like Brundage from asking the crucial question of why such rewards were offered to ancient athletes and what does it mean for modern Olympic sport? The answer to this question, in the context of ancient religion, however, is hardly a mystery. Athletic victors provided a valuable, community service by attracting the favor of the gods. In fact, it is precisely in this context that Socrates says he deserves the rewards given to Olympic victors for his own community service to Athens. He points out that the

---

[22] Avery Brundage, 'Why the Olympic Games' quoted in David C Young, 'How the Amateurs Won the Olympics', *The Archaeology of the Olympics*, (ed.) W. Raschke. (Madison: U. of Wisconsin Press, 1988) 55–78, 72. For more on Brundage's resistance to Olympic commercialism, see Barney, op. cit. note 21, especially chapter 4.

[23] Young, op. cit. note 22, 56.

[24] See, for example, Young, op. cit. note 22, 56–66.

[25] For example, Rodolfo Cremer, 'Professionalism and its Implications for the Olympic Movement', *Olympic Review* 26:14 (1997), 23–24.

[26] A point clearly explained by Young op. cit. notes 2 and 22.

Olympian victor only makes the citizens think they are better off, whereas his philosophical questioning truly improves them.[27] Socrates' skepticism about religious traditions (he has just been convicted of atheism) is the exception that proves the general rule that Olympic victors were valued and rewarded as community servants.

Furthermore, Socrates' did not advocate the abandonment of religion (he claimed that his own service to the city was directly motivated by the god), rather he sought a more functional and rational approach. Some say that Socrates' death was itself a sacrifice for the good of rational humanity generally. Unfortunately for the Olympics, when the IOC abandoned the religious function of sport, it lost the venerable tradition of sacrifice. Prompted by their obsession with amateurism to view sport as an exclusive and self-contained club, the Olympic Games ceased to look beyond sport for meaning. *Religio-athletae* made a religion of sport and when television money started flowing into the IOC, it was decided that those funds should be 'devoted to the future of amateur sport'.[28] While there is no doubt that the modern Olympic Movement was and is justified in securing its own financial survival, I contend that it should, like Socrates, have adopted a rational and functional approach to its religious heritage by committing itself to a humanitarian cause. The ideals declared in the 'Fundamental Principles' of the *Olympic Charter,* should be imagined and supported in concrete ways by the movement. Just as the ancients imagined that athletic victory would bring food, medicine, and conflict resolution to the Panhellenic community, we moderns should direct athletic profits toward providing food, medicine, and conflict resolution to our own world community.

Instead of this historically-sanctioned humanitarian turn, however, the movement experienced what Barney, Wenn, and Martyn call 'a philosophical shift', and under Brundage's successors, the IOC was transformed into a corporate entity with a commercial identity. Critics decry the commercialism of the games, but is it anathema from an ancient point of view? As a religious festival, the ancient Games were not a 'for-profit' operation. In fact, commercial activity – including the selling of food and drinks – was generally not allowed within ancient Hellenic religious sanctuaries or gymnasia. On the other hand, there were all kinds of vendors outside the *Altis* at Olympia selling all kinds of goods and services from the religious

---

[27]   Plato, 'Apology', *Complete Works*, (ed.) John Cooper (Indianapolis: Hackett, 1997) 36de.

[28]   David Lord Burghley, member of the IOC executive board, qtd. in Barney et. al. op. cit. note 21, 59.

to the decidedly unreligious. It seems to me that the real concern about commercialism in the Olympics is not so much that they sell Coca Cola, but rather that their *purpose* should be reduced to selling Coca Cola.[29] There certainly is a cultural paradigm under which modern sport is seen as nothing more than a television commodity and athletes view themselves as professional entertainers – have the Olympic Games become absorbed into this paradigm?

For their own sake, I hope not. Anything more than a superficial understanding of the economics of the modern Olympic Games will reveal that the source of their fiscal viability just is the complex of heritage, ideals, and higher purpose that 'over commercialization' seems to threaten. According to economist Holger Preuss, the Olympic aura, nourished by Olympic ideals, creates what he calls a 'globally valid ideology'. Preuss identifies this unique Olympic ideology as 'the basis for the power, the financial resources and the lasting existence of the IOC'.[30] In short, if the Olympics abandon their ideology and reduce themselves to a commercial entertainment product, they will no longer be viable as a commercial entertainment product.[31] By making a concrete commitment to humanitarian service, the Olympic movement, and sport more generally, can better embody its ideals, respect its ancient heritage, and ensure its long-term financial health. In this regard, some athletes have already taken the lead.

3. Reviving a Heritage of Service

The enduring and inspiring connection among Olympic sport, sacrifice, and service survives in a story that moves among Sicily,

[29] Supporters of the Olympic idea must recognize that the staging of the Games requires revenue that can come either from public or from private sources. Of these, the private sources are certainly preferable since sponsorship is voluntary and taxation involuntary. What is to be resisted is not the financial support of corporate sponsors and the entertainment industry, but rather the *reduction* of the Games to a commercial entertainment product.

[30] Holger Preuss, *Economics of the Olympic Games* (Petersham, NSW: Walla Walla Press, 2000) 248.

[31] Many in the Olympic movement apparently recognize this fact; Preuss characterizes the IOC as 'effectively fighting the issue' of over commercialization, op. cit. note 30, 257. Of course this statement begs the question of what an effective fight will be. No doubt it involves a clarification of and emphasis on the Olympics' so-called ideals, something we academics should be able to help out with.

Olympia, Athens, and Torino, between the 12th BCE and February, 2006. Let us return for a moment to the *Aeneid's* scene of Entellus' sacrificing his prize bull. Strange as it may seem at first glance, this act might be taken to symbolize an enduring ideal for both the social role of athletes and the social value of sport. To discover how, we may compare Entellus' act to another athlete's post-victory gesture at the 2006 Winter Olympic Games in Torino, Italy. After winning the gold medal in the 500 meter sprint, American speed skater Joey Cheek announced in the inevitable post-race interviews that he would be donating his $25,000 United States Olympic Committee victory bonus to Right to Play, 'an athlete-driven international humanitarian organization that uses sport and play as a tool for the development of children and youth in the most disadvantaged areas of the world'.[32] Cheek's gesture not only highlighted his inspiring personal integrity, it presented a welcome image of American generosity and compassion at time when their international reputation was more commonly associated with military belligerence and blind economic self-interest. Furthermore, Cheek's action gave his bitterly divided country something to agree about; it was an image of American virtue that everyone could rally around.

Understood simply and within the relevant temporal and cultural contexts, the connection between Entellus' ritual sacrifice and Joey Cheek's Olympic gesture becomes clear. In the tradition of religious, athletic, and specifically Olympic sacrifice, Cheek's donation provided personal inspiration, practical benefit, and a unifying spirit to the wider community. Indeed a second medal brought another $15,000 bonus, which Cheek also donated, this time challenging other athletes and sponsors to follow suit. The result was over $300,000 US earmarked to help refugee children in Chad and the Darfur region of Sudan. Said Cheek, 'I am thrilled that so many people watched my race and cheered for my teammates and me, but it means much more to be able to help someone else'.[33] Both Entellus and Cheek may be seen as heroes who put their athletic prowess in the service of their communities.

Joey Cheek is hardly the first modern athlete to sacrifice his spoils to a cause beyond himself. At Athens 2004, swimmer Otylia Jedrzejczak won Poland's first swimming gold then auctioned her medal to raise $80,000 for a children's hospital near her hometown.

---

[32]   Right to Play. 'Right to Play at a Glance', *Right to Play.com*. April 5, 2006, http://www.righttoplay.com.

[33]   Cheek qtd. in ABC News, 'Person of the Week: Joey Cheek' *ABC News.com*, February 24, 2006. April 7, 2006. http://abcnews.go.com.

Heather L. Reid

Jedrzejczak's story is quite explicitly one of religious-athletic sacrifice. After reading a book about a boy suffering from leukemia, she says she 'made a promise to god' that if she won the gold medal in Athens it would be dedicated to help children suffering from leukemia.[34] Just like an ancient athlete, she prayed for victory, won, and then paid her 'votive' as promised. It may even be the case that knowing their victories could help others gives some athletes that winning edge. Cyclist Lance Armstrong has attributed his success partly to the desire to help cancer survivors.[35] Professional athletes everywhere set up charitable foundations to support causes close to their hearts. America's National Football League has made a major public commitment to the United Way. Whether interpreted as divine intervention or simple motivation, the most sporting of all athletic advantages must be the athlete's awareness of his or her social responsibility.

Athletes who put sport in the service of their communities effect in our modern world the venerable benefits of ancient athletic sacrifice. First is the psychological benefit: inspiration. Not only were Cheek, Jedrzejczak, and others inspired by the opportunity to do some good in the world, their athletic success in turn provides inspiration to people engaged in a variety of struggles. The second benefit of sacrifice is more tangible. Like the roasted meat from the sacrificial animal, the money raised by athletes provides for the basic needs of people everywhere. Food and medicine, as well as the space and facilities to play are of immediate benefit, especially to children in refugee camps. The *Olympic Charter* declares play to be a human right.[36] Finally, athletic sacrifice provides for community bonding. Not only do the actions of philanthropic athletes unify their nations and communities, sport itself provides a public example of rule-governed, non-violent conflict resolution. By organizing soccer leagues in African refugee camps, organizations such as Right to Play have been able to cultivate peaceful tribal interaction among youths who had known nothing but sectarian violence.[37] Which brings us back

---

[34] Bud Greenspan, *Bud Greenspan's Athens 2004: Stories of Olympic Glory*, Showtime Network, January, 2006.

[35] Lance Armstrong, *It's Not About the Bike* (New York: Putnam, 2000), 160.

[36] International Olympic Committee, *The Olympic Charter*, (Lausanne, Switzerland: IOC, 2004) 11.

[37] Rachel Briggs, Helen McCarthy, Alexis Zorbas, *16 Days: The Role of Olympic Truce in the Toolkit for Peace* (London: Demos, 2004).

(Briggs et al. 61–2)

to the most ancient founding principles of the Olympic Games: the pacification and unification of diverse peoples.

Conclusion

Modern sport has shed its ancient religious function, not least because it serves a world community, which contains a variety of [often conflicting] religions. Cynics might say that the religious function has been replaced with a commercial one. Sport is a branch of the entertainment industry they say, its potential for social utility surrendered to its immense profit potential. A closer look reveals, however, that some of sport's ancient religious heritage survives in modern times. The Olympic opening procession, oaths, torch, and flame still evoke the Games' higher purpose as a community-building ritual meant to reward and inspire. As in Ancient Greece, the athletic contests attract large and diverse audiences, drawing attention to the movement's goals of humanism, justice, and peace – goals, after all, that are as much within our own power as that of any god. In effect, the Games are now praying to us. Enlightened athletes, officials, and spectators have the ability to uncover the educational and inspirational potential of athletics and bring them back to the fore. Athletes should be regarded neither as entertainers nor as revenue-earners, but as community servants whose personal sacrifice can and should benefit the others.

The gestures of individual athletes and small organizations like Right to Play are not enough, however. Modern sport organizations, especially the Olympic Movement, need to publicly commit themselves and their sponsors to concrete humanitarian goals consistent with their stated ideals, partnering as appropriate with established service organizations. Anti-Olympic campaigners may argue plausibly that the most effective humanitarian act the Olympic movement could perform would be to eliminate the Games. Olympic supporters, however, can respond with the vision of the Games' immense public profile being turned toward beneficial projects – as has been done with limited results in the area of environmentalism. If the Olympic movement commits itself publicly to community service, not only will it revive an important aspect of its ancient heritage, but it may well change the culture of sports in general. It's time that athletes and sports self-consciously abandon the modern commercial paradigm and return to their ancient and venerated roles in honorable public service. Olympic champions Otylia Jedrzejczak and Joey Cheek

Heather L. Reid

have shown that this is still possible. The connection between sport, service, and sacrifice is as old as contest itself.[38]

Morningside College
reid@morningside.edu

---

[38] An earlier version of this paper was published as 'Of Sport, Service, and Sacrifice: Rethinking the Religious Heritage of the Olympic Games'. *Cultural Imperialism in Action: Critiques in the Global Olympic Trust*. Eds N. Crowther, R. Barney, M. Heine (London, Ontario: ICOS, 2006) 32–40.

Chess, Imagination, and Perceptual Understanding

PAUL COATES

1. Introduction

Chess is sometimes referred to as a 'mind-sport'. Yet, in obvious ways, chess is very unlike physical sports such as tennis and soccer; it doesn't require the levels of fitness and athleticism necessary for such sports. Nor does it involve the sensory-governed, skilled behaviour required in activities such as juggling or snooker. Nevertheless, I suggest, chess is closer than it may at first seem to some of these sporting activities. In particular, there are interesting connections between the way that we use our perceptual imagination in sports, and also in chess. The same distinction between calculation and natural instinct applies in chess as it does in many physical sports.

Meanwhile, a proper understanding of the way perceptual imagination works in chess points to something fundamental about the way we understand the physical nature of the world. A good chess player's appreciation of the tactical and strategical aspects of a chess position involves an imaginative grasp of spatial possibilities. This understanding is mirrored in a straightforward sense in physical sports when a player anticipates a return pass in football, or places a shot in tennis.

But there are connections at a deeper level as well, between the way we see chess positions, and the way we see ordinary objects such as apples and chairs. Our understanding of the physical world has much more of a formal nature than we unreflectively appreciate. Seeing the difference between a ball and a cricket bat is analogous in many ways to understanding the difference between a bishop and a knight in chess.

2. Calculation and the Combinatorial Explosion

In order to fully understand the way good players see chess positions, we need first of all to clarify the difference between chess tactics and strategy.

doi:10.1017/S1358246113000258   © The Royal Institute of Philosophy and the contributors 2013

Paul Coates

Chess involves the calculation of tactical possibilities latent in a position, so as to work out what advantages may be achieved in a given situation – such as winning a piece, or forcing checkmate. If the position is otherwise equal, winning even one pawn is usually sufficient for a good club player to force victory.

But chess involves more than mere calculation. For in nearly all chess positions, the number of possible sequences multiplies at an exponential rate, the further one looks ahead. In an average middle game position, the player has around thirty single moves to choose from. For each of these, the opponent will, likewise, have around thirty replies. So in most given positions there will be getting on for a thousand possible full, one-move, sequences (one move by each player). To assess *every* possibility, even three full moves ahead, would require examining many millions of possible outcomes. Fully calculating the possibilities latent in a position is clearly not feasible.

Human chess players therefore have to be selective. They need to think strategically. At every stage they have to massively restrict the number of moves that they examine. Accordingly, they focus upon only those moves that might impact on the few select aspects of the position that appear to be relevant. To do this, chess players need to use *intuition*. Intuition enables them to assess which side has the advantage in a position, and what particular moves and general plans are worth exploring, and are likely to promote an advantage.

Chess therefore involves two main skills. The first is the ability to calculate sequences of moves accurately. This requires *tactical expertise*, or what cognitive scientists call the ability to '*search*'.

The second skill involves being able to assess positions and select the moves most likely to lead to positions that are obviously better. This demands *strategical proficiency*. Good players become experts in pattern recognition, developed through experience, and rely upon *intuition*, which, in this context, involves an ability to recognise common patterns of pieces as '*chunks*' or '*templates*'.[1] These units they associate with likely outcomes. Players will see a group of pawns as mobile or fixed, for example, or a king position as weak or well defended, or the possibility of a back rank mate, and so on.

Today, computers have reached levels at which they are capable of defeating world champions at chess. But computers play in a different style from humans. In short-term tactics they play perfectly. However, it proves very hard to programme computers to 'assess positions' strategically. They rely mainly upon what is called 'brute

---

[1]   See, for example, Chase and Simon (1973) and Lane and Gobet (2011).

force' – the ability to calculate literally billions of different positions very rapidly, so that they can compute in depth to around 8–10 full moves ahead, and with complete accuracy (the use of a large memory, for chess openings and endgame positions, also plays a role). However, their assessment of the resulting positions can sometimes be quite mistaken, as I shall illustrate in due course.

3. Chess and the Imagination

In both tactics and strategy, the good chess player makes use of his or her *imagination*, and I want first to distinguish various different senses of this term.

(1) *Basic imagination*:

In introductory books on chess, the nature of each type of piece is explained by diagrams indicating the legal moves open to it. Thus the bishop is characterised by the fact that it is only allowed to move along diagonal lines; the knight, by how it can jump to the opposite corner of a rectangle of 2 by 3 squares; and so on for the other pieces:

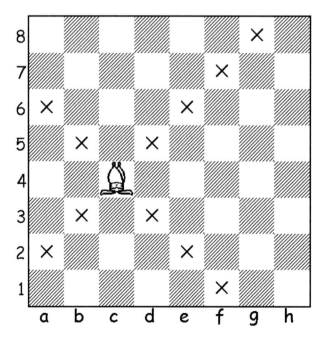

Diagram 1. Possible bishop moves indicated by the crossed squares.

Paul Coates

This already gives us a first sense of 'imagination', which I shall call the *basic* sense. To see a given chess piece as belonging to a certain type, such as a bishop, is to be aware of what squares on the board it can move to. This sense of imagination is closely related to Kant's important notion of the *Productive Imagination*.

As Kant argued, when I grasp the nature of a common-place object that I directly and spontaneously recognise in perception, I exercise a low-level classificatory concept. I cannot see, or otherwise perceive, an object – in a manner which involves some awareness of what I see – without having an implicit grasp of its different possible appearances. To see a black object on a chair *as* a cat necessitates being aware of how that object would appear from different points of view. The productive imagination imposes a unity upon different *spatial* perspectives of one and the same object.[2]

In a related sense, to grasp what type a chess piece belongs to – whether it is a rook, or king, and so on – requires an understanding of the legal moves permitted to it in the context of a game. In grasping *this* particular piece as a rook, I understand where it could move to on its next move in *this* particular position. The imagination imposes a unity on different *temporal* perspectives, so that two successive appearances of a rook on different squares are taken to be the play of a single legal move by one piece. The different overall positions are seen as belonging to one and the same game of chess, related sequentially.

When a competent player sees his opponent's rook on a certain square, he is thus prepared for it to move in certain specific ways. This basic imaginative grasp of the possibilities open to a piece is *constitutive* of understanding the type of piece it is. Moreover, the understanding of its legal moves is *all* that is essential to understanding the nature of a chess piece. The assignment of standard shapes to each type of chess piece is a merely contingent matter, and was regularised in the nineteenth century by the adoption of 'Staunton pattern' figures.

Precisely what is involved in this kind of imaginative seeing turns out to be a complex matter, and we will examine later on further aspects of seeing a chess position that are connected with this point.

(2) We are more used to thinking of the imagination in chess in two further senses, which need to be distinguished from what I have termed the *basic* sense. These have to do the use of the imagination in clever tactical sequences, and in more profound strategical plans.

[2] A modern development of these ideas is set out in Sellars (1978).

214

Chess, Imagination, and Perceptual Understanding

The beginner will have learnt what a knight is in terms of the way that it can move and carry out forks – by attacking two pieces at once, as in Diagram 2:

    1 Nf7ch   Kg7
    2 Nxg5

When we speak of an *imaginative tactical sequence* in chess, we have in mind the way that such simple ideas can enter into play, in more surprising ways. The proficient chess player, for whom the legal moves become second nature, instinctively guards against moves that straightforwardly lead to the capture and loss of an unprotected piece. The awareness of simple short sequences that result straightforwardly in loss guides the selection of sequences worth exploring further. Good players become familiar with forks, pins, discovered checks and other simple tactical devices, knowing what to avoid. But there is a critical balance to be achieved. While avoiding moves that lead to loss, the player must also develop a sense of the kind of situation that needs to be examined more closely. A move that appears initially unattractive may turn out to lead to greater gain.

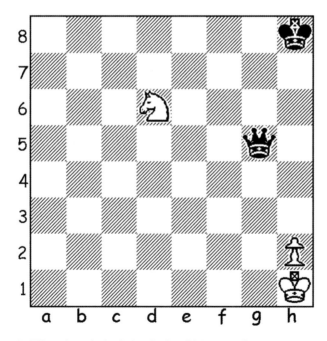

Diagram 2. The simple knight fork of king and queen.

Paul Coates

This second use of the chess imagination enables good players to discover effective moves that lesser players might overlook.

Here is a relatively simple example, from the end of the 10th Match Game between Petrosian and Spassky, first match, 1966 (Diagram 3):

Petrosian finished off the game nicely by playing:

    1 Bxf7ch   Rxf7
    2 Qh8ch!

At which point Spassky resigned, because of the forced sequence leading to a clearly lost position:

    2 .....   Kxh8
    3 Nxf7ch   Kg7
    4 Nxg5

In his famous game against Donald Byrne, played when he was only 13 years old, Bobby Fischer found a wonderfully imaginative tactical combination. Starting with a surprise queen sacrifice, he eventually won material after a forcing sequence of nearly ten moves (Diagram 4):

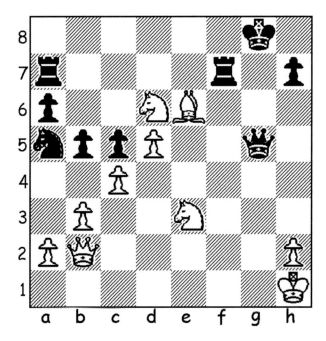

Diagram 3. Petrosian v. Spassky, First Match, end of Game 10.

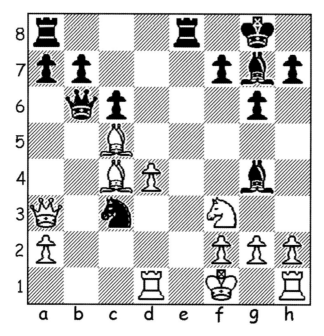

Diagram 4. D. Byrne v. Fischer, Rosenwald Trophy Tournament, US, 1956.

Fischer, playing black, achieved a won position by a spectacular combination as follows:

17....	Be6!!
18 Bxb6	Bxc4ch
19 Kg1	Ne2ch
20 Kf1	Nxd4ch
21 Kg1	Nxe2ch
22 Kf1	Nc3ch
23 Kg1	axb6
24 Qb4	Ra4
25 Qxb6	Nxd1

and with a rook and two bishops for a queen, Fischer had no problem in successfully winning the game.

In the Byrne-Fischer game, the actual combination itself is not too difficult for the average club player to follow. What was more remarkable was Fischer's imaginative ability in recognising the potential for the sacrifice in advance, and exploring its tactical possibilities. Imagination, in this *second* sense, involves examining

217

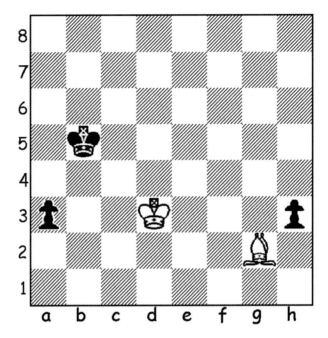

Diagram 5. Gratzer Endgame – queening threats: White to play and draw.

an unusual move or position, and seeing a tactical possibility that does not at first strike the player as obviously leading to an advantage.[3]

Here is another example of this kind of exercise of imagination, the end of a lovely endgame by Gratzer, in which the task is for White to find a way of forcing a draw (Diagram 5).

Although it is White to move, it looks initially as if one of the black pawns must go through to become a queen, in which case Black will win. It appears that White must first capture Black's pawn on h3, which then leaves the White king too far away to stop the Black pawn on a3 from queening. The sequence would be:

    1 Bxh3   a2
    2 Kc2   a1 = queen, and Black wins

---

[3]   In his pioneering research, de Groot (1965) distinguished between a player's initial exploration of the chess position, the selection of moves worth investigating in a given position, and a subsequent investigation or analysis of the actual tactical possibilities resulting from the move.

However, White has a remarkable imaginative resource, a move that at first glance seems hardly worth considering, but which achieves a draw. The main variation is:

    1 Bf1!! a2
    2 Kc2ch

the discovered check saves the day for White.

    2 ...   Kb4
    3 Kb2 h2
    4 Bg2

and with both Black pawns prevented from queening in safety, White achieves the draw.

(3) A third kind of imaginative ability is exercised when players consider the strategical possibilities in a position.

As we have already noted, the basic rules of the game stipulate which moves are legal. They are constitutive of chess. In a different sense, there are heuristic rules, rough principles that help players to select moves that will improve their position. Centuries of play were needed before players became able to articulate such heuristics, strategical rules such as:

> Capture with pawns towards the centre;
> Place rooks on open files, or on the seventh rank;
> Knights are better placed in the middle of the board than on the side;
> Aim not to move the same piece twice in the opening;
> Overprotect weak points;
> Don't let pawns become isolated;
> and many more.

These rules are not legal requirements. None of them applies in all situations. But on the whole, following them promotes success. A good player will have internalised scores of such rules, and will be guided by them in strategical play.

Diagram 6 shows is a famous example, from the tournament game Emanuel Lasker v. Capablanca, St Petersburg 1914, final tournament:

Here Lasker, as White to move, successfully carried out the strong strategical plan of establishing his knight in the heart of his opponent's position, by playing: Ne6. The knight on the 6th rank was, for Black, 'like a bone in his throat' in Kasparov's words.[4]

But there is room for a more creative use of the imagination at a strategical level, where mere heuristic rule-following becomes

---

[4]   Kasparov (2003), 212.

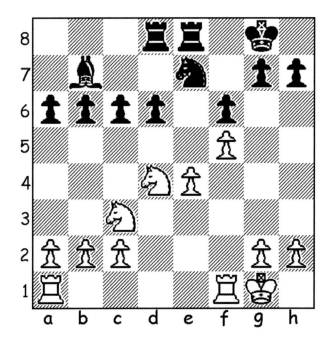

Diagram 6. Lasker v. Capablanca – White to play.

subservient to deeper aims. A nice example is given in another Fischer game, played against Matulovic in an international tournament (Diagram 7).

Here Matulovic had just played: 13 Bxe7, capturing Fischer's bishop. What might be thought of as the 'normal' move, the one that most averagely good players would automatically select, is a re-capture of the bishop by the queen:

13....   Qxe7

On the grounds that this would enable Black to castle his king into safety.

Fischer saw deeper into the position and realised that his king would be safe in the centre, and also that his queen would be needed on the queenside. He therefore played instead:

13 ....   Kxe7!

and a dozen moves later his choice was vindicated when they reached a position where his forces dominated the board (Diagram 8).[5]

[5]   After the moves: 14 Qd2 Nf6; 15 Bg2 Bb7; 16 Qd3 Qb6; 17 0–0 a5; 18 R(f)d1Ba6; 19 Qd2 R(h)c8; 20 h3 h5; 21 b3 Bxe2; 22 Qxe2 Rc3; 23 Rd3 R(b)c8; 24 Rxc3 Rxc3; 25 Kh2 Qc5; 26 Ra2....

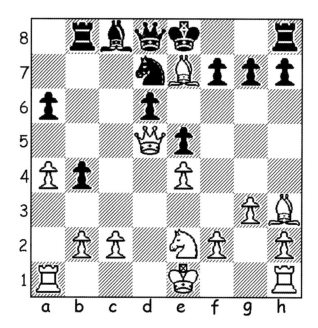

Diagram 7. Matulovic v. Fischer, Vinkovci, Yugoslavia, 1968.

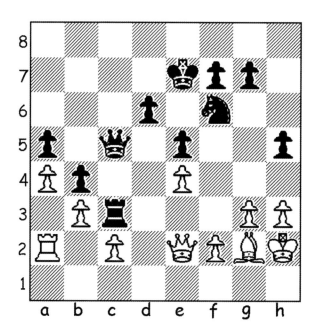

Diagram 8. Matulovic v. Fischer, position after White's 26th move.

Fischer won the game after a further dozen moves.

Here the imagination is being used in a different, creative way, looking more deeply into a position, and selecting an unusual move that proves to have beneficial long-term consequences.

Attractive as these examples of tactics and strategy are, the imaginative abilities they illustrate are complementary to an understanding of the rules of chess, rather than constitutive of it. Yet there is still a common idea involved. All three uses of imagination – in the basic sense of understanding how a piece moves, in discovering a tactical sequence, and in grasping the strategical aspects latent in a position – involve the subject considering future possibilities. Knowing that such possibilities exist enables a player to assess the potential of a position.

4. How Chess Players Think

Serious psychological investigation of the thought processes of chess players began with the work of Alfred Binet at the end of the nineteenth century. In 1946, the Dutch International Chess Master and psychologist, Adriaan de Groot, carried out a major study comparing the thought processes of top level Chess Grandmasters, who included world champions Alekhine and Euwe, with those of good club players.

De Groot's central finding was that the use of pattern recognition in soundly assessing positions was of greater importance than the ability to search accurately and to calculate positions in depth.[6] Of course, both abilities have to be well developed in a good chess player. At nearly all stages in a game a player will need to spend some time in careful calculation. But it is correct to say that chess players have to rely upon their intuitive skill in recognising patterns to guide their selection of the moves worth examining. It is this ability to select – usually in a matter of a few seconds – the few appropriate moves that merit further calculation that really distinguishes top level masters from averagely good players.

Current work on thinking in chess has upheld de Groot's findings about the central importance of intuition, or pattern recognition. Fernand Gobet summarises the findings of recent research as follows:

- Grandmasters are very good at the initial selection of moves worth considering, through pattern recognition, and they rely

[6] de Groot (1965).

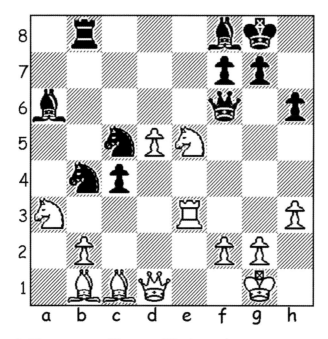

Diagram 9. Kasparov v. Karpov, Black to play.

heavily upon their use of intuition – that is by assessing and ca-
tegorising a move or position as strong or weak, without explicit
conscious calculation. They are also good at what is termed
'chunking': memorising typical groupings of pieces (empirical
tests on memory confirms this finding);

- The knowledge of typical position types, and the use of intuition and pattern recognition, are more important than the
  ability to search and calculate deeply in a position;
- Intuition characterises the thinking of experts all the way
  through the decision processes.[7]

Yet experts also rely upon their ability to calculate more deeply,
and slightly more widely, than average players. Gobet rightly criti-
cises the work of Dreyfus in this respect. Drefus over-emphasises
the reliance upon intuition by strong masters. He has claimed that
the expert chess player proceeds intuitively for most of the time,
rarely explicitly calculating sequences of possible future moves.
This simply does not match up with the experiences of experts.
Although they may intuitively, rapidly, and for the most part

---

[7]   Gobet (2012).

accurately, *select* the right moves to analyse, they still need to go through a *justification* process, in which the likely responses are quickly and carefully – and consciously – calculated. And at times a grandmaster may spend an hour or more calculating different variations in a given position. An example occurred in the 16th game of the third championship match between Kasparov v. Karpov in 1986.

In Diagram 9, with only one pair of rooks and a few pawns exchanged, there is a myriad of relevant possible variations that need to be examined. Karpov had a long think, for around a full hour, mainly devoted to deciding which knight to play to d3. In his book on the match, Kasparov devotes several pages to the ramifications of this extremely complex position, concluding that in eventually deciding to play: 25 ... Nbd3, Karpov selected the wrong knight to move to the d3 square.[8]

5. Seeing Positions and the Exercise of Concepts

In one respect, however, Gobet is misleading. He claims that, for the good chess player, the use of intuition precedes any conceptualisation. Now, it is true that chess players talk about having a good '*sight*' of the board, in swiftly and directly seeing the potential of a position. In this respect it has been claimed that at his peak, Capablanca was supreme. Reti complained that when he would show Capablanca a difficult endgame study that he had composed, the latter would instantly '*see*' the solution, almost before he had finished setting up the pieces. But it is a mistake to think of this kind of seeing as preceding the exercise of concepts by the player. Already, in seeing what the position on the board *is*, a chess player is employing classificatory concepts.

As we noted earlier, understanding the way a chess piece can legally move is internally related to, or necessary, for a grasp of which type of piece it is. It follows that what chess players call 'intuition' already involves the conceptual classification of specific pieces, and also of types of position. The exercise of this capacity is linked to an implicit grasp of the potential moves available to a piece. To see a piece as a knight in chess is to understand what it can do, to grasp its function.

This point is well illustrated by the occasional striking blunders perpetrated by even top grandmasters.

One tragic example occurred in a game between Petrosian – before he became world champion – and Bronstein (see Diagram 10):

---

[8]   Kasparov (1987). Kasparov's next move in reply also turned out to be an error.

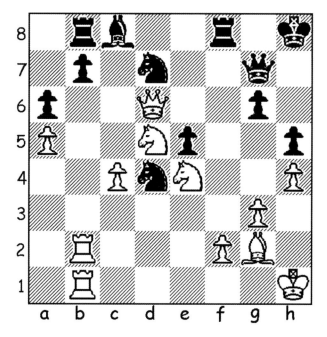

Diagram 10. Petrosian v. Bronstein, Amsterdam, 1956 – Black to play.

Petrosian had achieved a completely dominating position, and it seemed only a matter of time before he would win the game. Bronstein had been reduced to shuffling his knight around the squares: c6, d4 and f5.

In the diagram position, Petrosian had just played his queen to d6. Bronstein responded by making another knight move, 35 .... Nf5. Petrosian thought for a short while, and then blundered by:

36 Ng5??
and after the obvious reply 36 ... NxQ he resigned immediately.

Petrosian must in some sense have seen the black knight, but only as a black shape. It was, after all, there in front of his eyes for several minutes as he looked at the board, while he pondered his next move. Yet Petrosian did not see the knight piece *as* a knight; he did not see its potential moves, that it was attacking his queen.

Another very interesting blunder occurred in a game between Fischer and Geller (Diagram 11).

Paul Coates

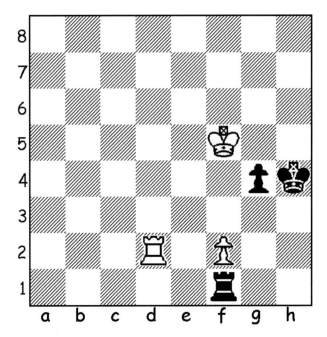

Diagram 11. Geller v. Fischer, Interzonal tournament, Palma de Mallorca 1970.

Geller was in a poor position. Being extremely tired at this point, he was relying upon the following variation, assuming that it led to an advantage for White:

```
67....        g3
68 fxg3 ch    Kxg3
69 Kxf1
```

The problem is that this variation contains *two* illegal White moves:

** 68: pawn (f) takes pawn (g3), check,

and

** 69: king (f5) takes rook (f1)!

Geller was conceptualising his king piece as a rook, a piece that, of course, moves in a quite different way. Geller was no longer seeing his king piece *as* a king.

These examples illustrate one essential feature of the way chess players see positions. For a player to conceptualise a rook piece as a rook, it is necessary that he sees the potential moves open to it – for example, that it might be moved along a certain file and capture a certain pawn. Thus conceptualising a piece involves a grasp of spatial possibilities – imagining, in the basic sense, the range of squares that it can legally move to. As we noted earlier, there is a sense in which the chess player is implicitly aware of the possible future appearances of the chess pieces on the board. Up to a point, this is correct. However, there are further issues that complicate the analysis of what is involved in playing a game, which require careful explication.

6. The Formal Nature of Chess

All perceptual experiences have two components. Firstly, they involve some kind of intentional component directed at an object, in virtue of which the subject focuses conceptually upon the nature of what is taken to be perceived. Experiences also contain a further, non-conceptual, phenomenal aspect. This second aspect is interpreted in different ways, either as the sensory *mode* of the intentional state, or as a distinct sensory *component*. In either case, it means that in addition to the intentional content, experiences involve a feature that is distinctive of perception, the awareness of phenomenal qualities.[9] These qualities are connected in some way to the external objects perceived.

In seeing a chess position on the board in an ordinary game, the player will entertain 'perceptual takings' about the game – perceptual thoughts, and intentions, involving the exercise of concepts focusing upon the pieces, their positions, and their possible future moves. Such thoughts will be guided by a visual awareness of phenomenal qualities, determined by the actual physical arrangement of pieces on the board.

If we consider any particular game of chess – for example, the sixth game between Tal and Botvinnik, in their 1960 world championship match – we need to distinguish three realms. First, there are the various concrete representations of the game, including the physical arrangement of pieces on the board in front of the players at the time of play; second, there are the players' visualization, thoughts, intentions and other mental states; but in addition to these two realms, there is a third realm, which includes the particular game itself, the

---

[9]   This sensory component is, in turn, interpreted in contrasting ways by the Causal Theorist and the Direct Realist.

focus, or object, of the players' thoughts, an abstract entity that is distinct from the various mental and concrete representations of it.

There are several (interconnected) reasons for distinguishing the objects belonging in this third realm from those in the first two. Firstly, for the experienced player, in thinking about the game they are playing, the precise physical details of the appearance of the pieces drop away as unimportant – one might, for example, play a chess game with pieces taken from two sets, where the pawns are of a slightly different height and shape.

Secondly, what essentially determines a piece's identity are the legal moves that are permitted to it. Awareness of the type of piece occupying a square consequently has a normative dimension. A piece is conceived as a knight, or a rook, and so on, in virtue of the fact that the player is implicitly aware of the different new positions it could take up; how it might appear on the board a move or more hence.

Thirdly, if the players are both playing blindfold, there may be no board, or a board whose only purpose is to act as a record of the moves and position reached. In playing postal chess, or on the internet, different players and observers will be looking at different boards, all of which represent the same position. When Spassky was playing a candidates' match against Korchnoi in 1977, he alternated between contemplating the position on the board in front of him, and studying (the same) position on the large display board situated at the back of the playing arena. If a game is adjourned, it may be renewed with a different set of pieces, and so on. If an actual set of pieces is used, these might get accidentally moved or damaged during a game. (Thus a player is permitted to say 'j'adoube', and to adjust the placing of a piece on a square.) The true position in the game will be reconstructed from the previous intended moves; it is not determined by where the pieces actually sit on the board.

For all these reasons, we need to distinguish between the identity of a particular chess game that is being played between two players, and the concrete physical structure that may represent it for them during any period of time. The 'real' chess game that they are considering is something abstract, a structure or model conceived in formal terms. This model has an abstract spatial structure, one that reflects what is in common to all the possible representations of the position. The structure represented is not to be understood as equivalent to any concrete region of physical space. It is not determined solely by the physical arrangement of pieces on the board, but by the joint intentions and actions of the players, as these are integrated into the wider intentions of the chess-playing community that decides the rules of the game.

Hence it is important to realise that, when the chess player focuses upon those aspects of the position that determine the actual chess game being played, their thoughts about the game are not, in a strict sense, directly *about* the physical pieces which visually prompt and guide them. Strictly speaking, the real focus of the player's thoughts is *not* the actual, static, arrangement of physical pieces on the board in front of him, but an abstraction from them. Their perceptual thoughts do not refer to the concrete position, but to something akin to a formal model. When chess players look at positions, understanding what they see, they *project* the more immediate awareness of the colours, shapes and position of the pieces on the board onto the abstract position that the physical pieces represent.

The actual physical pieces on the board are proxies that are used to illustrate the abstract structure contemplated. They can be used by the players to represent the position arrived at after each move. In seeing a position, the good player is guided by a non-conceptual *awareness* of the actual pieces' shape, yet *perceives* each piece in terms of its spatial role or function. He or she does not pay much attention to the phenomenal appearance of the piece. Blindfold chess players report that when they imagine positions in their mind's eye, they do *not*, for the most part, imagine the actual Staunton pattern shapes of pieces, but instead, conceive of them more abstractly, as radiating lines of force, corresponding to the way that they are legally permitted to move.[10]

In effect, chess is a branch of mathematics. Finding a forcing continuation in a position is analogous to finding a geometrical proof. The proof that the angles of a Euclidean triangle add up to 180 degrees is not about an actual diagram of a triangle that happens to be used to illustrate it, but refers to an abstract model (or set of models). In the same way, a thought about what is achievable in a given chess position refers to the abstract model that reflects what is in common to all equivalent chess positions.

It is also important to note that the abstract structure focused upon in a chess game is conceived in entirely relational terms. What is represented is a spatial arrangement, with pieces whose nature is exhausted by formally specified relational possibilities. The moral here is that when we conceive of a chess piece as such, the *intrinsic* character is not relevant. A chess piece can be made of wood, plastic, metal or old bits of kneaded dough. Its shape can vary,

---

[10]   See, for example, the classic work by Binet (1966). More recent studies confirm the finding that blindfold players imagine the chess pieces in terms of the 'lines of force' they exert: see Chabris and Hearst (2003).

likewise. An imaginative grasp of the future possibilities open to a piece is essential to our recognition of a piece for what it is. But the possibilities that in this way determine the nature of a piece are purely spatial. Only the potential relations of the piece to other squares and other pieces on the board matter. This idea, that the relational role or function of a piece is what is essential to our understanding of its nature, is one important feature that throws light upon the nature of our perception of everyday objects.

7. Phenomenology and Chess

The fact that our understanding of what is essential to a chess position refers to its formal, or abstract, nature contrasts with a paradoxical feature of chess to which I want to draw attention. Despite their abstract nature, from a phenomenological point of view, chess positions take on a vivid reality. From the good player's perspective, the pieces on the board come alive in a game. They are not treated merely as representations in some abstract formal system. Positions and pieces on the board can take on a meaningful presence, and have a strong emotional resonance. In part, the fact that positions take on significance has to do with practical goals, when a player strives to win the game. But in addition, the combinations that arise in practical play – and also in composed studies – can be assessed disinterestedly, in aesthetic terms, for beauty, elegance, wit and other related higher-level properties.

In his famous book, *The Luzhin Defence* – arguably the greatest novel about the game – Vladimir Nabokov captures some of these aspects of chess through his portrayal of the central figure of Luzhin, the doomed chess master whose thought processes, when playing blindfold chess, are described as follows:

> [Luzhin] saw then neither the knight's carved mane nor the glossy heads of the pawns – but he felt quite clearly that this or that imaginary square was occupied by a definite concentrated force, so he envisioned the movement of a piece as a discharge, a shock, a stroke of lightning – and the whole chess field quivered with tension ....[11]

Nabokov's description ties in nicely with the empirical studies of blindfold chess players of the way they imagine pieces in their mind.

[11]   Nabokov (1964) pp. 91–2.

Chess, Imagination, and Perceptual Understanding

In commenting on the final game of his return match with Euwe, Alekhine wrote of the capture of his opponent's piece as 'removing the *most hated knight* of the match', and such a comment is typical of the passionate way that players engage with the game. The chess style of Petrosian was characterised by the way that he would exert a 'python-like' grip on his opponent, depriving him of all counter-play. Nimzowitsch spoke of a passed pawn as 'a criminal, who should be kept under lock and key'; the passed pawn has a 'lust to expand'. In these, and in multiple other ways, the manner in which chess players talk about the game reflects the fact that chess positions are full of meaning for them, figurative meaning that goes far beyond a grasp of formal structure. This feature of the way that we see chess positions has implications for theories about perception and the nature of physical world.

8. Structures and Objects

There is one further aspect of seeing, or perceptual understanding, in chess that also throws light on the nature of perception in our every-day perceptual dealings with the world, outside chess.

As noted, in order for human chess players to avoid having to cal-culate excessively large numbers of variations, they have to restrict the possible moves they examine in depth. In order to do this, they have to bracket off groupings of pieces on the board that are less central to their main focus. The player needs to treat some groupings of pieces on the board as semi-permanent units, like complex objects, which have no direct bearing on the task in hand. If the immediate task is, for example, to find a direct sacrifice to expose the opponent's king to a possible mate, then the player may ignore pieces on the other side of the board, at least in a temporary way, while exploring the initial sacrificial possibilities.

An example here will illustrate what I mean, and clearly shows the difference between the way computers 'think' or compute in chess, and the way that humans explore the tactical possibilities in positions.

This is from a very interesting endgame study by Mihai Neghina, first posted on the internet in 2009. The position was initially pub-lished without a solution, accompanied by the claim that computers were unable to evaluate the position correctly (Diagram 12).

This position is a forced win for White. However, even after some introductory moves, the computer wrongly calculates that Black has a winning advantage:

Paul Coates

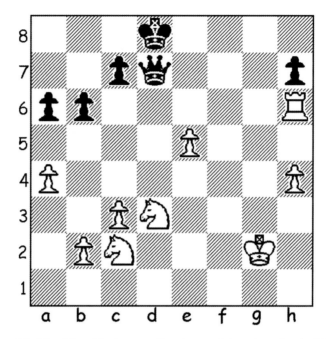

Diagram 12. Neghina Endgame Study position (version). White to play and win.

    1 Nd4   Qg7ch
    2 Kh3   Qxh6
    3 Nf4   Kc8

(Because of the threat of a knight fork on e6, if the knight on f4 is captured)

    4 Nde6   Kb7
    5 h5

Black has a queen for two knights and a pawn, normally a winning advantage for the side with the queen. The computer's verdict on this position is that Black should be able to force a win. But what the computer cannot do is assess the position in the way that a human can, as involving a piece-complex in which the Black queen will be trapped, and out of play – a key idea that the human player can trade on – and hence work out that it is White who has the advantage.

Diagram 13 gives the key trapping position, reduced to its bare elements.

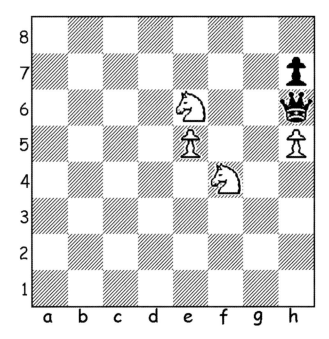

Diagram 13. Neghina Endgame Study: Trapping position.

The Black queen can make 8 moves in all, but they will all lead to her capture. It is very difficult to programme a computer to disregard this complex – at each move the computer will calculate these 8 possibilities, and their further ramifications, including over twenty possible replies by the White knights and the king. The possible variations multiply up to such an extent that they exceed even the computer's capacity for calculating billions of different positions.

The human player thinks differently. He, or she, can conceptualise the array on the right-hand side of the board as a semi-permanent object. The trapping piece-complex is treated as a stable unit. It can be imagined as a separate object, one that does not affect the play.

If the complex is treated in this way, it then becomes easier to ignore it when calculating the main lines, and analysing the best play for both sides. This results in White winning a crucial pawn on the queen side, so as to reach a won ending. The central variation continues: 5...c5 6 Kg4 c4 7 Kf5 Kc6 8 Ke4 b5 9 axb5ch axb5 10 Kd4 Kb6 11 Kd5 Ka5 12 Kc5 Ka6 13 Kc6 Ka5 14 Kb7 b4 15 Kc6 bxc3 16 bxc3 Ka4 17 Kc5 Kb3 Kd4 Kc2 19 Kxc4 and wins. It is only near the final stages, after around 10 or so moves, that the computer begins to assess the position correctly, as a win for White.[12]

There are two morals to be drawn from this example. Firstly, with respect to the differences between the way that humans and computers think, the fact that humans are able set aside piece-complexes, treating them as irrelevant to the immediate focus of play, shows something important about their imaginative resources.[13] Here the imagination works in a negative manner, by restricting the assessment of future possibilities, and by treating the trapping position as a fixed unit, removed from the immediate scene of action. The future possible moves within the piece-complex are, as it were, 'suspended' and removed from consideration by the player, at least on a temporary basis.

Secondly, it is a phenomenologically important fact that the structure which is treated by the player as a relatively stable object is a complex spatial structure. This structure can be interpreted as a high-level property of the chess game, and illustrated by a concrete arrangement of pieces on a board, but its essence is nevertheless something abstract and formal.

9. Implications and Applications

To summarise what I have argued so far:

1)   The imagination is exercised in different ways in chess. At the basic level, each piece is understood in terms of its spatial role. Players also exercise the imagination in further ways, in thinking through tactical sequences and assessing strategical possibilities, and in recognising larger structures, piece groupings that have different degrees of permanence and complexity.

2)   A player's grasp of a chess position is based upon an implicit or explicit awareness of the potential moves open to each piece: players envisage the different transformations of the position that will result from possible legal moves, generating different spatial arrangements of pieces.

3)   In thinking about a given position the player is *guided* by the representation of the position, either through seeing the

[12]   For discussion of this endgame study, see Josten (2010).

[13]   I am ignoring other differences between humans and machines that relate to the content and interpretation of chess moves, and the like. It is, of course, arguable that this constitutes a further dimension in which humans and computers differ.

qualitative aspects of the pieces on the board, or in imagining the positions of pieces when playing blindfold.

4) In a stricter sense, what the chess player grasps is an abstract model, a purely formal structure devoid of any intrinsic qualitative aspects, which is distinct from any concrete representation of the position reached in the game. In playing chess the player is dealing with what is at one level something purely mathematical: an abstract spatial structure governed by formally specifiable rules. Such structures are represented, for greater convenience, by arbitrarily chosen shapes on a board with a certain spatial configuration.

5) Yet the manner in which a good player responds to a chess position extends far beyond a grasp of its abstract spatial character. The arrangements of pieces on the board have phenomenological significance, and carry emotional charge. Although its essential aspects are purely formal, a chess position is seen as being richly meaningful.

The peculiar essence of chess as a game consists in this striking integration of two features of consciousness that are often considered to be starkly opposed: an *understanding* of formal or abstract structures, and an *awareness* of rich meaning, a meaning that transcends the practical goal of achieving a winning position.

These considerations about the way we grasp chess positions have important implications for epistemology. It is not only in playing chess (and similar games) that these two features of consciousness are combined. The structure of visual consciousness that is manifested in the case of seeing chess positions tells us something important about the general nature of perception. How we should analyse what goes on when a person plays chess has relevance to current philosophical disputes concerning the proper way to analyse the perceptual relation. The game of chess provides a model of our perceptual engagement with physical reality. In the concluding section of this paper I shall explain why this is so.

Much recent philosophy of perception has involved increasingly convoluted attempts to defend forms of Direct Realism (otherwise known as Disjunctivism).[14] The central tenet of this view is that experience is transparent, and that, in veridical perception, nothing mediates a subject's experience of the world. The subject is immediately aware of intrinsic properties belonging to the external physical

---

[14] Disjunctivism in its modern form stems principally from papers by Snowdon (1981) and McDowell (1982).

object perceived. An *irreducible experiential relation* connects the external object perceived with the subject's perceptual consciousness.[15]

Direct Realism has a superficial plausibility. It can appear to fit in with some of our common-sense convictions about our perceptual contact with the world. However, it faces two formidable objections. Firstly, there is the causal-scientific argument, developed by Valberg and Robinson. This turns on the point that both hallucinatory experiences, and also veridical experiences, are generated by exactly the same kinds of proximal brain states. Such states are sufficient, as the hallucinatory case indicates, to produce an experience *as of* an external world. The argument offers a good reason for holding that veridical experiences are *inner* states, which, like hallucinatory experiences, supervene solely upon the proximal brain state that is causally linked to the distal object perceived. It therefore follows that in seeing an object, I am immediately aware of the qualitative component of my inner experience – a phenomenal state of the same ontological kind that occurs in hallucination.[16]

The second objection involves a deeper metaphysical worry as to whether the Direct Realist theory is even coherent. What is an 'irreducibly experiential relation'? What kind of relation connects the subject's conscious experience to a mind-independent object? How does it fit into the natural world? It is difficult to spell out the Direct Realist theory in any clear way, so as to explicate the direct non-causal relation that is supposed to hold between the subject and the specific object he, or she, perceives. Without any positive account, there are no grounds to which the Direct Realist can appeal in order to specify which *particular* object is perceptually linked to the subject's experience, except grounds involving facts about causally related events. So Direct Realism becomes parasitic upon the causal account.[17]

The alternative to this view, the Causal Theory of Perception, holds that Direct Realism is misconceived. There is no irreducible *real* relation connecting a subject's conscious experience with any mind-independent physical item, which can make that very item phenomenally present in experience. The phenomenal redness that I am immediately aware of, when for example I stare at a juggling ball, supervenes on my brain state alone, and is an item logically distinct from that ball, ontologically in the same category as the green

[15] The phrase is from Hobson (*forthcoming*).
[16] See Valberg (1992) and Robinson (1994), and for criticism, Martin (2006) and Fish (2009).
[17] This argument is spelled out more fully in Coates (2007), Ch. 4.

after-image I will experience a moment later when I look away from the red ball onto a white surface. But to note this point is not to deny the fact that perception is also, in an important sense, direct. As Kant emphasised, there is a further component in experience, which comprises the exercise of low-level classificatory concepts. These concepts arise, without inference, in perceptual takings normally focused *directly* upon external objects and their features (surface or otherwise).[18] An *intentional* relation links the subject to the perceived object.[19] The awareness of phenomenal qualities causally prompts and guides our perceptual takings, which are about the external, mind-independent objects we perceive. The reddish shape I am non-conceptually aware of prompts me to see the object in front of me directly *as* a juggling ball.

The Causal Theory continues to meet with resistance. One objection to it interweaves semantical considerations about the content of experience with phenomenological considerations about the meaningfulness of our experience of objects. The charge is that the Causal Theory is unable to give a satisfactory account of how we come to have any kind of awareness of properties belonging to mind-independent objects, an awareness that forms the basis of our understanding of a rich and complex objective reality.[20] The Causal Theory thus appears to have the consequence that we are cut off from any knowledge of the intrinsic nature of physical things.

Part of the answer to this objection involves spelling out the structural realist conception of physical objects that, from a scientific perspective, is naturally allied with the Causal Theory. According to this conception, the intrinsic properties of objects are ultimately all primary qualities, qualities whose nature is essentially spatial. According to the form of structural realism originally outlined by Russell, the monadic properties that belong to a macroscopic object at a higher level of explanation are ontologically reducible. They

---

[18] It is of central importance in perception theory to distinguish the *directness* of manner in which the conceptual aspect of experience focuses upon the object, with the *immediacy* of non-conceptual, phenomenal, awareness of qualities that accompanies the conceptual aspect. These need not necessarily relate to the same entity.

[19] Note that to say this is not to endorse an intentionalist view of perceptual experience, since the intentional state is only one component of the overall perceptual experience.

[20] This objection appears to underlie McDowell's frequently expressed worries that a (Cartesian) epistemic divide between the subjectivity of experience and the external world has the consequence 'of putting subjectivity's very possession of an objective environment in question' (1986), 147.

can be accounted for in terms of spatial and causal relations between the micro-objects that constitute the higher-level structures.[21] Thus the nature of a certain kind, such as an apple, is explained in terms of its organic constitution, which in turn supervenes upon a certain chemical structure, and so on down to yet lower-level structures. What we understand, when we grasp the objective nature of an object, is something that can, in principle, be accounted for by reference to complexes of spatial structures connecting micro-objects, and the way that they causally interconnect.[22] However, we do not require full knowledge of these lower-level structures in order to have some understanding of the kind to which a given object belongs, so long as we have some knowledge of its causal nature. What we take to be the sensible qualities of objects in the world – the familiar colours, sounds, smells, tastes and feel of objects present to conscious experience – turn out to be states of our own minds, which we project onto the structures that we perceive.

By interpreting our perceptual grasp of the world along these structural realist lines, we can defend the Causal Theory against the charge that it is unable to explain how experiences have empirical content relating to an objective world.[23] Our formal grasp of spatial concepts allows us to form meaningful beliefs about the physical objects that transcend our experiences. Nevertheless, this appeal to our grasp of the essential spatial structure of the physical world does not exhaust the issues raised by the objection. There is a further dimension to the problem. The worry is that, on the structural realist account, we cannot do adequate justice to the phenomenology of our perceptual experience.

This deeper worry arises because, according to the Causal Theory, external physical objects can only be conceived of in austere formal terms, stripped of their intrinsic properties. The objection is that we are left with something that is only, at best, a grasp of a bare structure. Allegedly, this understanding fails to match up to our everyday grasp of the kinds of objects we encounter in perception. On the structural realist view, the notion of a physical object ends up as

---

[21] See Russell (1927).

[22] It may be that, at the lowest level, there are unknown intrinsic properties, as Langton (1998) and Lewis (2009) argue; alternatively, it has been argued that we do not need to posit monadic properties at the lowest level – structure goes all the way up, and down: see Ladyman (1998) and Esfeld (2003).

[23] See the defence of Russell's view in Maxwell (1970) and (1972), and also Lowe's vindication of Locke's views in his (1995) Ch. 3.

thin and attenuated. Yet the world that we engage with in our ordinary activities seems to be the very opposite of this. It is a world that is rich and complex, full of value and meaning. We encounter perceptually a multiplicity of complex natures, higher-level monadic properties, powers and norms.

However, from what has emerged about the way that we see chess positions, it should be clear that there is a good reply available to the Causal Theorist. As the examples from chess indicate, seeing (or otherwise perceiving) anything is always a complex affair. The way that we see chess positions is, to a large extent, indicative of how we see things in general. One component of visual experience – the sensory aspect of perceptual consciousness – involves something qualitative being immediately presented to the subject: an array of shapes and colours.[24] But the critical aspect of experience is the way that concepts enter into it. Experiences have a further component, which has intentional representational content. The patterns of pieces and squares presented in experience, when the player looks at the pieces on the board, need to be distinguished from the objects that are the focus of the chess player's higher-level cognitive attention, in which the pieces are taken to be related to each other according to formal rules that determine their potential moves. As we have noted, what the chess player sees, in the more inclusive sense, are abstract objects. In a strict sense, such objects are grasped in spatial terms, by virtue of the potential relations that the individual units bear to each other.

However, as the example of chess also shows, an essentially spatial grasp of an entity is compatible with that entity having a further level of meaningfulness for us. As has been argued above, chess structures can have a meaningfulness which goes beyond the merely formal. We perceive chess positions as containing relatively stable complexes of pieces, which can be considered, at least temporarily, as larger-scale unified objects. A chess player sees part of the board as a well-defended king's position, or a strong centre, a blocked pawn chain, and so on. We also noted that, despite the abstract formal nature of chess, pieces and piece-complexes are often conceived in value-laden terms, and they can take on a rich emotional significance. Parallel considerations apply to our perception of physical objects in general. In experience we intentionally represent objects around us as having shape, size, position and kind. Such features can be accounted for in terms of structure, resulting in the 'thin' conception

---

[24] The representational contents of this component can be accounted for in terms of Peacocke's scenario content.

of objective content. But in addition, the objective structures we interact with take on a much richer meaning for us. The strict, thin, account of content is compatible with a view of perception according to which experiences of the world have additional layers of significance. As in the example of chess, we directly perceive the physical world as comprising a wide range of different kinds of objects, instantiating rich and varied high-level properties, and permeated by value. The phenomenology of perception is compatible with an implicit understanding, in a stricter sense, of the relational structure of the physical world.

There is one obvious difference between our conception of chess positions and of physical objects, but it does not undermine the analogy I have been drawing. The abstract position that is the focus of my chess thoughts when I play a game of chess is conceived of as self-contained, unrelated to egocentric or allocentric space, and as causally inert. In contrast, the physical objects I see in my surroundings are potentially items I can causally interact with. This does not conflict with the structural view of objects. It means that my understanding of the nature of an object also comprehends an appreciation of the fact that my experiences of that object can undergo change as a result of changes in the object itself, and also as a result of my movements relative to it. An object of any given kind, such as an apple, will have a typical causal profile. In addition to understanding its essentially spatial nature, I have expectations of the different ways that an object will appear in different conditions, and how it will affect me.[25] I know that being hit by a hard cricket ball will cause me pain; and that biting into a ripe apple will cause me to have sensations of sweetness, and so on. This reinforces the conclusion that an essentially structural conception of objects is compatible with the rich experience of the world that is a feature of normal perception.

The conclusion suggested by these brief reflections is this. An analysis of the phenomenon of playing chess reveals something important about the general nature of perceptual experience, and of our relation to the physical world. Our perceptually based understanding of reality is of a world that has more of a structural character than we unreflectively appreciate. Our implicit grasp of physical objects has much in common with the kind of grasp we have of the spatial structures represented in chess positions. Seeing a chess position is in many ways like seeing in the ordinary sense; while conversely, our perceptually based understanding of the physical world has

---

[25] This point, again, goes back to the Kant's claims about the role of productive imagination in perception.

much in common with our grasp of the essential spatial character of chess positions.[26]

University of Hertfordshire
p.coates@herts.ac.uk

References

Binet, A. (1966) 'Mnemonic virtuosity: A study of chess players', *Genetic Psychology Monographs* **74**, 127–162. Translated from the *Revue des Deux Mondes* (1893), 117, 826–859.

Chase, W. & Simon, H. (1973) 'Perception in Chess' *Cognitive Psychology* **4**, 55–81.

Chabris, C. & Hearst, E. (2003) 'Visualization, Pattern Recognition, and Forward Search: Effects of Playing Speed and Sight of Position on Grandmaster Chess Errors' *Cognitive Science*, **27**, 637–648.

Coates, P. (2007) *The Metaphysics of Perception: Wilfrid Sellars, Perceptual Consciousness and Critical Realism*, London: Routledge.

Esfeld, M. (2003) 'Do relations require underlying intrinsic properties? A physical argument for a metaphysics of relations', *Metaphysica. International Journal for Ontology & Metaphysics*, 4, 5–25.

Fish, W. (2009) *Perception, Hallucination and Illusion*, Oxford: Oxford University Press.

Gobet, F. (2012) 'Concepts Without Intuition Lose the Game: Commentary on Montero and Evans 2011' *Phenomenology and the Cognitive Sciences*, 11: 2, 237–250.

Groot de, A. D. (1965) *Thought and Choice in Chess* (1st Ed.), The Hague: Mouton.

Hobson, K. (forthcoming) 'In Defense of Relational Direct Realism', *European Journal of Philosophy*.

Josten, G. (2010) *A Study Apiece*, Homburg: SAAR- Schach-Agentur.

Kasparov, G. (1987) *London-Leningrad Championship Games*, Oxford: Pergamon Press.

Kasparov, G. (2003) *On My Great Predecessors, Part I*, London: Everyman Chess.

---

[26] For helpful comments on an earlier draft I would like to thank Sam Coleman, Luciano Floridi, Peter Lane, and John Rose.

Lane, P. & Gobet, F. (2011) 'Perception in Chess and Beyond: Commentary on Linhares and Freitas', *New Ideas in Psychology* 29, 156–161.

Ladyman, J. (1998) 'What is structural realism?' *Studies in History and Philosophy of Modern Science*, **29**, 409–424.

Langton, R. (1998) *Kantian Humility*, Oxford: Clarendon Press.

Lewis, D. (2009) 'Ramseyan Humility', in David Braddon-Mitchell & Robert Nola (eds) *Conceptual Analysis and Philosophical Naturalism*, Cambridge, Mass: MIT Press.

Lowe, J. (1995) *Locke on Human Understanding*, London: Routledge.

Martin, M. (2006) 'On Being Alienated' in Gendler, T. and Hawthorne, J. (eds) *Perceptual Experience*, Oxford: Oxford University Press.

Maxwell, G. (1970) 'Theories, Perception and Structural Realism' in R. Colodny (ed.) *The Nature and Function of Scientific Theories*, Pittsburgh: University of Pittsburgh Press.

Maxwell, G. (1972) 'Russell on Perception' in D Pears (ed.) *Bertrand Russell: A Collection of Critical Essays*, New York: Anchor Books.

McDowell, J. H. (1982) 'Criteria, Defeasibility, and Knowledge', *Proceedings of the British Academy*.

McDowell, J. H. (1986) 'Singular Thought and the Extent of Inner Space', in Pettit, P. and McDowell, J. H. (eds) *Subject, Thought, and Context*, Clarendon Press: Oxford.

Nabokov, V. (1964) *The Luzhin Defence*, London: Weidenfeld and Nicolson (With thanks to the Nabakov Estate).

Robinson, H. (1994) *Perception*, London: Routledge.

Russell, B. (1927) *The Analysis of Matter*, New York: Harcourt, Brace.

Sellars, W. (1978) 'The Role of Imagination in Kant's Theory of Experience' in Johnstone, H. W. (ed.) *Categories: A Colloquium*, Pennsylvania: Pennsylvania State University.

Snowdon, P. (1981) 'Perception, Vision and Causation', *Proceedings of the Aristotelian Society* **81**, 175–92.

Valberg, J. J. (1992) *The Puzzle of Experience*, Oxford: Clarendon Press.

Index of Names

Achilles 67–68, 108 n.9
Adams, Robert 40, 121 n.21, 127
Adkins, Arthur 112 n.14, 124, 127
Agathon 120
Ajax 67–68
Alexander (the Great) 110
Ali, Mohammed 67
Alvarez, Al 150
Amphidamas 67
Antilochus 67
Apollo 200
Aquinas, Thomas 30, 34
Aristotle 28, 30, 31, 33, 36, 41, 42, 71, 99, 102, 105, 117 n. 18, 124 n.24, 125 n.25, 126
Armstrong, Lance 208
Athena 68, 200
Atherton, Mike 72, 74, 168
Attwood, Julian 149
Augustine 117, 114 n.16

Bach, Johann Sebastien 76
Bäck, Alan 38–39
Bannister, Jack 176
Beckham, David 67
Bentham, Jeremy 94–96, 98
Binet, Alfred 222, 229 n.10, 241

Boardman, Peter 66, 151, 156
Bodhidharma 18, 21 n.13
Bonaparte, Napoleon 110
Bonington, Chris 149, 152
Botvinnik, Mikhail 227
Boycott, Geoffrey 183
Bratman, Michael 187, 195
Bristow, Eric 181
Broad, C.D. 114, 115, 117, 127
Bronstein, David 224, 225
Brundage, Avery 203, 204, 205
Brutus 10
Buddha (Siddhartha Gautama) 21, 23
Butryn, Ted 130
Byrne, Donald 216, 217

Caesar, Julius 9, 10
Capablanca, José Raúl 219, 220, 224
Chaplin, Charlie 155
Chappell, Greg 160
Cheek, Joey 32, 36, 197, 207–209
Christ 121–123 (see also 'Jesus')
Churchill, Winston 105, 106, 128
Colton, Nick 49

Constantine, Lebrun 172
Cowell, Simon 119
Cox, David 147
Crippen, Fran 65
Cumberbatch 172

Dares 199
Davids, Fakhry 170
De Coubertin, Pierre 68, 202–203
De Groot, Adriaan 218 n.3, 222
Dennett, Daniel 12
Dixon, Nicholas 7, 14
Dodds, Dickie 164
Donald, Allan 72, 74, 168

Edmonds, Phil 182
Edwards, S.D. 140
Einstein, Albert 155
Elliott, R. 4, 13
Enke, Robert 73
Entellus 199, 200, 202, 207
Epeus 67
Eumeleus 67

Fagan, Patsy 181, 182
Falstaff 110
Fischer, Bobby 216, 217, 220, 221, 222, 225, 226
Flintoff, Andrew 104, 163
Foe, Marc-Vivien 65
Fosbury, Dick 5

Index of Names

Fox, Robin Lane 68
Franco, Francisco 110

Gaita, Rai 112, 128
Geller, Efim 225, 226
Gobet, Fernand 212
n.1, 222, 223, 224,
241
Goebbels, Joseph 110
Gollwitzer, Peter 41
n.31, 188, 189, 195
Gower, David 176
Graf, Steffi 182, 194
Gregory, Richard 12
Gumbrecht, Hans
80–81, 91, 92 n.13,
94, 98

Hamlet 119
Hanson, Norwood
Russell 12
Haraway, Donna 130,
131, 134, 142
Hargreaves, Allison 66
Haston, Dougal 155
Headley, George 172
Heidegger, Martin
132
Helen (Illiad) 108, 169
Henman, Tim 66
Herzog, Maurice 147
Hillary, Edmund 87
Hitler, Adolf 110, 111
Hobbes, Thomas 117
Hobbs, Jack 168
Hogan, Ben 181
Holton, Richard 187,
190, 195
Homer 66–71, 107–
110, 112 n.14, 121,
127 n.27, 128, 199–
201

Horace 148
Houston, Charlie
147
Hume, David 22, 75,
101 n.3, 128
Hunt, John 147
Hutton 169

Insole, Doug 164

James, C.L.R. 172,
173
James, Daniel 65
Jedrzejczak, Otylia
207, 208, 209
Jesus 120
Job (biblical) 65
Johnson, Leavander
65
Jones, Carwyn 30 n.2,
32 n.6, 140

Kallis, Jacques 184
Kant, Immanuel 92,
114, 124, 149, 214,
237, 240 n.25, 242
Karpov, Anatoly 223,
224
Kasparov, Garry 219,
223, 224, 241
Keillor, Garrison 107,
128
Kempis, Thomas 119
Khaneman, Daniel 47
n.3, 48, 49 n.5
Knoblauch, 'Chuck'
182
Krein, Kevin 56,
57–59
Kurz, Toni 66
Kurzweil, Raymond
131–133, 141

Lachenal, Louis 59
n.32, 147
Lamba, Raman 65
Landeweerd, L. 140
Langer, Bernhard 181
Lasker, Emanuel 219,
220
Lawrence, D.H. 66
Lee, Brett 163
Lenk, C. 140
Leyland, Maurice 166
Lillee, Dennis 165,
168
Loland, Sigmund
135, 136
Lorca, Federico
Garcia 65
Luzhin (*The Luzhin
Defence*) 230

MacAloon, John 202,
203 n.19
MacIntyre, Alasdair
31–32, 102–105,
108, 109 n.10, 113,
118, 124, 128
Mallory, George 49,
66, 156
Mann, David 179,
180, 196
Matulovic, Milan 220,
221
McGrath, Glenn 164
Mead, Margaret 152
Medlycott, Keith
182
Mejias, Ignacio
Sanchez 65
Menelaus 67
Messner, Reinhold
152, 156
Miamoto, Musashi 18

Mill, John Stuart 94–
96, 98
Miller, Keith 73
Milton, John 76
Morris, Thomas 41–
42
Murray, Andy 71
Murray, W.H. 123,
128
Mussonlini, Benito
110

Nabakov, Vladimir
230, 242
Nadal, Rafael 71
Neghina, Mihai 231,
232, 233
Nietzsche, Friedrich
107, 117, 119
Nimzowitsch, Aron
231
Nisbet, Robert 135
Noel, John 149
Novotna, Jana 182,
194
Nussbaum, Martha
118, 128

O'Donnell, Phil 65
Odysseus 67–68
Olivier, Sydney
172
Opening, Reti 224
Orwell, George 74

Paris (*Illiad*) 108
Pascal, Blaise 74–76
Patroclus 67–68
Paul (saint) 121
Petersen, Kevin 66
Petrosian, Tigran 216,
224, 225, 231

Pistorius, Oscar 138–
141
Plato 29–30, 34, 76,
102, 118 n.18, 120–
122, 125 n.25, 201,
204, 205 n.27
Pollini, Maurizio 93
Ponting, Ricky 104–
105
Prasanna, Eripalli 164
Preuss, Holger 206

Radcliffe, Paula 134
Ramprakash, Mark
175–177, 183, 194–
195
Rawls, John 150
Reid, Heather, 68
Richards, Viv 170,
171, 172
Roberts, Andy 168
Rooney, Wayne 67
Rousseau, Jean-
Jacques 152
Ruth, Babe 107

Sailor, Pam 134
Sandham 168
Sartre, Jean-Paul
117
Sasser, Mackey 181
Semenya, Caster 140
Senna, Ayrton 65
Shankly, Bill 65
Sidgwick, Henry
125–126, 128
Simoncelli, Marco
65
Simpson, Tom 65
Smith, Mike 168
Smythe, Frank 149
Snead, Sam 181

Socrates 110 n.11,
120, 122, 124 n.24,
127, 204–205
Soho, Takuan 19, 27
n.29
Spassky, Boris 216, 228
Stalin, Joseph 110
Stocker, Michael 124,
128
Suits, Bernard 5, 6, 9,
86 n.9, 131 n.4, 133,
142

Tal, Mikhail 227
Tasker, Joe 66
Thomson, Jeff 165,
168
Tresthcothick,
Marcus 73
Tversky, Amos 47 n.3,
48

Van Hilvoorde, I. 140
Vaughan, Michael 92
Venables, Stephen
149
Virgil 197, 199–200

Walton, Kendall 69–
70
Warne, Shane 170,
175, 176, 177, 180,
183, 194, 195
Watson, Tom 181
Wenger, Arsène 37, 72
Wheldon, Daniel 65
Whillans, Don 155
Williams, Bernard 99
n.1, n.2, 113 n.15,
114, 124, 128
Winnicott, Donald
166, 173

Index of Names

Wittgenstein, Ludwig 76, 84–86, 98

Wolf, Susan 124, 128

Woods, 'Float' 172

Woods, Tiger 141

Wordsworth, William 146

Worrell, Frank 172

Yeats, W.B. 109

Young, David 204

Zedong, Mao 110, 111

Zeus 108, 202, 203

Zidane, Zinedine 67